sailing at the *edge* of *disaster*

sailing at the *edge* of *disaster*:

a memoir of
a young woman's daring year

Elizabeth W. Garber

Toad Hall *editions*

ISBN: 978-1-7369925-5-5

First Edition 2022
Biography & Autobiography / Personal Memoirs

Cover design and book design by Liz Kalloch
Ship image painting by Abe Goodale

For Kim and Pogo, and my brother Woodie

A note to the reader:

This is a true story, as best as I could reconstruct, of the last sail of the *Antarna* in 1971-72. The ship now sails as the magnificent *Sea Cloud*.

For the fifty years since we left the ship in Panama, I held onto my photo album, journal, letters home, parent letters from the school director, and Kim's journals. I couldn't have recreated Kim's voice in this book without her journal, recent emails and calls.

I am telling my version of the story, recreating what happened from my memory and from several years of asking old friends from the ship what they remembered. I keep learning new stories from my shipmates.

I use the first names of students and teachers who gave me permission to name them and include their stories. The Director speaks from her parent letters and in the memory of her students. When I include students, teachers, or crew I was unable to track down, I use fictitious names. If a person is a publicly known figure, I use their name. Names and identifying characteristics have been changed to protect the privacy of certain individuals.

The book, *Sea Cloud: A Living Legend,* by Kurt Grobecker and Peter Neumann (Collectors Books Limited 1991), includes a chapter about the Oceanics School on the *Antarna* which verifies the story I tell here, but as my crewmates agree, it has many inaccuracies.

In the beginning I was so young and such a stranger to myself I hardly existed. I had to go out into the world and see it and hear it and react to it, before I knew at all who I was, what I was, what I wanted to be.

—Mary Oliver

The cure for anything is salt water—sweat, tears, or the sea.

—Isak Dinesen

This will end up being the most educational year in most of your lives.

—Stephanie Gallagher, Director of the Oceanics School

Contents

Prologue

Fall 1971
In the Rigging

"I can't." My legs wobble on the rope rung digging into my sneakers. I hold on to cables running up along the mast over one hundred feet above the ship's deck. I close my eyes for a second but that makes everything worse; my chest thuds, my body trembles. I try to speak up; me, the pitiful teenager frozen in the rigging, "I can't do this." I don't care how pathetic I sound.

The crewman on the second platform above me leans over the edge and gives directions. "Reach up one hand over your head to seize hold of these shrouds. Then the other hand. Pull yourself up onto the platform." His voice is upbeat. "You can do it." My hands are sweating, my knees threaten to give way, and he sounds so fucking positive.

All the way up this rope ladder I face the massive steel mast and chant, I can do it, I can do it, like a ridiculous Little Engine That Could, and I'm okay, until I get here.

I'm on the main mast of our school's four-masted square-rigger for sail training. Today everyone is required to climb up and over the second platform in the rigging. *I'm supposed to lean my whole body out at a ninety-degree angle over wide-open empty space? What if my arms let go? There's nothing under me for one hundred feet before the deck.* The mast moves, a slow sickening sway. I glance down at the docks, boat yards, and the causeway to Miami, when nausea catches in my throat.

Dad's voice slams into me, like a loud speaker turned on in my brain. *You are weak. You've never learned to work.* My hands shake and my grip starts to slip. His voice tears into me, pummeling, his words a one two punch, before he knocks me with a hook. *You'll never amount to anything.* I tremble, barely hanging on. I close my eyes, and my head slumps against the rope rungs.

Coming to the ship was my escape. But Dad knows exactly how to break me. I can't hold him at bay up here. My arms are weakening. I just can't do it.

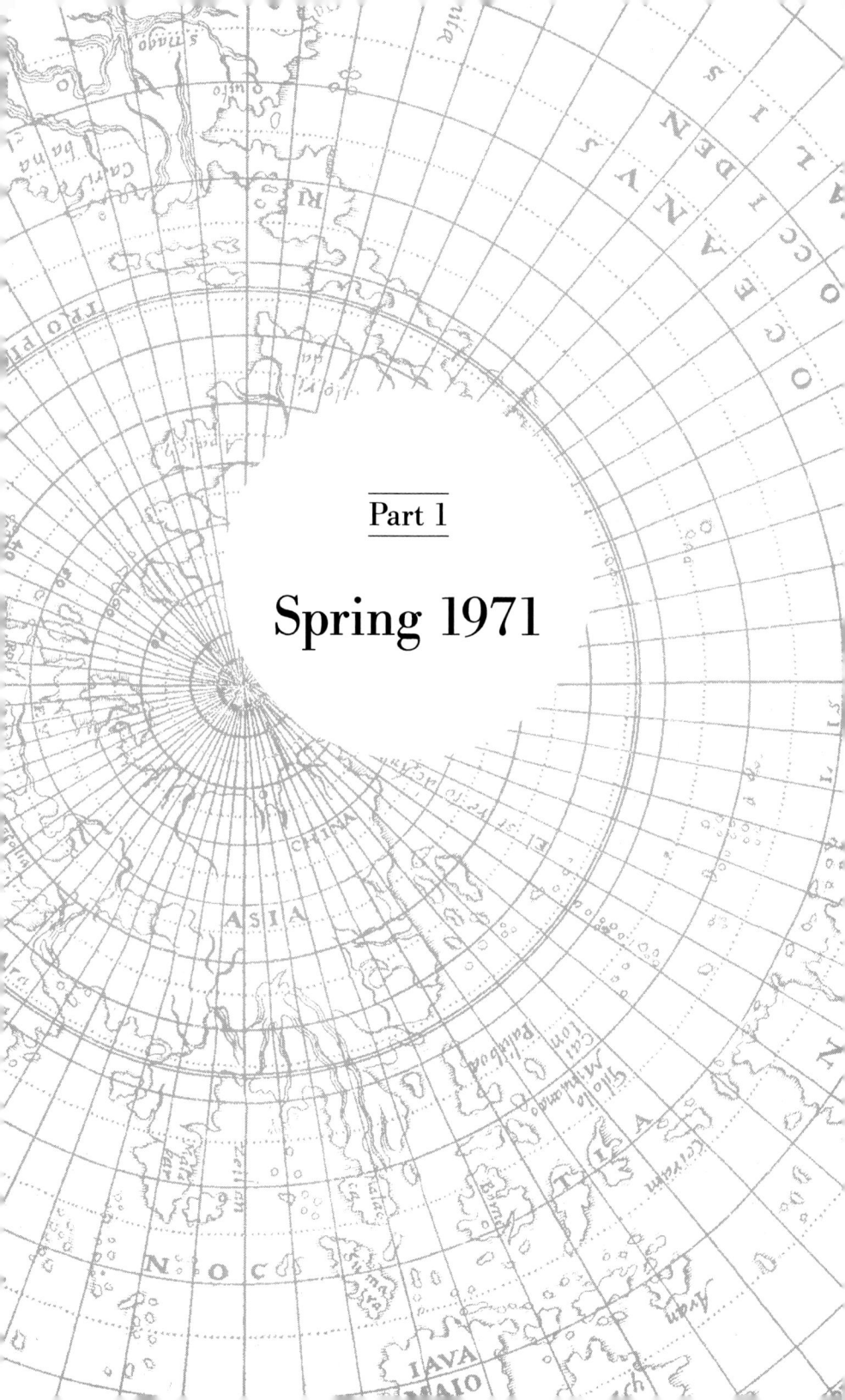

Part 1

Spring 1971

At the Dinner Table, Glendale, Ohio

Dad had some idiot plan to send me to Katharine Gibbs secretarial school in New York City so I could work my way through college. Sylvia Plath even mentioned that school in *The Bell Jar* as the destination for those perfectly made-up '50s girls in twin sets and pearl necklaces. Oh God, I would die there. I simmered in silent fury. I would not be a secretary for anyone. Or a stupid housewife. But I had no idea what I wanted to do with my life, except read Plath, and get out of school so I could write something that might mean something.

There was a bang outside and I jumped. I leaned toward the wall of glass beyond my desk in time to see a fading wisp of white smoke. I rolled my eyes. "That little shit is messing with gunpowder again." My four-teen-year-old brother, Woodie, was in trouble. He was always getting in trouble. He joked about how he'd been paddled over fifty times in middle school. How was that possible?

Slumping back in my chair, I pulled my skirt down with both hands so it covered my ass, a maneuver I practiced over and over all day as I changed classes at school. I glowered at any asshole who might look and whistle at my long legs. Thinking of them, I fumed. Pigs. I crossed my legs, and checked to make sure I didn't have a run in my favorite black tights. I looked at the sheet of paper in my portable typewriter splattered with whited-out corrections. My term paper on prison reform was due tomorrow. *Oh shit.* I'd have to type that page over.

Five years before, when our family had moved from an old Victorian to the glass house, we'd all thought it would be so cool to live in a modern house that my dad designed. We didn't know then that we would live in a construction site for two years, in the middle of two acres of bulldozed earth. We worked for five years, every weekend and all summer, first on the house, and then landscaping our dad's elaborate gardens. At fifty-eight, my dad was barrel chested, strong and bald; dripping with sweat when he climbed down from his small bulldozer. He entertained visitors with his big booming voice: "I'm having the time of my life. And my children are learning the value of good hard work." We'd glance at each other in our dirty work clothes with tight smiles. *Yeah, sure.*

•

I ignored my paper and my brother's suburban bombings of plastic model cars, and snuck back to Plath. Her words were a relief. *I felt very still and empty, the way the eye of a tornado must feel, moving dully along in the middle of the surrounding hullabaloo.* While I read, I ran my fingers through my eyebrows and eyelashes until hairs fell out. Then I stuck them into wet globs of Elmer's white glue on a small square of cardboard. The glue set up clear, like petrified amber but with traces of me caught for all eternity. Which was actually how I'd felt ever since Dad announced he would not allow, NOT ALLOW, me to go to college. "You are too immature to go to college, young lady. I won't waste money on you going to some hippie school where they shut down classes for anti-war protests."

Months away from the end of senior year, when I'd thought I was escaping from home, Dad had somehow weaseled into taking control of my life again. It wasn't as bad as the previous winter; yet, you never knew with him. Everything could always change on a dime.

Last Christmas, in a crescendo of fury, he'd pulled me out of school because I disobeyed him and refused to break up with my Black boyfriend, Alvin, after a year of dating. Alvin was my first boyfriend, a broad-shouldered, award-winning gymnast, who was chased after by so many girls. We'd fallen for each other because of how we loved to read and talk—about the *Tibetan Book of the Dead*, about the novels we read in English class, about life—and he made me laugh. Dad declared he wasn't racist, but this was the time in my life for studying and not wasting it with a boyfriend. He added, like an afterthought, that it was too dangerous for us to be a biracial couple. When Dad really got worked up, he demanded to know where Alvin had touched me. Was I still a virgin? I didn't even have to lie. We still were.

For the entire two-week holiday break, I was forbidden to leave home while Dad lectured me for hours at a time. About my disobedience. My failings as a person. My lack of moral integrity. Outside on a dark night, Alvin and a friend lay in the snow with binoculars, watching our house lit up like a white-gleaming jewel box, the long sliding glass walls revealing all of us, as if we were characters in a play. The others moved numbly around the house, but I burrowed into the orange Womb chair, where I stared at the floor or at the dark mirrored walls of glass, while a fury ground into my belly. I hated my dad. Occasionally I lashed out with sarcastic attacks. But he didn't stop yelling, day after day for ten days. It was the scariest he had ever been. He seemed possessed with a self-righteous fury that he was doing this to save me from myself. His orders held me hostage, and no one could save me. Certainly not my insecure mom, who was nearly twenty years younger than my dad, and seemed to fade and recede more each day. He got louder and louder until I went silent. I didn't know if I would ever speak again.

Finally, Mom escaped up the hill to ask our minister to come to our house and do family therapy with us—me, Mom and Dad, and even my two younger brothers. For two days we sat in a circle in the long glass room, as the minister led us through exercises to listen and then repeat back what each person said. Somehow my dad finally believed that I had listened to why he was scared about the dangers of Alvin and me being in public together. And he was made to listen and repeat what I said, rather than yell at me. Listening this hard gave me a headache, but a miracle happened: Dad let me go back to school. I could see Alvin, but only in odd-numbered groups. I agreed to stop attacking my dad with sarcastic zingers. He agreed to stop yelling. And then it was over. Suddenly we were out of a family nightmare.

Back at school, Alvin and I were ecstatic; our passion escalated, and our mission was to find a safe place to spend the night to lose our virginity. But even though we succeeded, and we were tender and loving that last winter of high school, a creeping fog of depression dragged me down, and eventually pulled me from Alvin more stealthily than my dad's orders.

•

There was another bang outside the window and a telltale wisp of smoke. I leapt to my feet. "Mom!" I ran to the kitchen with the practiced air of a complaining older sister and leaned on the counter. A line of copper pots hung over her head as she chopped an onion. I was such an annoying tattletale. "Woodie's using gunpowder to blow up his car models again." I was trying to get him in trouble because I didn't think he should use gunpowder. Not that I really worried about him.

She smiled wearily. "Oh, Elizabeth, relax. As long as he doesn't blow off his fingers. And I made your brother swear he won't." She laughed. "He's fine."

My mom was a lenient, 1960s kind of mom when my dad wasn't around. When she was at home alone with us, she had the attitude of "Do what you want all day, and get home for dinner." When we worked in the garden with her, she made the work fun. We'd weed the corn, thin carrots, or pick beans, laughing and teasing each other. At forty, she was thin and strong, wore dangly silver earrings, and had a pixie haircut. Everyone said she was so beautiful. I grimaced. No one ever said I was beautiful, except Alvin. My friends said my mom was "so real," like when she complained about menstrual cramps in front of my boyfriend. I was mortified to talk about periods. But overall, life was pretty good until my dad came home, when she'd go mute, and we would be on our own, without protection.

My eyes teared from the onion and frustration. "But Mom, I learned in chemistry that gunpowder is unstable and dangerous."

Her voice was calm as she scraped the onion into a skillet. "There are lots of dangerous things we have to face in our lives. I trust your brother's basic ability to make a decision." This was her mantra with us. "I trust your ability to make a good decision." I bet she'd read this in Frankl's *Man's Search for Meaning*, which she kept in her VW bus and read while she waited for us at school or at the orthodontist. She ignored me and added a chunk of butter to melt.

I rolled my eyes. "But what if we were doing something really dangerous? What would you do then?"

She held up a leek before she sliced it. "Look at this. You can tell it's spring. Time for vichyssoise." Mom specialized in changing the subject. She ignored what was really going on, and tried to distract us from conflicts with Dad. She pointed at the recipe. "Even though the *New York Times Cookbook* says only use the white part and only white pepper, I don't want to waste the green part of the leeks." Mom was slowly breaking the domestic rules she'd grown up with. Changing recipes was the beginning. She didn't wear white gloves when she drove to Cincinnati to go shopping anymore. No stockings on hot days under her shorter skirts. She sautéed the leeks before pouring in chicken stock and adding potatoes.

I scowled. "Spring means everyone's getting into college except me. Alvin was accepted by University of Michigan at Ann Arbor."

"That's where your grandmother went to school. Would you please make the salad?"

I groaned and grabbed ingredients out of the fridge. I was sobered thinking about my grandmother. She was in her junior year in college when her parents were lost at sea, their ship torpedoed by a German sub in 1915. I always felt sad about her becoming an orphan at twenty. She never talked about losing them, but when we visited her on her farm in upstate New York, she talked a lot about her father whom she'd adored.

Once I'd been a girl who adored her father, when we talked about architecture and modern art. But everything changed when we built our house. It was the end of our childhood. From then on, everything in our lives was focused on building our house and gardens. Suddenly, Dad seemed to love us only if we were hard workers. My youngest brother was only six, worked hard and received all the praise. Woodie and I, at nine and twelve, were relentlessly criticized, no matter how hard we worked the next five years. I was closer to my mom then. With her, we could be honest and complain about Dad and all the work. But I also felt like I had to protect her, like she was one of us. I imposed on myself an unwritten rule that I couldn't get mad at her, because she stood between us and Dad. What would we do without her?

I washed salad greens, and chopped apple, walnuts, and blue cheese to add to the salad. The glass door into the Great Room slid open and Woodie came into the galley kitchen reeking of sulfur and smoke. I put down my knife. "You're using gunpowder! Isn't it against the law?"

At fourteen, Woodie was slight for his age. He tucked his chin-length hair behind his ears and laughed at me. "I'm doing chemistry experiments. I mortared and pestled potassium nitrate, charcoal, and sulfur. It worked. Perfect proportions, if I say so myself."

"Why are you blowing up your models? You spent so much time making them."

He shrugged. "Don't care about them now." He was trying to goad me. "I just built them for sniffing the glue anyway."

"No, you didn't. You loved those models!" I followed him into his bedroom and looked up on the bookshelves that used to be crowded with plastic model cars, and planes. Only a few were left. Then I looked at the two-foot-long sailing ship on his desk. I glared at him. "You aren't going to blow up your square-rigged ship, are you?" He'd worked on it for a long time, even running threads for rigging the masts.

"Of course not. I'm not stupid." Then he glowered. "Or maybe I will. I don't care."

He followed me back to the kitchen. I said, "You're the stupid one if you blow it up."

He opened the refrigerator and stared inside.

Mom tried to distract us. "So, Woodie, how was school today?" It was the wrong question.

"The Vice Principal has it in for me. He called me into the office over my hair." He took a big gulp of milk out of the bottle. Mom grabbed it away from him and closed the fridge. "He told me it's too long. Said I have a bad attitude." He rolled his eyes, his voice angry. "But he has done nothing to earn my respect. The bastard."

My brother and I had very little in common, except we were both bookworms. When Woodie read, he couldn't be roused, even when we yelled at him. Only shaking him would get his attention. We teased him about always carrying another book in his back pocket. But I wondered if he always had to have the next book ready to escape into.

Mom ran the blender. The loud rumble interrupted all conversation, as she added cream to the steaming vichyssoise. She was distracted. "Damn," she muttered when hot soup splattered her hand. She wiped her hand on a tea towel and looked at the clock. "I'm behind on everything today." She glanced at the dining room. "Woodie, time to set the table. Your dad's almost home."

My youngest brother, Hubbard, arrived from playing baseball down the street. At twelve he was nearly six feet, taller than Woodie and more confident. He towered over his friends and seemed to be the leader of their adventures. He disappeared into the bathroom to wash his hands.

Dad's Jaguar accelerated up the driveway, the extra rev of the engine as he pulled up to the door of the garage and beeped the horn. He was down there, waiting for someone to open the garage door.

Mom was instantly anxious. "Who's going to open the door for him?"

Woodie nudged me. "You do it."

I pushed back. "No, you do it." We poked each other and laughed.

The horn beeped again. Mom was urgent. "Come on. Fast. Run. Whoever's going to do it! Go!"

I dashed to the door. Woodie called out with a grin, "You lose."

Mom sent him off to wash and put on clean clothes for dinner. "Don't want your dad to smell that gunpowder! Drop your clothes in the washing machine and close the lid." We were a well-oiled machine, hiding our life from our dad, sneaking behind his back and his rules, when we could. Even though television was forbidden during the week, we watched *Laugh-In* when he was gone on Monday nights. Alvin and I beelined to my room after school when no one was home.

I ran down the exterior stairs, dashed into the basement, and pulled up the garage door before he beeped a third time. He revved the engine again before driving in. Then he climbed out of that low-slung white convertible. I loved everything about this car. The red leather seats, the wooden steering wheel and gearshift handle. I sighed, gazing at the car before I faced my dad. He was wearing a khaki dress coat over his Brooks Brothers suit. With his red bow tie and black framed glasses, he was the picture of a modern architect. Long round tubes of building plans filled the narrow ledge back seat of his XKE. He was an imposing man. "Hey, Sugar, give me a kiss." I gave him a quick peck on his wind-chilled cheek. We both admired the Jag. Sometimes I was so comfortable with him, as if a strange amnesia slipped over me. I'd feel a surge of love for him again, and forget our battles.

"Someday I'll let you drive this, but your shifting has to improve. Once you can double clutch down, I'll let you give it a try. But don't hold your breath. This baby is my pride and joy!"

In person, it was as if we'd been in a truce lately, like play-acting the old days when I adored him. Our house was finally finished, and the gardens finally met his expectations. He wasn't cracking the whip all the time. When my friends came over, Dad was on his best behavior, and he talked about the old days when he had raced cars. He'd play new jazz records and talk about his buildings under construction. He seemed like the coolest guy. Our house was now spectacular, with modern furniture and sculpture and paintings. Of course, Dad chose it, and arranged it all. He even picked out Mom's clothes and her jewelry. Sometimes I went out at night into the garden and watched the house, glowing like a lantern in the dark. No wonder my friends thought I had far-out parents. Except Alvin who saw right through my dad.

But once Dad lectured and yelled, the spell would break; I'd harden my heart and shut down again into hating him.

•

At night, the long glass walls became silvery mirrors, where I watched my family at the dinner table, reflected. That night Dad unfolded a full-page article from the *New York Times*. "A friend at Literary Club gave this to me because he knows I love to sail. It's about a high school for boys on board a square-rigged sailing ship." His face was intent, and his bald head gleamed under the ceiling lights, as he explained that the directors, a filmmaker and his young second wife, were at their wits' end to get his children interested in education. He glared at Woodie. "Then they had this great idea, a school on a ship." He lifted up the paper, adjusted his trifocals, and read aloud. "'The students are learning navigation, songwriting...operating the launch, oceanography, math and climbing the rigging.... They are learning how to work—and they are learning how to learn.'"

Woodie sat on the edge of his chair, listening and guarded. Head down, his hair fell over his face.

Dad said, "This would be the best way for Woodie to develop some integrity and learn to work hard for a change." My brother slumped down to avoid the attack.

I asked my brother, "What are those books about the sea that you read all the time?"

Before Woodie could mumble "Horatio Hornblower," Dad interrupted to say he had always dreamed of sailing around the world.

Sitting upright, Hubbard asked Dad, "Are you going to go to this ship school?"

"No, this is for Woodie, to get his life in shape."

Mom wanted to hear more. "What kind of ship?"

I cleared the table, listening with vague attention, as I thought about retyping my paper and when I would call Alvin.

Dad said, "I talked to the director already. She sounds terrific, but she's overwhelmed with calls since the article. I decided I had to take action. She wants to interview Woodie. Says he's the kind of student they're looking for." He turned toward Woodie. "I'm sending you to New York for an interview next week."

Mom looked stricken. "He's only fourteen. He's never been on a plane and wouldn't know how to find his way in a big city."

"Not a problem. I'm sending Elizabeth, too."

I turned, startled. "Me? Go to New York to help Woodie get to his interview?"

Dad's intent gaze now focused on me. "I think this school will be the answer for you, too. I told her I had two problem kids."

I snarled inside. *Me, a problem kid?* Because I didn't obey all his orders? When he ordered us to work, I worked. When he forbade me to get my ears pierced, I didn't dare disobey. But give up my boyfriend? No way. Did that mean I was a "problem"? At school, the problem girls rode around in cars with boys, wore thick eyeliner and bright lipstick, and smoked dope or got drunk. I'd never been drunk or stoned. I was even too uptight to dance to rock and roll. I didn't know how to lighten up and have fun. I was a problem kid?

But as Dad talked, I kept my face neutral and flat, careful not to start a fight.

"Stephanie is interested in meeting you, too."

"Who's Stephanie?"

"The director—she's a dynamo."

I was confused. "But it's a high school and I'm graduating."

"Oh, you wouldn't go as a student. She needs a librarian and tutor.

You would work for room and board. Can't beat that, since Woodie's tuition will really cost us. But she has to meet you first, before this is settled."

I was dazed. A sailing ship on the ocean? I'd only seen the ocean once, when I was a little kid. I remembered how the waves knocked me over. Dad might love boats and sailing, but it had never been my dream to sail on a boat at sea.

Mom asked, "Can't we think about this and find out more about the school?" She was shrinking into her chair like a scared child. She had to be very careful about saying anything when Dad was wound up with one of his "inspired" plans.

I remembered when he took us all sailing for the first time, when we were about eleven, eight, and five. He'd decided a racing catamaran was the perfect family sailboat and he took us out for our first sail on Lake Erie when gale warning flags were snapping. The two narrow hulls sliced through the crashing grey waves, we were soaked through from the spray, and he sailed so tightly into the wind that one hull lifted out of the water. My hair whipped across my face. I loved looking up at the taut white sail, the way the boom flew across the deck as we came about, before we caught the wind again. He yelled at me and my little brothers to pull on ropes. My dad put me in a canvas sling trapeze attached with ropes to the mast, so I could lean out over the water, holding on with my toes to the edge of the hull. I looked back at my little brothers, grinning in their orange life jackets, and my dad "higher than a kite"—but when I glanced at my mother, her face was white; she was terrified and hanging on for dear life. At that moment, I was my Daddy's brave girl, flying in the wind, and I dismissed her as a boring scaredy-cat. Only years later would I remember that she didn't know how to swim, was frightened to even put her face into water, probably because her grandparents drowned at sea.

Dad handed Mom the article about last year's ship. "They're still looking for the right ship for next fall." Then his voice made it clear his decision was already made and final. "It's settled. The tickets are paid for New York. You fly next Tuesday for interviews."

Woodie and I glanced at each other. Was this for real? Fly to New York City on our own? We'd never traveled anywhere on our own.

My brothers and I cleared the table, rinsed dishes, and filled the dishwasher while our minds whirled. Hubbard joined Mom to work on his homework at the kitchen table, like any other school night. Woodie and I tiptoed into his room, spread out the newspaper, and read. He pointed to the photo of two boys climbing a rope ladder up a mast. "I've always wanted to do that." Our usual negative comments about Dad quieted as we read about last year's school ship sailing along the coast of Europe to Africa, then crossing the Atlantic to the Caribbean.

I whispered, "It sounds like we might get out of here." After feeling so trapped, so controlled, suddenly a door opened. I could actually escape and have a new life. And leave home. But I couldn't trust it yet. I let out a bitter laugh. "I bet he's thrilled he finally figured out a way to separate me from Alvin." I added sadly, "But we're already going our separate ways."

My little brother looked wary, but wistful. "I've always dreamed of running away to sea."

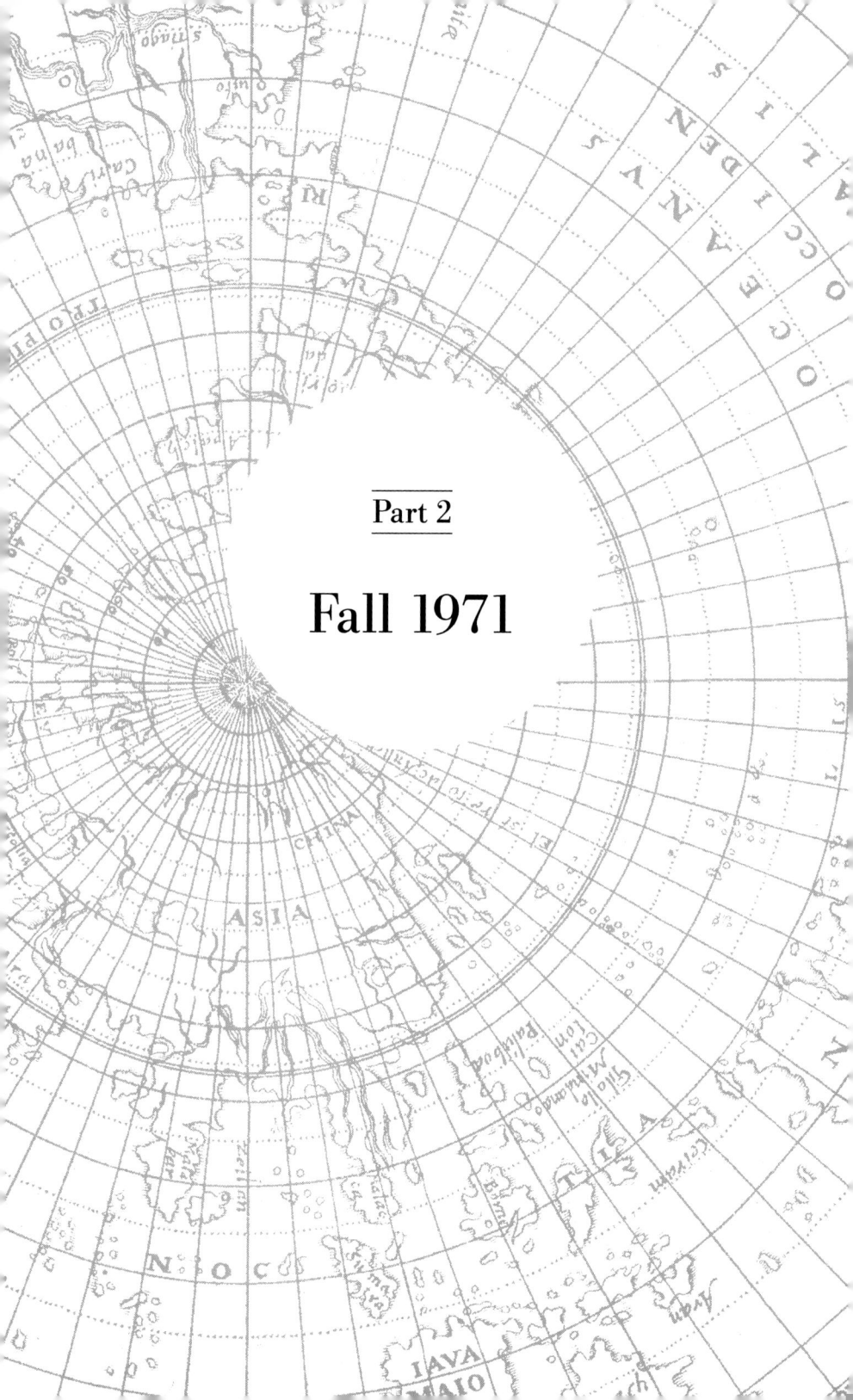

Part 2

Fall 1971

In Port of Miami, Florida, On Board the Antarna

From the Oceanics School brochure: *The OCEANICS proposes that teens be "kicked out" of their comfortable numbing environments and into the real world with its natural highs and natural lows and natural in-betweens.*

The taxi from the Miami airport drove slowly through a maze of metal shipping containers stacked three high. I clutched my sweaty cash, and asked again, making sure I was in the right place, "Ashbury Docks? The *Antarna*, yes?"

The driver pulled to a stop on an open dock, and through the windshield I saw a rust-streaked hull and a line of portholes. When I stepped out, it towered over me, a four-masted ship I'd only seen in a black-and-white photograph from the 1930s with its thirty sails filled with wind and the hull slicing through whitecaps. I gasped. "Holy shit."

The ship was swarming with boys: teenaged, shirtless, long-haired boys lined the railing and milled around on the dock, and a lot of them seemed to be watching me, a skinny seventeen-year-old girl in a white linen jacket and short-shorts, with new sandals and freshly shaved legs. I blushed from all the attention.

A couple of tall guys with ripped jeans ambled down the gangway of the ship and walked toward me. They were tanned, dirt-stained, and grinning. "You're here for Oceanics, right?" I could only nod. "Cool," they said, before they hoisted my duffel and backpack from the trunk of the cab and carried them up the gangway and down the deck.

I followed them, holding on to the railings until I realized how greasy they were and let go. But at the slight sway of the ship, I grasped on again. I made a mental note: Don't wipe the grease on my good clothes. Midway, I paused and looked down at the narrow chasm of dark water between the dock and the hull. I shivered—this was the ocean. I was a Midwestern girl; this was only the second time I'd seen it.

At the top of the gangway, a guy showed me the logbook. "You sign in and out every time you leave or return to the ship. Put down the time, too." I glanced at my watch and then I leaned down to write—Elizabeth Garber, October 9, 1971, 2 p.m.—while all around me was the hot smell of sweat and the noise of boys. Talking, laughing, goofing around. And my dad sent me here because he thought I was too immature for college!

As I looked down the long deck of the ship, it was a girl, striding toward me, who seized my attention. She was tan—a hardworking, ground-in-dirt, farm tan—shorter than me, and she moved like a strong-muscled animal, as if propelled toward me. People slid out of her way. Her unbrushed hair was truly dirty blond, held in place with a couple of barrettes, clearly not for looks but for work. Was she going to run me over?

She stopped in time, then squinted at me. "Hey, you're Elizabeth, the librarian. I met you when I came for my interview. I'm Kim." Her voice was husky and strong, and everyone turned to listen when she announced, "I've gotta take a shit."

My mouth involuntarily pursed, a twinge of reaction I'd been unable to hide. My cheeks flushed with heat, which clearly amused her. She looked at me piercingly. "As soon as I get back, I'll show you the girls' quarters." Her feet pounded down the metal gangway to shore, making it clang and jolt. She called back to me, "Hey, we're roommates." Then she raced across the dock, leaping over tar-dripping buckets and tangles of discarded metal and rope, until she disappeared into a concrete-block building.

Of course, I remembered her. It was a month ago in New York, at the school office where I had worked with our energetic young director, Stephanie, all summer. I was her assistant, sending off parent letters about departure dates. I included packing lists: six dark blue T-shirts, six blue jeans, heavy wool sweater, foul-weather gear, and more. And reminders: Make sure your children's passports are up to date. I added students to our roster—so far forty-three boys and, since the school had decided to go coed, six girls. I answered the phone. "Yes, we have room for a few more students." They interviewed with Stephanie and I handed them packets as they left. We'd been a team all summer. Stephanie went over and over our numbers, enrollments, teachers, funds.

Then this wiry girl arrived to meet with Stephanie. Kim and I checked each other out with narrowed eyes, assessing our differences. I sat at the typewriter, with long smooth brown hair, in a Jones of New York dress Stephanie had given me, while Kim wore a wrinkled shirt and jeans, with blond curls shoved behind her ears. She and Stephanie disappeared into the back office for a long interview. She left without a glance at me. I tried to read Stephanie's face to see what she thought of this girl.

She tapped her pen on her desk. "Kim's important. She has a strong spirit. I gave her the job to keep everyone's attitude upbeat and positive."

Hiding my pang of jealousy, I asked efficiently, "How much tuition?"

"Complete scholarship."

I pursed my lips, and shook my head as I wrote her name on a fresh file. Kim. I was in competition with her already.

•

The rumble of a refrigerator truck compressor brought me back to a cacophony of noise: hammers beating metal, vibrations of engines, and out in the harbor of Miami, cargo ships headed out to sea sounding their deep horns. Tugs and ships churned wakes. I craned my neck to look up into the *Antarna*'s soaring masts.

Even with all these people milling around me, and even though I was standing on the deck of a sailing ship for the first time in my life, I was still distracted by Kim. I'd never known a girl who said she had to take a shit before. I felt conspicuously weak and pale from working all summer at the office.

A tall guy near me stuck his head into a doorway where a current of hot oily air poured out, and shouted, "Hey, Woodie. Your sister's here." The guy looked at me and explained, "He's one of the grease monkeys down in the engine room." He gestured toward a deck bench where some skinny boys with long hair in filthy blue jumpsuits were smoking. Ah, they were grease monkeys.

I peered into the doorway where a metal ladder descended into a dark, smelly, deafening realm. I held onto the heavy door handle until I realized how greasy it was and pulled back my hand. Where could I wipe my fingers? I stepped back as an oil-streaked teen emerged, his shoulder-length hair held in place by a red handkerchief headband. I didn't recognize him.

"Hey," he said with a lackluster voice. "You finally got here." It was Woodie. He was so dirty his skin looked grey. He gestured with his head toward the bow, like he was embarrassed to talk to me in front of the others.

As we walked forward, I gushed. "The ship is so beautiful. Are we really close to leaving?" We reached the quiet foredeck where a mast, as big as the trunk of a mature oak, was surrounded by a waterfall of heavy lines on all four sides. I looked up past the yardarms, and I couldn't even see to the top of the mast, but I knew the facts. "Foremast, right? Goes 170 feet above the deck."

Woodie nodded. "I'm going to climb the main mast someday. Even if it kills me to do it. Once you get to the top, you can hold on to a line, wrap your legs around it and slide down from the top. Crazy!"

"Oh, Woodie, you aren't doing anything dangerous, are you?"

"What on this ship isn't dangerous?" His face was serious, with none of his old sarcasm.

"What do you mean?"

After a couple weeks on the ship, he seemed older than his age. At home he was a dreamy boy with his nose in a book, or a bitter boy blowing up model cars. Now he'd adopted a tough mask, living among the boys down in the rows of bunks lining the forward compartment of the ship. He worked down in the engine room with engineers. "I like the work and especially the respect and appreciation." He added, "It's a nice change after Dad."

I asked about the other boys.

"They're mostly OK here." One guy had tried to push him around, but he'd pushed him back and no one had messed with him since. "My new motto is: It's better to fight once and get beat up, but not get picked on again and again." He added, "Wish I'd learned that back in middle school. Would've saved me a lot of grief."

I tried to stay upbeat. "So how are classes?"

"Classes? They haven't really started, but how can I go to some stupid class when there's so much work to do? None of the engine room guys will go to class." At my disapproving look, he said, "Let me explain."

We sat down on the deck and leaned back against the railing. "Rumor has it," he said, "the last crew on the ship wasn't paid, so when they left, they flooded the engine room with salt water." He grinned. "I can appreciate their act of revenge, but it's made a terrible mess for us." He explained that no one noticed for a few days. Then the owners drained the water and had the engine room spray-painted so it looked new and clean when Stephanie and her husband, Chick, took the tour. "At this moment, there are no working water pumps, no electricity, no engines, no galley, no working heads. Almost nothing works on the ship."

Ever the bossy older sister, having worked with Stephanie at the headquarters of the school, I was certain that I was still privately in the know about what was really going on. All summer we were on a mission to make this school happen. I'd slept on a mat on the narrow aisle of the Oceanics School office. I typed and retyped the proposed itinerary: from Miami, through the Panama Canal to the Galápagos Islands, back through the canal, along the coast of South America, across to Africa, into the Mediterranean, and then up the European coast and back across the Atlantic to New England. Stephanie was a wizard at calculating dates and distances to sail. I couldn't believe I'd actually get to sail across the ocean.

Now that I was on the ship, I had to protest my brother's claims, out of loyalty to Stephanie and the school. "But the owners promised the ship was only two weeks away from sailing."

He was dead serious. "I know I'm only fifteen, and all I know about sailing ships came from reading books about the Napoleonic Wars." He looked at me intently. "But I can tell you, we're in big trouble."

"But Woodie, it can't be that bad."

"Let me give you the real introduction to the *Antarna*." He grasped my hand, pulled me to standing, and we climbed ladder steps to the upper deck leading to the bow. He pointed to the dock alongside the ship, where a very long heavy metal pipe lay in a tangle of wires and ropes. "Let me introduce you to our bowsprit. Some German freighter knocked it off a year or two ago." Now, he fumed. "And the owners haven't gotten around to fixing it yet!" I remembered the old photograph of this ship sailing in the 1930s, when it was a private yacht built for Marjorie Merriweather Post, the wealthiest woman in the world at the time. I looked at the bow, searching for the beautiful bowsprit; the long spar that extends forward with stays attached for sails. Nothing was there. I looked back at the severed limb down on the dock.

"Doesn't anything work?"

He shrugged his shoulders, and a smile slipped across his face. "Well, we haven't sunk yet. But, that's still possible."

"But Woodie, if it's really dangerous, should we go home?" But the moment I imagined home, I clenched inside. This school was our escape. Being home for a week after the summer in New York reminded me. No matter what was happening here, it was safer than home. This ship had to sail.

His answer was swift. "Hell yeah, it's dangerous, but I won't go home. No way. I'm actually having a great time." He grinned.

•

As Woodie slouched back to the engine room, Kim hurried up the deck toward me. "I'll show you our cabin." Her saying "our" gave me a little thrill.

We walked down the opposite side of the ship away from the crowd at the gangway. "Which side of the ship is this, port or starboard?" I asked.

She turned to face the bow, her voice confident. "Here's how you get oriented." She put out her arms, waving to the right, then the left. "Starboard is the longer word, for right side. Port is the short word for left. I'm so used to it now, I hardly have to think about it."

We strolled toward the stern, under white metal walkways that offered shade from the afternoon sun. I studied the mahogany walls and doors, brass-trimmed portholes, brass round lights, and doors with plaques: SHIP'S OFFICE, RADIO OFFICE. The wooden deck felt wide like a little promenade. She pointed out a shady room visible through brass trimmed windows. "That's the fancy dining room and living room that go with the staterooms part of the ship."

"Have you been in there?"

"Hell, no. That will be for donors someday. We're the crew. I wish I was up in the fo'c'sle with the boys in the bunks." When I looked confused, she said, "That's the nautical way to say forecastle, the bow of the ship where the sailors live. Then I'd really feel like a sailor too. Us girls, our bunks are in the Maid's Quarters." She groaned. "I hate that. I'm not anybody's maid!"

A strange moment of dizziness scared me, like I'd almost lose my footing. I reached out my hand to the cabin wall. She smiled. "You'll get used to it. We learn to sway a little and move with small waves that hit the ship at dock. In a few days you won't even notice it. But when we get out on the ocean, it will be awesome!"

"Hey, what's that?" She caught my right hand and held it up to look closely at the ring on my index finger. It was a silvery cube of iron pyrite, with a wrapped silver wire ring that held the small stone in place.

It was the second time someone had taken my hand to look at the ring. When I came home from working in New York, my dad grabbed my hand and scowled. "What's this? Damn poor design and why wear a ring on that finger?" He'd pushed my hand away, disappointed in me.

I smiled at my ring, to answer Kim. "It's fool's gold. I gave it to myself, as a kind of declaration of my independence."

She nodded. "I like it."

She glanced at her watch. "Yikes! I gotta hurry. I'll show you our quarters." We cut across an open deck to the port side and stopped at a metal door. "These are watertight doors. See how they bolt? That's so a storm won't send water down the steps. But stuffy as hell down here if we shut it." My bags were in a pile where the boys had left them. Kim hauled my backpack and stepped over a foot-high threshold. I thumped my duffel down the ten steep steps while I held onto the railing with one hand. These were the girls' quarters, with a carpeted floor and the welcome sound of female voices from three open doorways. Kim eyed me. "Are you neat or messy?"

"I'm kind of neat." We both laughed—the answer was obvious—me in my linen suit and Kim in a filthy T-shirt and ragged jean shorts. We took an immediate left and walked into a tiny room with a porthole between two narrow bunks.

She grinned. "It would be a disaster if you were as messy as me." She motioned for me to stand back so she could scoop armfuls of clothes—bathing suit, underwear, towels, and shoes—off my bunk and the narrow aisle between. She dumped it all on her bed and wrinkled her nose as she sniffed the air out the porthole window. "Here's our lovely view." She pointed to the dock and stacks of steel shipping containers, three and four high. "Someday we'll see the sea out our porthole, but we'll have to bolt it shut if there's rough water, so waves don't crash in." She opened a narrow door and showed me a tiny metal-walled room. "This is our 'head.' Bathroom. But there's no water, so don't forget and use it by accident! You have to run for the bathrooms on the dock. A holy pain in the arse, if you ask me. The boys can pee off the fantail after dark, but not us girls." She rolled her eyes wearily. "Gotta go to my mess duty. I hate how they make the girls work in the galley so much. I wanna do real work to get this ship ready to sail."

I noticed a speckled black-and-white steno notebook open on her pillow, with scrawling messy handwriting in a mixture of bright felt-tip colors. "You keep a journal?"

She flipped it closed and shoved it under her pillow. "Yeah. Everyone wants to read what I'm writing, but I don't show anyone."

"I write in a journal too. I wouldn't show anyone what I write either."

She nodded, then bounded out the door and up the stairs. The room was suddenly quiet, and I plopped down on my bunk. I was both relieved to have a moment to myself and revved with excitement. I hoped she liked me.

I changed out of my linen suit, opened my duffel and pulled out a pair of blue shorts, a Mexican embroidered blouse, and sneakers. Then I gathered my sweaty hair back into a ponytail. I wanted to blend in but not look boring. I was already comparing myself to Kim. She was so—what? Lively and confident, compared to me. I felt humbled by something imposing about her, like she would always be ahead of me.

Even though I'd sent off packing lists to all the students from the school office, I had not followed the requirements. I did not have the required navy T-shirts and new blue jeans. I didn't have the Norwegian yellow heavy foul-weather gear or sou'wester fisherman's hat like in a painting of sailors in a terrible storm. They didn't sell those in Ohio. I'd packed my embroidered blouses, my Indian embroidered shirt with hood, my canvas pants with leather lace-up instead of a zipper. Unusual clothes were my way of saying "This is who I am." I couldn't bear to dress like everyone else if they were all wearing blue T-shirts and jeans.

Once I'd shoved my stuff into a few cupboards, I stretched out on my bunk. With the door closed, the bare metal-walled room seemed timeless. Maids had slept here forty years ago. As I relaxed from the rush of the day, an old sadness seeped into my body. I couldn't remember when I hadn't felt sad. When I stopped working hard to be friendly or helpful, this was what I sank back into. Did it come from trying to help my mom, or to keep my dad happy? I was so tired of feeling like I had to save other people.

Tears pricked my eyes, and I blinked them back, confused. I'd left home today. I'd wanted to go, but suddenly I missed my mom, my room and my favorite books. Everything was so different here. I wanted something to feel familiar. Then I remembered. I had my weird little brother here. Comforting, in a way.

All summer at the New York office, I knew the inside scoop on the school, the students, and teachers. I made Stephanie her cups of coffee all day, with the right amount of cream and sugar. I'd hand her the mug while she talked on the phone. When she winked at me, mouthing, "What a love," I felt a rush of pleasure. I listened to her phone conversations with parents, as I learned to answer the same questions when I fielded calls. Working with her, I'd never felt so important or appreciated. I was so busy and ahead of the game. But since I'd arrived at the ship, I already felt so behind. Everyone else knew what was going on. I was no longer living in Stephanie's shadow. In the hubbub of voices, I was plain old sad me, all over again. The girl whose father wouldn't let her go to college. I couldn't tell anyone that my dad sent me. It would sound like I was some kind of loser sent to reform school.

I remembered my journal. The first day I met Stephanie, she said, "I have something for you." She pulled out a thick, red, tooled-leather-bound book with the year 1963 embossed on it in gold. She'd found it in a box of donated books. It had empty lined pages, an old-fashioned gentleman's diary. She looked at me seriously. "This is for you to write the story of your year at sea. You need a book worthy of telling the story."

I cracked open the journal to the first page, found a pen, and wrote *October 9, 1971. I arrived on the* Antarna. This was what I wanted, time to write and read. So much to write. Where would I begin? Then a bell rang. I closed the journal and slipped it under my pillow.

In the hall, the girls came out of their cabins and said hello. Some of them looked vaguely familiar. I said, "Hi, I'm Elizabeth, from Ohio. Did I meet you at the office in New York?" What else could I say about myself? As we clomped up the steps, I talked to each one, repeating their names and where they were from. I kept them straight by their hair. The girl with curly brown hair to her shoulders was from Connecticut. Shy Jane with a short bowl haircut was from Michigan. Another girl with long straight blond hair was from Montana. "Wow," I said, "I've never met anyone from out west." The petite girl with almost waist-length hair was from Cincinnati. I said, "I'm from Cincinnati, too." Lisa with the sweetest smile and wavy brown hair was from Minnesota. I asked, "There are a lot of students from Minnesota. Do you all know each other?"

She laughed. "Oh, yeah," she said, with a distinctive lilting accent.

As we walked up the deck, I studied them closely. Did they shave their legs? Some yes, some no. Did they wear bras? Yes and no. I looked at each girl as we walked, and wondered, who would be a good friend?

A young boy ran up to the girls, with a Beatles thatch of hair and a wide grin, and he burrowed his way into the center of us as if he was trying to get away from someone. Two girls fussed over him. "Richie, how'd you get soot all over you?"

A tall black man in his thirties hurried after Richie, lecturing him. "If I ever catch you up in the smoke stack again . . . You have no idea how dangerous it is up there."

Richie feigned innocence. "I was just exploring the ship, Karl. I didn't know it was off limits." Karl shook his head and walked off, clearly irritated.

I realized who this towhead was. Stephanie had told me to give special attention to Richie Meeker, the son of TV actress Mary Tyler Moore. At fourteen, he was our youngest student, and he already seemed to be an expert at wiggling out of trouble. It soon became unspoken but clear: everyone knew who he was, and he knew we knew, and although none of us mentioned it, we watched out for him protectively.

As soon as Karl disappeared up the deck, Richie dashed in the opposite direction.

One of the girls leaned toward me, and murmured. "A limo delivered him. The driver stacked his bags on the dock and drove away." She looked around at the other girls, who nodded. "Everyone was watching from the railing."

Another girl picked up the story. "Karl was on the gangway." I knew Karl had just finished his four years in the Air Force, and was our scuba and photography teacher. "Richie looked at him like he was supposed to carry his stuff. Karl said, 'Get off your butt and carry your bags.' And Richie did." She shook her head. "Oh, Richie. He's a rascal." We smiled to each other, unified in a feeling of older sister warmth.

We followed the kid ringing the dinner bell as he walked. We girls stuck together as we edged through the boys milling around the deck. One by one the line of girls climbed down a steep metal ladder deep into the ship. I faced the ladder and held on tightly to the railings on either side. Pushing after us, a torrent of boys slid down the railing like it was a fireman's pole; some faced the room, their arms stretched backward like wings, and halfway down, they leapt into the air, to land with a crash. The noise in the metal-walled mess hall was deafening with fifty sweaty teenagers talking, laughing, and hooting. Teens filled the benches around a grid of metal-topped tables, with a lip that I realized was to keep plates from sliding off in storms. I didn't know where to sit but Lisa, the sweet girl, slid over and let me in on her bench.

"Listen up!" a man shouted over the hubbub. It was Ron, one of the teachers, tall and lean with no shirt, shoulder-length curly hair. "Meeting first, then food." The students grumbled. I remembered he'd graduated from Harvard and had asked for a weekend leave for a home football game. "Stephanie's been meeting with the teachers today to see how you guys are doing." Excitement rustled through the crowd on hearing her name. I hoped to say hi and get her special wink.

Ron said, "Quiet. I know it's discouraging that the ship's not ready to sail."

A boy shouted, "You got that straight!"

More grumbling followed. Ron said, "She'll be meeting with the owners and working on what needs to be done to get us out of here."

Another voice called out, "Like everything!" to a chorus of laughs.

"She'll give an update at muster tomorrow." Glancing at his notes, he added, "The refrigerator truck stopped working and no one noticed until it was too late. So that load of food some of you moved the other day went bad." A huge groan. He stayed upbeat. "So tonight we have turkey sandwiches, salad, and watermelon. Have a good dinner." He left quickly, escaping the next wave of complaints. I guessed then that I hadn't missed out a lot from being sick last week and arriving late.

Kim slid in next to me. She was done with food prep. "Those poor cooks. All the power comes from an extension cord from the dock, and the water comes from a hose." She raised her plastic glass. "Tastes like rubber. But drink up!"

Lisa asked me, "So how'd you get to this school?"

"That *New York Times* article last spring." I looked around the table. "Who else?"

A chorus of voices around our table said, "Yeah. Me, too." They said their names as they nodded to me, but I forgot them instantly.

"My dad roped my brother and me into this. He never asked if we wanted to go." I let my voice go sarcastic, how I talked in high school. I mimicked an old guy's voice. "'I'm shipping you off to shape up and work hard.' Dad thinks it's some strict sail training school." I gave a mock salute. "'Aye aye, Sir.' Wouldn't he die knowing it's a crazy hippie school."

A soft-spoken guy my age smiled across at me. "I'm Pogo. At my interview, I begged Stephanie to let me come. I had to sell my sailboat and paint houses all summer to raise enough money. I saw you when I had my interview."

Flustered, I said, "I saw so many come and go. Everyone blurs together. But I could probably recite your address. Did all of you come for the interview?"

Lisa shook her head. "It was too far to come from Minnesota. I talked to Stephanie on the phone."

A big guy laughed. "You missed out on going to the office? The Penthouse suite!" The others joined on the shared joke.

Lisa blushed. "What do you mean?"

As they told their stories of arriving at the office, I remembered Woodie and me, on our first taxi ride, from La Guardia to Manhattan. We'd never flown before, and had never gone to a big city on our own. The taxi let us off in front of an elegant Upper East side apartment building and I asked the uniformed doorman for the Oceanics School. He pointed us across a marble floor to the elevator. "Push the Penthouse button." We rose upward, our wide eyes reflected in polished brass, expecting luxury offices, but the door rumbled open to a grey hallway lined with closed doors. We stood there confused, until a door swung open and a few teenaged boys spilled out. "Hey, you're looking for us, right? The Oceanics School?"

Woodie and I were ushered into a narrow long room, the walls lined with shelves of stationary, brochures, envelopes. Three boys sat stuffing envelopes at the long wooden desk that ran the whole length of one wall. Then an assured young woman stepped forward and beamed at us and shook our hands. "I'm Stephanie Gallagher. You must be Woodie and Elizabeth." Compared to the long-haired boys in sloppy clothes, Stephanie was beautifully dressed in a fitted short dress, with glossy black hair. She smiled warmly, like she was including us in a secret. "You have to excuse our office. My husband Chick and I rented out our apartment downstairs. We've put everything we have into the school. We live and work up here. It's perfect, really." With an infectious enthusiasm, she cast a spell that drew me in from the start.

My interview was first while Woodie hung out with the students from the previous year. I followed her into a small room with a view of a roof garden, and she admired the macramé purse I'd spent hours knotting from white butcher twine. "You'll have to teach that on the ship." She leaned toward me, her eyes attentive, and asked a question that broke me open. "What's really important in your life?"

My miserable story poured out. Dad wouldn't let me go to college. I was caught between Dad's orders and Mom surviving in silence. I struggled with depression. I wanted to write. Books were everything to me.

"So, what do you read?" She invited me to tell her everything.

I showed her a little notebook I carried, with my reading list in the back. She took the book and ran her finger over my list. She was really paying attention, not like most adults who only glance at what teens do.

She looked up. "Camus's *L'Étranger*." She had a good accent. "Did you read it in French?"

"I started in French but had to finish it in English. My French isn't good enough yet."

"I've hired a native-born French teacher for the school. Lovely woman. Keep working on it." Then she ran her finger down the list. She smiled knowingly, "*The Harrad Experiment*. An experimental college with co-ed dorm rooms, right?"

"Yeah. I was trying to figure something out . . . " I paused awkwardly. "I was trying to decide if I should lose my virginity."

"Did the book help?"

"Yes," I answered with a wry smile. And she left it at that. I liked that. By the end of the interview, Stephanie seemed to know me better than I knew myself.

"You have to leave home. Come to New York and be my assistant for the summer." She mapped out my new life. I'd catalog the school library, be librarian on the ship, tutor writing, and yes, teach macramé.

My interview was both a confession and a seduction. I left devoted to her. All the other pressures in my life dissolved. Depression, worry about college, rebelling against my father, the sad slipping away from Alvin. All of that would recede. I was going to New York to be Stephanie's assistant.

When Woodie and I left Stephanie's office, the boys crowded around us at the elevator in the grey hallway. "You'll have a blast on the ship. A trip of a lifetime." They laughed uproariously, as if they knew a secret. "You'll never be the same."

•

At dinner down in the mess, I said, like I was telling a joke, "You guys come out of the interview with Stephanie in a kind of daze. Like you're stoned." I sounded like I was making fun of them, or like I smoked pot, which I didn't. I'd tried once but I didn't know how to inhale.

Kim was huffy; her voice fierce. "I loved my interview with Stephanie.

She's inspiring. I came here because I believe in her and want her school to work." She pushed off from the table, cleared her dishes, and left with the others.

I wanted to back up and explain what I meant, how the interview changed my life, but it was too late. I had a choice to make. Would I keep up my high school repertoire of striking out with sarcasm to sound smart? Or would I risk letting out my vulnerable self? Would people like me?

I watched Kim move around the crowded compartment. She tousled the hair of the younger ones and wrestled with a tall awkward boy. She put her hands on another boy's shoulders to give a mini shoulder massage. Watching her, I realized in a flash how cold my family was. We didn't reach out to comfort each other; we hardly ever touched. Sure, my brothers and I gave elbow pokes or punches for fun, but even when I left to fly to the ship, my mother gave the briefest of hugs, and my dad pounded on my back before lecturing me to work hard. I watched Kim and wanted her to ruffle my hair or throw her arm around me, like a sister.

•

After dinner, I walked back toward the stern, and passed the large open deck between the main and mizzen masts—I was starting to get some of these nautical terms straight. There in a circle were about ten teachers—a mixture of men, mostly in their twenties with longish hair and mustaches, a few women in shorts and peasant tops—and in the middle, looking organized and smartly outfitted was Stephanie, in red—her power dress. She was organizing her teaching team. So much weighed on her. It was a thrill to see her again.

I studied Stephanie with the practiced skill of a teenaged girl. Her glossy black hair was always brushed smooth, into a knot at the back of her neck. Her skin was pale with only a touch of blush, mascara, and rose lipstick. Stephanie was a dervish of activity and talk, in her rotating collection of bright dresses, stockings, and pumps. Even though I'd worked for her all summer, slept on the floor of the office, and greeted her every morning, I knew so little about her. She was driven to pull this school together and that's all we talked about. I was sure I had a personal private connection with her, that she relied on me, that she knew me. I think a lot of us felt that way about her.

But none of us knew she was only twenty-five, or that she had married at 19 to a wealthy film maker twenty years older who was hardly ever around while we were running the school from the attic office. I didn't know she'd gone to a Catholic convent school and had only a smattering of college. I don't think anyone in the school knew any of these things about her. She was someone who was consumed with visions of creating experiential educational opportunities on ships. She talked with so much self-assurance and momentum, that we all assumed too much about her expertise. Except perhaps the families who didn't sign up their children after their interviews, and my mother who met her briefly on a trip to New York the winter we were on the ship. My mom, even fifty years later, still glowers at the mention of Stephanie's name, claiming "I knew she was a flimflam artist the moment I met her. I didn't trust her for a minute. But your dad found her enchanting, and I couldn't say a word."

For me, she was my Pied Piper and I would follow her anywhere. Her array of sprightly outfits, in contrast to our wrinkled hippie clothes, were for me a radiant statement of her confidence. None of us had any idea what her youthful lack of experience would cost us.

I stood out of sight and watched them huddle closely together, note-pads on their laps, serious and intent. A murmur of voices, a few students' names. I wanted to tiptoe up and touch her shoulder for a quick hello, but I didn't dare interrupt.

I followed a group toward the stern where a group of boys were playing "Rocky Racoon" on their guitars. A lot of people were sprawled on a wide, curving continuous mahogany grid seat. When I leaned over the railing, the water was about fifteen feet below. Kim plopped down on the bench next to me. "See these holes in the grid? When waves in a storm crash up here, the water flows through the seat."

I bit my lip. Waves hit that high? I stuck my fingers through the spaces in the grid. She pointed to the three forward masts in a line toward the bow. "See how those masts have yardarms for square sails to hang down?"

I answered flatly, "Yeah, I know that." I wasn't stupid, I'd been studying the drawings of the ship.

She pointed to the last mast. "This is the jigger mast, which has a big gaff sail, the spanker, that extends out, called a fore and aft sail. This type of rig is what makes this ship a barque."

Instantly, I did feel stupid. I didn't know any of those terms.

She sighed happily. "Someday we'll have these sails up." She gazed up into the rigging, her face dreamy but her voice powerful. "It will be amazing." As Kim spoke with such certainty that the ship would sail, I let my little brother Woodie's dire predictions slide away. I didn't want to believe the ship was a wreck and dangerous. I wanted to believe what Kim and Stephanie believed. I latched on to their certainty.

Kim sprawled on the fantail seat now, her arms stretched back, her tangle of blond curls blowing in the breeze. "What a cool scene."

I sat stiffly with my knees together, watching everyone talking. She pointed to a spot on deck near the porch of the Smoking Room. "That's where I sleep outside every night. A lot of kids crash out here. Like a big sleepover party."

"I'll sleep out here too."

Next to us were the guitar boys and a girl. A tall, skinny guy with a huge tangle of curly hair was awkwardly funny, with a dry, flat voice. "Don't pay attention to my playing. I'm so bad at this. I'm Ted. I met you at the office."

Sitting very close to Ted was Jane, the shy girl with the bowl haircut who leaned over her guitar—they were clearly a couple. They were joined by some other boys who turned their backs to Kim and me. I sensed a vibe that they were a closed group.

Suddenly I was exhausted by the long day. I needed to sleep. People unrolled sleeping bags along the deck and spread out sheets and pillows. I hurried down to our cabin, collected my stuff, and my journal. I guessed everyone slept in their clothes.

•

Back up on deck, I chose a spot along the deck porch and spread out my sleeping bag. Looking up, I was surprised to see my brother. He sank down next to me, leaned against the wall with his knees up. He sniffed and kept his head down.

"Hey, Woodie, you okay?"

"No." He leaned his head down further and wiped his eyes with his sleeve.

"What happened?"

He spoke quietly, his voice cracking. "One of the teachers, Mike, told me I had a bad evaluation so far. Stephanie said if I didn't improve my attitude and stop being so negative . . . " He paused as if he could hardly say the words, ". . . she's sending me home."

He stopped and put his head on his knees. In a while he lifted his eyes, and looked at me, terrified. "I will die if I go home. I mean it. I have to stay." He pulled his arms around his chest.

Woodie and I hadn't ever mentioned what happened the day before he left for the ship. We wanted to scour it from our minds, but the threat of his being sent home brought it screaming back.

•

Late September, I'd flown home to get organized. Woodie was all packed and flying down to Miami early—the second student to arrive at the ship. Dad went on and on at dinner that night about how thrilled he was that we would get strong this year, develop our muscles. He announced that he would document before-and-after effects of our year on the ship by taking photos of us naked. He held up a Polaroid camera. "I bought this specially for the photos. First thing in the morning before Woodie's flight."

My brother and I glanced at each other and glowered. This was bull-shit. But we knew nothing we could say could make any difference. Dad's announcement dampened dinner, and the old feeling of suffocation came racing back. I couldn't wait to leave.

I went into Woodie's room after he'd gone to bed. He was lying on his back adjusting little dials on the new camera he'd bought. Dad had finally paid us the money he'd promised for our years of landscaping.

I sat on the end of his bed. "How's it been around here while I've been gone this summer?"

"Hell." His voice was flat and he kept his face behind the viewfinder on the camera while he turned the focus of the lens.

"You mean as bad as ever, or worse?" I asked, trying to get more information from him.

He sat up, and snapped his camera into the leather case. "Well, it was the usual this summer, with him getting on my case. But by the end of the summer, he went ape-shit crazy. But he wasn't going after me anymore, he was on Mom's case. About what a bad irresponsible mother she was. How going to college was changing her, and he wouldn't put up with it." He sighed. "That kind of shit, for hours every night, and Mom sat there, and didn't say a word. Hubbard and I would sneak out after we cleared the table and washed dishes, but even in our rooms, we could hear it."

He blew out a long breath of air. "That was the worst part. You couldn't escape his yelling any place in the house and sometimes it was during the day. Hell, I almost considered going back to high school while I waited to go to the ship." He added, with a thin smile, "Naah. I wouldn't do something that stupid." He looked at his bookcase. "I reread all my books to keep from going stir crazy. But tomorrow, I'm out of here." He lay back down on his pillows and rolled on his side. "Poor Mom, she has to stay."

I tiptoed out of his room and into mine.

Early in the morning, Woodie had his backpack and duffel bag loaded into Mom's VW bus for the ride to the airport. But Dad was ready to take pictures. He'd moved the dining room table so he had a clear space for us to stand. We both hid in our rooms, but we couldn't get away. Dad yelled "Let's get these photos done. Woodie first."

My fifteen-year-old brother walked into the dining room with its long glass walls in his underpants and stood in front of the wall. "For crying out loud," Dad said, "take off your underpants. This is to see how your body changes with puberty and how your muscles develop from a year of good hard work."

I waited in my underwear with a towel around me until he called. I saw my mom standing at the kitchen counter with a sponge in her hand, frozen, looking down.

Dad barked at Woodie. "First shot, forward. Profile right. Back view. Left profile. Okay, you're done."

Woodie raced past me to his room naked and slammed the door.

Dad shouted, "Elizabeth, your turn."

I called from my bedroom, "Do I have to take off my underwear?"

His voice cut me off. "You shouldn't have to ask that question. The body is a beautiful thing. There's nothing to be ashamed of. Haven't I been telling you that your whole lives?"

Seventeen years old, I came out with a towel around me, unwound it and set it on the table before I stood with my back to the wall. My twelve-year-old brother, Hubbard, was put in charge of the photos as they developed. He'd turned so his back was to me and he kept his head down. He was not going to the ship, so he didn't have to have his photos taken.

My father lectured. "Stop hunching over. Stand up straight. Be proud of your body. You are a beautiful young woman. All right, forward shot."

I stared across the room cutting off from my body in an old familiar way. He barked. "Turn, profile."

I chanted inside my mind. *I will freeze my body.*

"Turn. Back view."

I repeated my old mantra. *I will feel nothing.*

"Profile. Done." The camera whirred and spat black-squared photos.

He said, "Now that wasn't so bad, was it?" I grabbed my towel and ran back to my room. He called out to both of us, "When you get home next spring, we'll take a second round to compare."

My brother was dressed and standing in his doorway next to mine. We stared at each other. Woodie growled. "Over my dead body will he ever do this again."

We whispered the same words to each other. "That bastard. I hate him. I hate him."

After breakfast, right before Woodie was taken to the airport, he snuck into our parents' bedroom, stole the Polaroid camera, and hid it in his knapsack.

I hugged him goodbye. "See you in a week."

Dad sat in his chair, listening to jazz records, as my mom and Woodie drove down the driveway.

●

My brother and I never told anyone the bad stories. Stephanie didn't know what the threat of being sent home meant to him.

Woodie said, "I searched the ship until I found Stephanie and I told her I will do anything I can to stay. I will do the hardest jobs. I'll be positive. Just tell me. I can't go home." He sniffed as his eyes teared up again. "I begged."

He stared up into the rigging and rubbed his cheeks. "She says she believes me. I can stay on provisionally. But I have to go to classes. She's taking me out of the engine room. I'm to work on the rigging with the deck crew. They'll review how I'm doing in a few weeks." He looked exhausted, like an old man with the weight of the ship's failings on his shoulders.

Woodie put his head between his knees. I remembered how Kim was affectionate with the boys at dinner. I reached my hand out to pat his back, awkwardly, and I let it rest there and he didn't shrug it away. I didn't think I'd touched him much since he was a baby, except for little punches. At home, we were so isolated. We didn't have a couch like families who snuggled together when they watched TV. We would sit on Dad's modern office chairs at tables or on our beds. Dad told people who lived in the houses he designed that they couldn't have couches because they didn't work with the design of their house.

After a sigh, Woodie said, "I'm going to sleep on my bunk." I quickly pulled my hand away.

I thought about him as I lay on my sleeping bag looking up into the rigging. We grew up in rooms next to each other, watched each other across the dinner table, and rolled our eyes with exasperation over the same family craziness. But how much had we actually talked to each other? Maybe this was the longest we'd ever spoken. I hadn't been the kindest older sister, immersed in my own world, complaining about what he was doing, instead of trying to understand him. But he'd trusted me tonight. Would we be there for each other if we needed help on the ship?

•

Lying on my sleeping bag, even though I was looking into the masts and ropes above me, I was still back at home, remembering my own secrets I'd never told anyone, not even Alvin. But I wondered if my brother had known something wasn't right, since he slept in the room next to mine. From the time I was fourteen to sixteen, my father came into my bedroom on nights when Mom was away at college classes or meetings, and he gave me "backrubs" and "front rubs." He told me to take off my nightgown and lie naked while he massaged my back and then my front. I wonder if my brother overheard my dad complimenting my developing body as he stroked me. Dad assured me he would never touch my breasts or genitals but I knew I couldn't say "No, I don't want a massage." Instead, I froze my body when he touched me. I declared to myself in a silent cold fury, *I will feel nothing*, when his hand stroked below my waist, across my belly and hips and thighs. Until I finally pleaded, "I have school tomorrow. I have to go to sleep," and he'd finally leave.

I shivered as I lay on deck. I closed my eyes, and shook my head to get the memory out of my head. My brother and I had both escaped. Now that we were out, we would not go back, no matter what happened.

I lay there on the wooden deck with sleeping teens scattered around me. I pulled a sheet over me as the heat of the day cooled and the night darkened. I glanced up and saw the moon through the rigging. It jolted. *What happened?* The ship looked absolutely still, but the moon jumped again. I sat up, startled. I whispered to a guy lying on his sleeping bag nearby. "Do you see what the moon is doing?"

His arms were behind his head. He turned his head towards me and grinned. "Yeah, kind of crazy. The ship's rocking in the water. We don't even feel it. But it makes the moon look like it jumps. Damn cool. I can't wait to watch the stars jump around when we get out onto open ocean."

I lay back down and pulled up the sheet and listened to the warm night in a vast working harbor. It wasn't very dark. On the dock, street-lights shone on the stacked shipping containers. On the ship's walls, round wall lamps glowed like faint moons. I spotted Kim sitting nearby, writing in her journal.

How could I have forgotten? I jolted upright, pulled out my red leather journal, and opened to the first page. Where to start? Kim was scrawling furiously across the page. I couldn't let her get ahead of me.

•

A bell rang relentlessly. I pulled up the sheet, burrowed under my pillow to make the sound go away. A boy shouted, "Morning! Wake up you idiots! Time to get going." I jolted awake and sat up, disoriented. Around me at the fantail were lumpy piles of students in sleeping bags, their hair a tangle. Our covers were damp with morning dew from a chilly breeze off the water. I looked up at the jigger mast and boom gleaming in morning light reflected off the water. Some students staggered to standing but many didn't budge from their covers.

Someone yelled at the guy with the bell, "Oh, shut up, already! I heard you the first time."

Another person said, "Someone should shoot that guy." Laughter spread across the fantail. This was morning on the *Antarna*.

I leapt up and rushed: bedding and journal to the cabin, changed my clothes, brushed hair, ran down the gangway to the bathrooms on the dock, and finally in the crew mess hall I spooned down cold cereal. I joined the students on the foredeck for morning muster a few minutes early. Teachers and students leaned against the railing, milled around, or slumped half-asleep on coils of rope. Everyone looked rumpled. The boys looked like they hadn't brushed their hair for days. I rolled my eyes. How ripped and ragged can jeans get and still stay on? Their T-shirts smelled ripe. "Boys," I grumbled to myself. The girls clustered together. We looked fresh, our hair brushed, except I couldn't find Kim. I scanned the deck until I saw her perched on the top step of the ladder to the upper foredeck writing in her journal. I thought, *Wow, she's more serious about her journal than I am. So far.*

The hot sun was already beating down. Lanky Ron, the social studies teacher, in T-shirt and jeans, wiped sweat off his forehead and commenced with roll call, going down the line of names. Some were serious, while others worked the crowd for a laugh. "Yep." "Here." "Shouldn't be here." A few snickers and the boy bowed. How would I get to know all these people?

Some names were followed by long silences until someone explained. "He was on night watch." Or, "He's in the galley." Or, "He's still sleeping, couldn't wake him up." Names I'd typed in New York came to life and I remembered some of their stories. The First Nation brothers from Drift-pile, Alberta. The three Exeter guys who'd gotten kicked out a week before graduation because they had beer in their room. A wiry guy with a muscle T-shirt and the first tattoo I'd ever seen, a little anchor. I'd overheard him talk about fighting in Vietnam, but why would he be here? Then I remembered his file—he was eighteen, and just out of high school. Was he lying?

The roll call continued. I answered, "Here."

My brother followed me from across the deck, "Yes, Sir." He received a few laughs, but his voice was serious.

Stephanie had told me last summer that she was building a community with the right balance of positive students to bring up the negative ones. Listening to how they answered roll call, I could hear the boys who were sneering with attitude, the "I don't care, don't give a shit, you can't make me" ones. Stephanie had told parents, "The school isn't ultimately about sailing, it's about changing their lives."

I looked up into the rig of the foremast. The school was also about this ship and sailing. Would I ever be able to climb up there? I couldn't imagine I'd ever go out on one of those yardarms to stow the sails. I shivered. It was not time to climb the rigging. Not yet.

At the end of roll call, Stephanie slipped in next to Ron, radiant and smiling, in her blue dress with little white anchors. Her tortoise shell sunglasses were pushed up on her head. She held a thick sheaf of papers and called out, "A new student arrived last night. Zip." Everyone looked around but no one answered. "Anyone seen Zip?"

One kid said, "I signed him in on the gangway last night."

Another boy said, "I showed him to his bunk, but he didn't sleep there."

A kid snickered, "Smart idea if you ask me."

Stephanie sent Ron to look for Zip. Her voice was bright and strong. "We are ready to begin. We've had tremendous good fortune to get us to this point, and everything indicates we have fair winds ahead." Even though this sounded like the usual going-back-to-school speech, something was so compelling about Stephanie that even the snarky boys paid attention. She looked at each of us, and her eyes caught mine for a second. "The teachers tell me the community is getting off to an excellent start." She introduced the teachers. Tall Karl in fatigues. A petite blond actress with pigtails who directed plays. The elegant French teacher with a scarf. As she kept introducing the teachers, I connected their faces to the bios I'd typed. They announced their subjects: Mythology and Dreams, Math, Art, Oceanography, Native American Studies.

Stephanie caught my eye. "We have a student librarian and tutor, Elizabeth. She did a great job this summer organizing our five-thousand-book library. She'll get that set up very soon." She beamed at me and I was thrilled to have her notice me, but I was shy when the crowd looked at me.

She changed the subject, staying upbeat. "Now as for the ship, although she's not ready yet, our *Antarna* seems as eager to go as does the community!" She brought the ship into a personal relationship with us. The crowd murmured, but she maintained an engaging smile. "A certain amount of patience will be required. We have some good work to do, which is a great learning opportunity for us to get to know our ship. Then we'll be off, before you know it." The doubters stayed quiet, for now.

•

I remembered her in New York as she spoke persuasively, on the phone or in person, or rapid-fire typing, letters, proposals, information sheets. A magnetic force drew us in, students and parents, teachers, and so many donors. Stephanie's dynamism captivated her students to volunteer, and to sleep on her office floor, like me. We probably all thought we were her special assistant, her most valuable, most attentive, most attuned to what she needed, handing her the right letter when she needed it, or a fresh cup of coffee, thrilled by that special flash of a Stephanie smile.

One night in New York, Stephanie left a poem she'd written on my pillow. "When it seems as though you're all alone/ and maybe you really are/ for a time . . ." She wrote about how we have to leave home or we will lose what we want to hold on to. How the cold, outside world didn't know me yet, and that the world "like you . . . is afraid." My eyes filled with tears. How could she know how afraid I was? Here she was working so hard, but she took time to imagine what it was like for me in the office. "As the hectic days go by/ I see you working hard/ and I know you're being brave/ for I remember when I left home/ and almost died." She took the time to let me know that she understood me, and that meant the world to me.

•

I moved to the shade under the officer's bridge. I leaned against the white bulkhead, wilting in the muggy heat. I watched Stephanie and the crowd from there. Then I noticed a red-headed muscular guy with a backpack ambling up to stand in the back.

Stephanie was mapping out the hiring plan. "There are only a few truly qualified officers and seamen for ships of this sort. During the summer season, they are employed on sail training ships until October. My husband, Chick, is in Europe now, meeting with crew as soon as their ships dock. To draw on the best, we must be willing to wait. We have a temporary skeleton crew here to oversee our preparation for sailing."

She ended with a flourish, her voice on an upswing. "Who wants to volunteer to prepare the bowsprit to install? I need a team of students to scrape and paint it with red lead paint." A group of boys and girls stepped forward to volunteer. She applauded them. "That's great. You'll be working with our rigger. Meet down on the dock after muster, for tools, masks, and gloves. Have a great day on the ship!"

She turned the muster over to Mike, the mythology teacher, who looked kinda cool with a trim mustache, a white shirt, khaki pants, and a Panama hat. He carried on with class announcements. Stephanie rushed past me to the red-haired boy. "Zip! I expected you to call from the airport yesterday. How did you get here?"

He answered with an amused smile. "I took a couple of buses and walked. No problem." I was impressed—it was no big deal for him to walk miles carrying his heavy pack and duffel? I was fascinated with his confidence, remembering he was only sixteen.

Stephanie asked, "Where were you last night?"

"That bunk room was a bit stuffy for a boy used to a cattle ranch in the Sandhills of Nebraska." He talked with what I guessed was a Western drawl. "My apologizes for causing a stir."

Stephanie was so relieved she gave him a hug. "I'm so glad I don't have to call your mom and say that you're lost."

Zip smiled. "Don't worry about me. I'm never lost."

Meanwhile, Mike sped through the announcements. "Who's serious about learning scuba diving?"

About eight boys, including Zip, threw up their hands, and yelled, "Yes!"

Mike directed them. "Meet up with Karl and Peter at the bow. Muster's over. Everyone to the sign-up board."

Then Stephanie turned to me, flashing her winning smile before glancing at her checklist. Her voice was fast and businesslike. "Glad you've settled in. I need you to tutor a student. Have you met Richie yet?" I nodded with a smile. "He needs English and creative writing. And the library is a top priority. What's happening with that?"

I stammered. "I don't know where the boxes of books are."

Her voice rattled off my assignment. "Find where they're stored. Bring a few boxes to the mess hall. Novels, sea stuff, books about knots and ships, navigation. These students need books. Figure out where to set up the library. Keep me updated on your progress." And then she was gone.

My breath caught in my chest. She had a school to run, owners to meet, a sailing contract to hammer out. My time inside the private world of the New York office as her assistant was over. I was now a crew member, a student, a tutor, and librarian. I had to prove myself to her.

As the students dispersed, Kim appeared. "I'll show you the watch duty assignments. Everybody has watch jobs for two to four hours a day for a week. Working in the mess, or in the galley, or on the gangway, or when you wake people up." She smirked mischievously. "I can't wait to wake everyone up and get revenge on some of those asshole boys!"

Kim was talking to me! I was thrilled. Maybe I hadn't blown it last night. I bubbled with excitement. "Do you know what classes you're taking?" I rattled off mine: "I'm going to try snorkeling, never done it. Advanced French. And Mike's class on mythology and dreams. I can't remember my dreams, but I want to. And, of course, photography. This sure is a different kind of school. What about you?"

We walked down the deck, our heads close as we talked. She slid through the crowd, studied the watch duties, and reported back to me. "You're on galley with me. Welcome to the grease palace!" We scrawled our names on class signup sheets.

•

I discovered the books were in the shore office, under the lock and key of Mrs. Roberts, a dour middle-aged woman with tight-permed grey curls who worked for the owners of the ship. I introduced myself. "I'm the school librarian." She looked me over suspiciously. I persisted. "I cataloged thousands of books this summer." I wanted to inspire her to trust me and show her I was serious. "Where can I set up the library on the ship?"

She shook her head. "There's no place to set up a library." She was clearly possessive of the ship and was not thrilled to have us running around on board.

I gulped. "There has to be a library." That's why I was there on the ship. I had to make it happen. For the time being, I hauled out a few boxes before Mrs. Roberts once again locked the storeroom. A few of the students helped me haul them up the gangway and down the steep ladder into the crew mess.

When I rushed into the galley for lunch prep, the French chef glowered at me and spoke with a thick accent. "You're late." He had no patience. "Do the library on your own time. Watch duty comes first."

We cleaned the galley before they cooked lunch. In the hot metal room, one bulb hung from the ceiling on an extension cord, and a garden hose was secured by a rope from the porthole to the sink. Pots of water steamed on the stove. We scrubbed accumulated grime off counters and shelves, and scraped mold off the walls and floor while the French and Mexican cooks argued over the menu. Since the fresh food had rotted in the refrigerator truck, their menus had to be thrown out too. Their thickly accented misunderstandings were spiced with swearing but they finally decided: more sandwiches and powdered lemonade; buy food one day at a time; and no big orders until they could trust the refrigerator truck. For dinner: spaghetti for seventy-five, pasta sauce, and garlic bread.

I tried to cheer up the French cook by asking if we could make vichyssoise. I made sure to pronounce it right. He smiled for a moment, but then scowled. "No leeks until spring, and no chives in this uncivilized place." With a dramatic miserable shrug of his shoulders, he asked, "How could we chill it? *C'est impossible.*" In New York, Stephanie raved to the parents about our food expert, who had studied with health food guru Adelle Davis and would plan healthy meals on the ship. Little did we know the difficulties.

The art teacher, Jill, with long brown hair and an Indian scarf around her head, approached the cooks. "Could you cook a big pot of brown rice for lunch and dinner? Some of us are on a rice diet. It's very cleansing."

The French cook asked, "That's all you eat, rice?" The cooks agreed begrudgingly, but after she left, they shook their heads and shrugged, unified for one moment by their opinion of the hellhole galley, ruined food, and hippie diets.

When I was released from galley duty, I opened library boxes on a crew mess table. As students arrived, hot and sweaty from work, they swarmed around the piles. "Hey far out, Herman Hesse novels. Holy shit, all of them!" "A book of knots, perfect for what I need." "Solo circumnavigating the world? Dibs on that one." Books were passed around, and the boxes emptied. I was thrilled when they said, "We need more books." I was determined to find a place to put the library I'd organized.

•

In late August, Stephanie had sent me on a commuter flight to Watertown, New York, to catalog the books from last year's school, stored in a Victorian carriage house behind the home of supporters of the school. A taxi dropped me off at a large old house on a tree-lined street. A middle-aged woman showed me to the barn in back, where wide doors were propped open to reveal a mountain of boxes, four long folding tables, and a chair. I would sleep in the long-ago chauffeur's quarters, with a saggy metal bedstead, a rust-stained bathroom, and a hot plate. The phone on the wall, the owner impressed on me, was for emergency use only.

"I'll check in with Stephanie a couple times. May I call my mom to let her know where I am?" She stiffly allowed that I could. We devised a system. If a call was for me, they'd have the caller phone right back and I was to pick up. In my most earnest voice, I promised, "There won't be any calls. Stephanie is so grateful I can stay here." Then she left, and I was alone.

After the frenetic activity at the office, I was daunted by the silence in this barn and the nearly two hundred boxes. I'd created a modified Dewey decimal system for stickers on the spine, ordered an ink stamp to print *Property of the Oceanics School*, and envelopes to paste inside the back page, and devised a system of cards for checking out books. I hoped to be done in a week. Each box was a chaotic collection. I sorted books in rough categories on the long worktables: novels, history, math, navigation, sea stories, and a junk pile of old magazines and student notebooks, the detritus of the last school year. Outside, the rumble of a lawn mower, children on bikes, a basketball bouncing a few houses away. Finally hungry, I walked down the street to a mom-and-pop store for apples, a box of Rice Krispies, bananas, milk, and a sandwich. I unpacked and sorted under a dangling light bulb as night settled in, until I crashed and slept on the creaky narrow bed. I was up at dawn for more cereal and another day of books.

Mid-afternoon the phone rang. When it rang again a minute later. I lifted the wall phone, ready to say hello to Stephanie, but my father's voice barked at me. "You have a job to do young lady. You are disobeying me and disappointing Stephanie."

"What are you talking about?"

"Don't think I don't know what you are up to! You are turning your work time into a secret meeting with Alvin."

"Dad, what are you talking about? I haven't seen him all summer."

"Don't lie to me!" He was in one of his furies.

"Dad, stop!" I was firm. "I'm in a barn by myself. I'm working on library books. I am not supposed to use the house phone. I don't know what you are talking about. I have to get back to work."

"Don't you hang up on me!"

"Dad, this is someone's home phone. I have to get off. Goodbye."

I hung up and sat down on my folding chair; dazed, slammed by his fury, and confused. What in the world was going on? I'd sent a postcard to Alvin saying I was going to upstate New York, nothing more. "Oh God, Dad is nuts again." What a relief to be far away from his craziness all summer. I sliced open more boxes of books for a few hours, when two teens, a muscular black guy and a lanky white guy with backpacks walked down the driveway. I glanced up confused, slow to recognize Alvin's broad grin and our friend Terry's crazy hooting laugh. "Surprise! We found you!" Alvin threw his arms around me, his face so happy and hopeful to see me.

My heart sank, but I tried to look happy. "Oh, wow, gosh, how'd you get here?"

They grinned. "We hitched! You won't believe all the crazy rides from Ohio!" They recounted their exploits, laughing and carefree. "Your mom told us where you were. We snuck out and no one knows we're here."

I shook my head sadly. "Oh yes, they do. Dad's already gone ballistic."

"What?!"

The house phone rang again. I motioned them to be quiet, praying it wouldn't ring again. It did. This time it was Alvin's mom. "You put that son of mine on the phone right now."

I handed Alvin the phone and watched the joy and excitement of their surprise wash out of his lovely warm face. He turned his back on us, hunched over the phone, muttering single-word responses, before hanging up the phone. He turned back to us, deflated. "Can you believe it? She and your dad tracked us down. We are eighteen years old, and they're treating us like children. She's threatening to not pay my college fees if I don't get my ass out of here this minute."

The man of the house came out. "You're inconveniencing us with all these calls." He looked suspiciously at the two young men. "And who are these people?" I apologized profusely. "My old friends decided to surprise me." I tried to justify their visit. "They wanted to say goodbye before they start college. It's almost night. May they stay here and leave first thing in the morning? They have sleeping bags."

"Just this once," he said, but I could feel his disapproval as he walked back to the house.

I was so sick of our parents' drama since Alvin and I started dating two years before. I called home preemptively. "Dad, Alvin and Terry just arrived. It was a surprise. They'll leave in the morning." Then I grew fierce and clear. "Absolutely do not call this phone again. It is only for emergencies." Dad interrupted me, but I was firm, "They are leaving in the morning."

His voice rose. "Don't tell me what I can and can't do."

"Dad, these are *Stephanie's* friends who are letting me work here." I knew that her name alone would hold him in check. "You are intruding on her friends. Don't call here again. Goodbye."

But after I hung up the phone, I was exhausted from the storm of Dad's fury. I'd let down my guard. Alvin called his mom and told her the plan, and hung up quickly. I sighed. "So much for your sweet surprise." We walked into town for pizza. I looked at them on either side of me, and said, "Hey, we're the Mod Squad again, like last year." But the old joke about us looking like the TV trio fell flat. We were all sad, knowing it was our last walk together. Alvin was packed to leave for Ann Arbor. Terry had discovered the Bahá'í faith and was moving to Boston.

That night Terry slept on the garage floor, and Alvin shared my narrow creaking bed. We held on to each other, our last night together, feeling the fury of our parents. I confessed, "I can't make love." I didn't know if I could explain it. I loved him, but I wasn't in love anymore. His mother and my father had worked so hard to drive us apart "for our safety." I woke early and watched him sleep. We'd grown up together, learned to think and express ourselves, and had loved each other. When he woke up, we stroked each other's faces, tears running down our cheeks, hugging each other, with no words left to say.

After they walked toward the highway for the long hitch home, the barn was empty and cold as I ate my bowl of cereal. I turned up the radio as I sorted books, The disc jockey played Carole King's "It's Too Late" too many times that lonely week, until the books were packed for shipping to the school and I returned to the intensity of Stephanie's world.

•

After galley cleanup from lunch, I felt coated with grease, I collected my bathing suit and towel for snorkeling class. I walked across the causeway with about fifteen students to an aqua-colored motel that the school rented for classes, use of the pool, and showers. I changed into my bikini then slipped into the pool to join the class. Our teacher, Peter, who had a walrus-style mustache, handed out masks and breathing tubes. "Spit on the inside of the lens. Then rinse it off a little to keep it from fogging up the lens." He put on the mask and fit the mouthpiece, took a breath, and blew a firm blast of air to clear any water out of the tube. He was serious: "You could choke if there's water in the tube. That's all there is to it. Go for it!"

As I pulled on the mask, I imagined snorkeling over coral reefs watching multicolored fish, but the mask steamed and I couldn't see. I tried on the mouthpiece and blew out the water in the tube, but the moment I placed my masked face in the water, I panicked. I couldn't let myself breathe in and out of my mouth into the tube. Fear gripped me. How could I be sure the tube didn't have water in it? I pulled my face out of the water, wrenched off the mask, and gasped for air through my nose and mouth. I tried again: mask, mouthpiece, tube, face in the water, breathe through the tube, but then panic slammed me again.

When I was five, the ocean crashed over me at Nantucket. How I fought against the sucking pull of water after it knocked me into the sand.

I'd floundered, my arms whipping with nothing to hold on to, until I'd pushed myself to standing, choking on salt water.

I looked up at the pale blue sky to calm down. Okay. I'd try it again. But this time after the jolt of fear, I was nearly crying. I could almost hear Dad yelling at me to put my arms over my head, lean forward, and dive into the pool from the low board. I stood there shaking, as he lectured, and I whimpered, "I can't," until I finally climbed down off the board. He walked away in disgust.

The old feeling and voice in my head came back. "I can't do it." I couldn't put my face into the water. What was wrong with me? Why was I so afraid to breathe through the tube?

Peter swam over and reviewed the instructions. He was tall and tan, and they called him Fish. He seemed so at home in the water. I didn't want him to see how upset I was. I couldn't let anyone know how afraid I was. So I pretended. I nodded while he explained patiently, and I acted like I was following what he told me. I was relieved when he moved on to help another kid. I looked around, and hoped that no one had noticed me. I pulled off the mask and put the gear on the side of the pool. I watched the others snorkeling, like a little flotilla of submarines with their breathing tubes sticking out of the water. Once I'd relaxed, I was actually happy to float in the clean warm water in the sun. It was OK. No one was going to yell at me because I couldn't do it. I didn't have to learn everything. I could choose what I wanted to learn.

•

After dinner, the Mythology and Dreams class students gathered in old leather chairs around a table in the Smoking Room off the fantail. This group of students seemed interesting and serious: Ted and Daniel of the Exeter boys, Zip, Kim, Pogo from Maine, and a lanky boy with a quick smile. Mike introduced us to Carl Jung's life and work. He showed us photographs of a circular stone tower Jung had built, paintings of sacred circles called mandalas, and Jung's journals. I ran my finger over his illuminated handwritten journals, and over paintings of his dreams. I'd never seen anything like this.

Jung's journal drawings cracked open a doorway into a rich inner world I hadn't even imagined. I thought of what was valued at home, our glass house and modern furniture and abstract art. This world of dreams was so different. Mike spoke to us, saying, "You,"—and he paused to emphasize the word as he looked around at all of us—"You can connect with your inner world like Jung did." This was what I yearned for. But my spirits sank when he said, "All you have to do is start writing down your dreams."

Disappointment sank through me. I never remembered my dreams. Was this class going to be another thing I was crummy at, like snorkeling?

He asked, "Who remembers their dreams?" Half the students raised their hands and the rest of us wavered, not sure if we did. I looked down, disappointed in myself. Was there anything I was good at?

I'd had vivid nightmares since childhood—as vivid as a movie. I would follow a beautiful path through a leafy wood and slowly all the tree roots would turn into snakes, until the ground was writhing with them. I'd wake up, heart pounding.

Another nightmare happened at my grandmother's old farmhouse in upstate New York, my favorite place to be. In the dream, the house was filled with my cousins, aunts, and uncles. At night, when everyone was asleep, a fire would start burning in different parts of the house. I'd try to help people out, but I couldn't save anyone. I'd end up watching through French doors as the library and music room filled with flames, and I was frozen, helpless with fear.

Mike said, "Your assignment is to write down your dreams for the whole year."

Oh, no. I wanted to take this class, but what if I couldn't do the homework? Others also looked worried. One boy asked, "My dreams vanish right away. I can't remember them."

Kim agreed. "I remember a dream long enough to tell someone but then it's gone."

Zip wasn't worried. "I forget my dreams, but later, something reminds me of it, and I remember it."

I sank, discouraged. "I think I only have nightmares. Those aren't real dreams, are they?"

Mike looked at me thoughtfully, stroking his mustache, thinking before speaking. "They are a kind of dream that ends in the release of strong feelings, of fear or anxiety or anger." I nodded and looked down.

Mike asked, "How many of you think you never dream?" I joined a few of us holding up our hands tentatively. He smiled at us with certainty. "I promise you that you do dream and that you *will* start remembering them. As you go to sleep, say to yourself, 'I want to remember my dreams and I promise that I will write them down.'"

Our homework was to start a dream notebook and write down our dreams every night. He explained it might not happen right away, but he promised us that by the end of a month "you'll remember dreams almost every night." He added, "Don't worry. Your dreams will come." He beamed at us, like a magician. Then he paused and looked serious. "Your dreams are private. No one should look at your dream journal, unless you want to share it."

As I was leaving class with Kim and Pogo, Mike saw my ring, the silvery cube on my index finger. "Fool's gold?" He glanced at me. "That's perfect. Do you know about the tarot deck?"

I shrugged. "Not really. Fortune-teller cards, or something?"

"They're an ancient deck of symbolic cards that map out the hero's journey." He pointed to a copy of Joseph Campbell's *The Hero with a Thousand Faces*. "The first card is The Fool. An innocent figure, gaily setting off on his or her journey, having no idea what will come." He smiled. "Like all of us on this crazy ship. Remember in Shakespeare: 'A fool thinks himself to be wise, but a wise man knows himself to be a fool.' It's a powerful place to be, The Fool." He waved and left the room.

After class, Kim and I climbed down the ladder to our room, closed the door, and collapsed on our bunks. "What a day!" The dockyard light streaked through the porthole on to the dark cabin bulkhead. With no electricity to switch on, I enjoyed a strange comfort in the darkness, even though we knew so little about each other.

Kim chewed on her thumbnail. "So you grew up in Ohio? A town or the city?"

"I grew up in a village outside of Cincinnati." I told the same old story. "My dad's an architect and he designed a modern glass house. We moved into an unfinished shell and lived in it for a couple of years until we finished building it."

"You're kidding!" She sat up and looked at me intently.

Did she think this was weird? "Yeah, studs for walls. My brothers and I slept in one room and a curtain separated us from our parents. Every weekend a carpenter came and our whole family built the cabinets, and closets, and desks." I paused. Should I tell the upbeat version our family always tells, or did I want to tell what it was really like for me? I sighed. I didn't want to lie anymore.

"Our childhood ended when we built the house. All we did was work for years. My brothers and I had to beg to play with our friends. Dad would yell at us and say we couldn't stop until the day's jobs were done."

"We did the same exact thing."

"What do you mean?"

"My mom met my stepdad. He had two girls and she had us three girls. We all moved into the house he was building. It was a shell of plywood and glass, modern too. It had a toilet and water for the kitchen. I loved it. I learned to work with tools and build things. He always made things so fun for us."

Now it was my turn to stare at Kim. Did I love the work? I wanted to explain what I did. "I was good at trimming the walnut veneer cabinets. I sanded and oiled a million miles of wood!" But did I feel happy or proud of it? Dad made us feel trapped at home on weekends. I didn't want Kim to think I was a complainer but I had to be real, if I wanted a true friend. "But it wasn't fun. He always lectured us and made us feel that we weren't ever doing enough. He always said we had bad work habits, even though I don't know any other teens who labored as hard as we did every weekend."

Kim was caught up in her own memories. "We built a lot of stone walls and I got really good at it. He put in a bridge over a stream leading to the front door. But we played too. My stepdad made us swings and a trapeze."

I felt sad, thinking about my dad and the years of building his house and gardens. "My dad sucked most of the joy out of the work. Still, it's an awesome house. Especially the Great Room when it snows outside the long glass walls."

Kim nodded and went back to chewing her nails. "Our house is cool too. But our Great Room isn't done. No fireplace, only a stovepipe hanging from the ceiling." Her voice had a sadness to it that I didn't fully notice then. Later I'd wonder how she spoke of the house yet didn't say her step-dad wasn't there anymore. She didn't betray what she wasn't ready to talk about. We grabbed our sleeping bags and journals and soon were asleep on deck.

The next morning came in a rush—someone rang the bell, and we ran off into another day. When I was standing in line waiting for muster, I turned to Kim and asked, "Any dreams?" She grimaced and shook her head. I shook my head as well, but I was determined. I somehow believed that having real dreams would drive away the nightmares. I was also sure that dreams would somehow connect me to a deeper life where I could be more real, and where I would know what I was really thinking and feeling. I felt strangely peaceful. I was certain: dreams would come to the surface, and I'd remember them and write them down.

•

Stephanie showed up at muster in a yellow-and-white dress, her hair sleek in the morning sun, exuding enthusiasm as she pitched an important job.

"Our next priority is the water system. We have to clean out our potable water tank before we can run clean water through the system." The team needed to siphon out the dirty water, scrape down the rust in the tank, and then seal the tank surface with cement paint. I tried to imagine a tank big enough to carry all the water needed for a ship at sea for a long time. She said, "It's a dirty job and we need volunteers. Don't sign up if you get claustrophobic in tight spaces. It's a tank you have to climb down into." I smiled, thinking that she talked like a used car salesman. The worse the job, the more exciting she made it sound. "Volunteers?"

No one stepped forward. Her voice was strong and clear. "Okay, we need volunteers. This is essential to get the ship out to sea." Shy Jane stepped forward, with her flash of a smile. "Thanks, Jane." Then another awkward pause, and my brother Woodie stepped forward. Steph gave him a nod. "Good choice, Woodie." My brother looked down but straightened his shoulders. Then a few others. Ted, the Exeter guy who played guitar; Pogo; and a few other guys. I knew I couldn't do it. I'm horribly claustrophobic in tight spaces, which thank goodness gave me an excuse, because I didn't want to get so disgustingly dirty.

After muster it was time for my first tutoring session with Richie. Before everyone dispersed to their jobs, I asked Karl, the scuba teacher, "Any idea where I can find Richie?"

Karl laughed. "Who knows where that boy is hiding! He's the laziest kid I ever saw." He shook his head. "Never knew a boy more determined not to work. He hides all over this ship. I found him inside the smokestack tower." We looked up to the enormous white stack, rising ten feet above the second story aft of the bridge.

Karl looked exasperated. "Fortunately, there's a screen to keep things from falling in and to keep hot sparks from flying out. Crazy kid." He ran his hand through his short afro, shaking his head. "We found him in the chain locker having a nap. If they'd used the motor to move heavy chains to lower the anchor, he'd have been crushed." Karl finished, "So, no, I haven't seen him. But watch out when he gives you that innocent little smile! He's up to something."

I intercepted Richie as he strode up the gangway. "It's time for our tutoring session at the Smoking Room." Once we sat in the leather chairs, he laid his head down on his arm and started doodling.

I said, "Let's start with creative writing. What do you like to do?"

He lifted his head and gave me a charming grin. "Get out of stuff I don't want to do." When I eyed him seriously, he said, "Okay, I like to drive. I steal my mom's Jaguar whenever I want." He sat up straighter, asserting himself.

"Richie, you're only fourteen." But he'd snagged me on one of my favorite topics and I had to ask. "What kind of Jaguar?"

"XKE. It's red. Convertible."

"That's so crazy. My dad has a white one. He won't let me drive it yet."

Richie stared at me. "Why do you wait for him to let you? Just take it!"

I groaned. "You don't know my dad!"

He stretched out his legs like he was in the car and showed me how he'd pretended to drive until he could hold down the pedals. Then he'd take off driving in the Beverly Hills, but the police always caught him and took him home. "Mom tries to be angry at me. Makes rules to punish me. But I know how to charm her." He grinned his adorable smile.

"Richie! That's a great story to write." I was trying to entice him to want to do something. People had probably been doing that his whole life.

He looked serious, and appealed to me. "I'll start writing if you get me some water. I'm so thirsty."

Of course, I fetched him a glass of water, idiot that I was, and of course, he was gone when I returned. Only his name scribbled on a crumpled piece of paper.

•

I was discouraged. I had to tutor Richie because Stephanie depended on me, and I needed her approval to justify being on the ship. And then the library—I felt a clench of pressure. I had to find a place for the library. I dashed down to the dock before lunch for more books. Mrs. Roberts looked up from her desk, clearly annoyed. "You again?" I apologized and explained that I needed more books. "Hurry up, I'm about to leave." I located the boxes of books on navigation and sailing, and books on Jung for the dream class, and I called for help to haul them to the crew mess. But now I found library books left on benches, tables, on deck, and on the floor next to bunks. I gathered them up and returned them to the mess. Where would I put the library? I searched through every compartment on the ship that wasn't locked, but there were no empty shelves anywhere.

When I saw Richie at lunch, he raised his water glass to me and flashed his charming smile, like a dare. Richie: I, Me: 0. To him it was a joke, but a pressure weighed on me. I had to prove myself to Stephanie. I had to tutor him, and I had to find a place for the library.

Woodie and the water tank crew arrived for lunch. They'd rinsed off with clean water and were still dripping when they climbed down the ladder. They acted loopy, bumped into each other, and laughed, as they loaded their plates with sandwiches and filled glasses of lemonade.

"How's it going in the water tank?"

Woodie explained the job. "We set up a hose to siphon out the rusty water to dump it into a drain on the dock. No wonder all the water lines to the heads and galley are foul."

Jane ran her hand over her rust-splattered arms. "We wire brushed the walls."

"It messes with your head down there," Ted said, "especially after you start to get woozy."

I was worried about them. "You have to stay safe!"

Ted laughed. "If we were going to stay safe, we wouldn't have stepped onto this ship!" He added with cheer, "But mateys, we are 'Salty Dogs!'"

Pogo tied a red bandana around his head to hold his chin length hair out of his eyes. "I nearly passed out in there. Jane and Matt pulled me up the narrow steel ladder and shoved me out the tiny crawl hatch. It's a good thing we're scrawny." He explained how they worked in teams, rotating out every twenty minutes or so. "I guess I stayed in too long."

I envied their enthusiasm as they headed back to work. None of us seemed to notice how we had become accustomed to danger. After dinner, as a crowd gathered at the fantail for photography class, Kim and I wrote like mad in our journals, trying to cram in everything important. Kim sprawled her legs wide like she'd climbed off a horse, while I sat primly with knees together. Then Zip, the red-headed farm boy with wide side-burns, let loose a long loud belch, and Kim and I both looked up. I was appalled and she was thrilled.

Kim let loose a huge belch, and she and Zip went at it like a battle of bullfrogs. Kim was competitive and determined to surpass Zip's belching. The crowd of adolescent boys loved the duel. I was disgusted. Nice girls are not supposed to burp. I must have looked like I had a lemon in my mouth. When Kim glared at me, I was sure she'd written me off as a stupid prissy girl.

When Karl called out, "So who brought a camera?" the belching stopped on a dime. About twenty students and a few teachers on the curved bench faced Karl, who wore fatigue pants and the cleanest T-shirt on the ship. "We start with the basics, so you'll know what you're doing." After the first technical hour, once I'd learned how to use the dials and settings on my new camera, we focused on composition.

I squinted through the lens, holding the heavy camera with my left hand while focusing with my right. I crouched, moving forward and back. Peering through the camera gave me permission to get up close to people. Looking through the lens was liberating. I could stare at people, and zero in on them through the lens, and I didn't feel self-conscious or shy. I shivered with anticipation. I was going to capture the year on film, *and* in my journal. I loved that word, *capture*.

It was getting dark by the time we put away our cameras. The guitar players hunched over, working on Dylan's "Like a Rolling Stone." They practiced until the chords were right, and they started quietly, singing along.

I lay back on the fantail with the others, like spokes on a wheel, fanning around the stern of the ship. I didn't even know who all these kids were, but we joined in, singing together. A wave of contentment spread through me as the stars came out. I heard the song like I'd never heard it before, because now I was living "Like a Rolling Stone," no longer having a home, carried along in an unknown that we were creating. Maybe this school could feel really better than home. I joined the voices around me, gently singing with the guitars, and the words settled over us lightly like the evening dew.

•

The next day when the water tank crew collapsed on the benches for lunch with their plate of sandwiches, Pogo tried to express his wonder. "You've never seen dark like this." He was fascinated. "You know how when you wake up in the dark, that after a while your eyes adjust and you begin to pick out details." He shook his head. "But in the tank, the darkness sucks up all the light. I wave my hands in front of my eyes and see nothing."

Jane laughed, and crinkled her nose under her John Lennon-style round metal frames. "When we climb down the ladder, it's like the darkness eats up the light."

They had to feel their way in the darkness with their hands on the walls. Pogo made the work sound so interesting, "The walls of the tank feel like tree bark with scales."

Woodie no longer sounded negative. He was getting into it. "It's like the tunnel in *The Hobbit*, in the dragon's mountain."

"That's it!" Pogo agreed.

My brother teased me. "I bet you still haven't read *The Hobbit*! I'm sure there's a copy in those library boxes of yours!"

I was a reading snob. I didn't read fantasy; I was into serious literary fiction. I shrugged to show him I was waffling, but not convinced.

Pogo was unexpectedly firm. "If you're interested in Carl Jung's philosophy, you'll see all the elements of the hero's journey in *The Hobbit*." Understanding this felt really important to him.

"OK," I conceded. "You guys convinced me."

•

After dinner, a group of us gathered at the fantail as the sunset faded and the sky turned a deep blue. Ted's unruly curls covered his face as he leaned over his guitar, playing the haunting tune of "Wooden Ships" by Crosby, Stills & Nash. I hummed along.

Pogo stared at the rigging, "I wonder if that song inspired all of us to come."

"How do you guys all know each other?" I asked.

Pogo shrugged. "We met painting a house in Maine last summer."

Ted looked up from his guitar. "But it really all began the day I ran into Daniel on the path from the library at Exeter." He smiled wryly across at Daniel. "You got us all into this mess." Daniel looked up from a Jung paperback and nodded in his serious philosophical way. Ted nodded. "He told me he wasn't going to college but was joining a program on a school ship and sailing across the ocean. I thought it sounded cool and said maybe I should do that."

I was incredulous. "You made a decision, just like that?"

"I had to break it to my parents."

"How did that go?" I was amazed. He told his parents what he wanted to do? No one else in the group acted as if this was unusual.

"Not as badly as you might suspect. I wrote a heartfelt letter to Stephanie, making my case to be admitted. She loved my letter so much, she included it in her marketing literature." Ted met Pogo house painting. Then he met Jane. "She was a science whiz interning at a genetics laboratory nearby.

Jane giggled. "He talked all of us into going to Oceanics. I used every cent I'd saved working odd jobs through high school to get here." I learned Jane was working class from Detroit, and had never seen the ocean until this summer in Maine.

Pogo drove to New York to convince Stephanie he would be a great asset for the ship even if he had no money. He worked overtime painting, sold his sailboat, and his parents agreed to pay his airfare. "My parents were happy to see me leave my girlfriend." He looked embarrassed. "She's twenty-five and was my French teacher."

Ted grinned. "Hard to imagine Pogo as the focus of gossip all over the island." Pogo looked down, clearly embarrassed. But I was strangely relieved. His story meant I wasn't the only kid sent here to break up a couple.

Ted finished, "So now you've been introduced to my posse. Good thing I brought them, because this school sure is a weird group of rag-amuffins and misfits." We all looked around at each other and nodded in agreement.

Then Pogo asked, "What about you, Elizabeth, what was your life like before the ship? How did you end up here?"

My mind blanked out. I'd settled into listening to everyone else talk. When someone asked me to talk, I sometimes didn't know what to say. I preferred asking questions. I latched onto the myth of my old life. "I live in a village in Ohio full of big old houses. We live in a glass house my dad designed and we built. We have big gardens and grow our own food. My mom makes bread and is involved in prison reform. My dad used to be a racing car driver." People always responded to that. I distracted attention from myself with stories about my dad. But I was missing from this picture. I was defining myself by my parents and what they did. I didn't even know what to say about myself. I felt so boring compared to everyone else.

•

When the water tank team emerged from sealing the tank on the final day of the project, they shivered in the heat. Pogo said, "The cement paint gets so hot when it cures. It's freezing out here!" Jane, Pogo, Ted, and Woodie brushed cement streaks on each other's chests, as they laughed and posed for the photographers practicing with their new cameras. They seemed oddly heroic to me. Would I have kept working at a hard miserable job for as long as they had? Maybe my dad was right about me, that I didn't persevere, that I didn't have a good work ethic.

•

Darkness settled after a long day, and a lot of us sprawled on the fantail bench. I watched the masts and lines above us as the stars came out. Some older boys started telling stories and asking questions; their voices, some deep or raspy or giggling like they were high. I couldn't identify who was talking, but it didn't really matter, it was just cool to listen to voices in the dark.

"Think there are ghosts on this ship?"

"Maybe, if you think of the guy they put in the refrigerator."

"Who got put in our fridge?"

"Generalissimo Trujillo, dictator of the Dominican Republic."

"No shit, he was a bad dude, death squads and stuff. How did he get in our fridge?"

"He was assassinated. But his family stole his body, and a lot of gold, and they snuck him aboard the ship, when it was called the *Angelita* after his daughter. The ship sailed towards Spain. But there was a revolution on the island and the new government ordered the ship back."

"Where do you hear this crazy stuff?"

"Alfonso, the chief engineer, knows all the stories. Actually, the General was in a lead-lined coffin."

"I still don't want to eat food from the refrigerator."

"Don't worry. None of them work anyway."

"OK, so do you know why we have such big freezers?"

There was a pause, and I ventured to speak up. I'd heard this from Stephanie. "Marjorie Merriweather Post of Post cereals, had this ship built, in 1931 in Germany, during the Depression. With so many big freezers they so could go sailing for half the year and eat fresh frozen food. And get away from those depressing food lines."

"Humm. Rich people. They live in another world."

"Like how we are living?"

"Not exactly. We're the peons working our asses off putting this ship back together."

"You got that right."

"So, do you think there are ghosts?"

"I don't want to think about it. I'm going to sleep."

The SEA CLOUD Sail Diagram

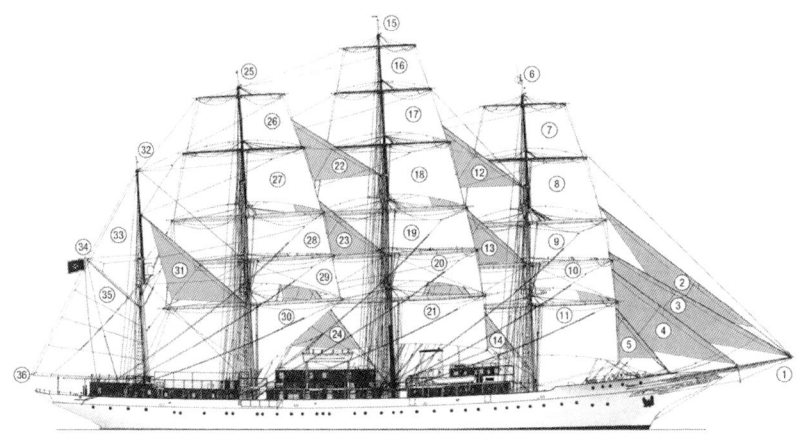

1	Bowsprit	13	Main Topgallant Staysail	25	Mizzen Mast
2	Flying Jib	14	Main Topmast Staysail	26	Mizzen Royal
3	Outer Jib	15	Main Mast	27	Mizzen Topgallant
4	Inner Jib	16	Sky Sail	28	Mizzen Upper Topsail
5	Fore Topmast Staysail	17	Main Royal	29	Mizzen Lower Topsail
6	Fore Mast	18	Main Topgallant	30	Mizzen Course
7	Fore Royal	19	Main Upper Topsail	31	SpankerTopmastStaysail
8	Fore Topgallant	20	Main Lower Topsail	32	Spanker Mast
9	Fore Upper Topsail	21	Main Course	33	Spanker Gaff Topsail
10	Fore Lower Topsail	22	Mizzen Royal Staysail	34	Spanker Gaff
11	Fore Course	23	Mizzen Topgallant Staysail	35	Spanker Sail
12	Main Royal Staysail	24	Mizzen Topmast Staysail	36	Spanker Boom

A few days later, after muster, Stephanie addressed us again, sunglasses covering her eyes against the morning glare. "Four years ago, this ship was restored in Italy to the tune of one and a half million dollars. The teak decks were replaced."

I looked down at the oil-stained filthy deck. This ship was perfect four years ago? Now it looked like a ramshackle old mansion; the mahogany cabin walls were peeling; the metal hull was streaked with rust.

"The rigging on the four masts was replaced, and the hull was scraped and painted. But when the ship arrived in Miami, U.S. Customs charged import duties on the value of the whole ship. The owners didn't have that kind of money, so the ship was impounded and has sat here ever since."

It was hard to believe that after all that work in Italy, the owners left it sitting for years rather than pay the duty. That was so weird. No wonder they were so happy when Oceanics came along to lease the ship and Stephanie said she'd pay the import duties and repairs. They'd get their ship fixed up and the school would get to sail it. What a great arrangement for everyone. But then I groaned to myself. All we had to do was get it going again!

Stephanie introduced a middle-aged man in worn jeans, with a knife strapped to his belt. "We hired David, with years of experience on square-rigged ships, to climb aloft, inspect the rigging, and assess the impact of four years of tropical weather."

The day before, we'd watched him climb the rigging on each mast, to the very top and back down again. He said to us, "Take a look at the ratlines." I squinted to look up at the hundreds of ratlines that formed the climbing rungs on each mast. His voice was strangely flat and firm. "The ratlines are rotting. Many gave way as I climbed."

I gasped, and my chest tightened. He said, "I've got a math problem. If you add up all the rigging, and the ratlines, how much rope does a ship this size require?" All our heads strained to look from one mast to the next to the next. Some people mumbled numbers. All I could think was *oh, shit* instead of calculating anything.

A younger boy called out earnestly, "A lot."

Another said seriously, "Miles. Miles of rope."

David nodded. "That's about right. Miles." The weight of his words sank into me and through the crowd of students and teachers. His face was serious. "All the running lines need to be replaced." I stared at the vast web of lines from the masts to the railings. "At sea, the strength of the lines means the difference between life and death. When the rigging begins to rot, wooden blocks and tackles up in the rigging can tumble down in a storm. These are called 'deadeyes' for a reason."

I spotted several wooden blocks in the ropes high above us. I'd never known fear on the ship until now. The mood on deck sobered.

Even Steph looked daunted. She said, "No one goes aloft until the ratlines are replaced. All students, teachers, and crew will learn to splice." We looked around at each other. We're the ones who are going to do this work? "The splicing will be done on deck and a trained team will work with David in the rigging. Go collect your sheath knives and wear them on your belts. Take off any rings and necklaces. You don't want them caught in the lines. In fifteen minutes, you'll meet with David on the mizzen deck to learn to splice." Then she beamed. "This is all part of the greatest year of your education."

Pogo and Ted were energized. "This is definitely salty." The rest of us hurried to our bunks, bewildered. I put my fool's gold ring away in a drawer. I pulled out my knife and fastened the sheath on to my belt, like I was putting on a costume. How could I make any difference with the ship's rigging? I didn't care how positive Kim was, or what Stephanie promised, the sheer volume of the miles of ropes above us in the rigging weighed on me. We'd never get this boat sailing.

Fifty students, ten teachers, and a few of the crew crowded around David, our bosun. We sat, knelt, and stood, to watch and listen. "You'll learn to do this so well you'll be able to do this in your sleep." A quick smile flashed across his kind, worn face.

He laid out the five tools we needed: a rigging knife; a sharpening stone; a "fid" (a pointed conical piece of wood); a "marlin spike," which looked like a very heavy nail about six inches long; and a sturdy, large-eyed "whipping needle." "Think safety at all times. Keep the knife in your sheath on your hip when not in use. Before you lay aloft to climb the rigging, your knife must have a lanyard, a thin line attaching it to your sheath." I imagined a knife falling from the rigging. I nodded, humbly, yes.

I mimed the angle at which he held the knife as he cut a length of rope. "This is how you'll make a ratline. You'll make a loop in the rope to weave the strands of rope back into the body of the rope." He worked slowly, plying the spike to open up spaces in the twisted rope. I glanced around and everyone was attentive. He wove in the strands of rope, with a thick needle and tarred twine. An idea struck me. I loved hand-sewing. I'd made my clothes since eighth grade and was really good at macrame. This was thicker rope. I bet I could get the hang of this.

David showed us how to climb, stepping up from the rail onto the lowest part of the rig heading up toward the mast. He talked to all of us as he took his first steps upward. "It's like a ladder: you don't hold on to the rungs, or in this case the battens, called rat boards, you hold on to the rails, which we call shrouds, on either side." On the deck, I mimicked his movements. He pointed up to the first platform. "After you get there, the rest of the way up into the rig is climbing on rope ratlines. That's what we have to replace."

Woodie nudged me; his face excited. "Going up there is my idea of a good time."

I couldn't imagine I'd ever go up there. I studied David's every move as he climbed from the first platform straight upward toward the second platform. He stepped on a ratline and the rope gave way. His foot sank into empty space, while he held on, three or four stories above us. Many of us gasped. I grabbed on to Woodie's shoulder.

By the time David climbed back down to the deck, he faced a subdued audience of students and teachers. David admonished us. "Your lives are in each other's hands. You have to splice these ratlines perfectly. They can't be sloppy or loose. Your lives depend on the ratlines."

My first attempts, the splice was lumpy, the strands fighting against me. They didn't want to be forced through the rope. But by the third try I'd begun to get a feel for how to bend the rope with the twist rather than fighting against it. Then the strands snuggled in together, a successful splice. I liked the oily texture and smoky smell of the whipping twine as I pulled it tight to secure the splice. David watched as I finished. "Nice job. You're ready to splice ratlines."

"Thanks." I flushed with pride and looked down at my splice, the elegance of the interwoven rope. My obsession with macramé, knotting butcher's string into belts and purses for years, had paid off. I glanced around the deck to see how others were doing. Some kids had tangles of rope in their hands. Others struggled to get the spike through the rope twists. David moved slowly around the deck, squatting down to guide a student as he worked. I spotted Richie with a ragged mound of tangled ropes. With an expensive knife, he was still working at it. Even though the work was daunting, I felt a glimmer of hope as, one splice at a time, we became the crew.

I had no interest in climbing up the ratlines. I was more afraid of heights than I was afraid to snorkel. But I was a splicer.

•

After lunch, I joined a group of approved splicers, where we were handed measured pieces of rope. To escape the afternoon sun, we retreated under shade and sat cross-legged and talked while we worked. I didn't feel as shy. I asked Rick, a clean-cut guy with short hair, "How did you get here?"

He was thoughtful and serious. "I was so disgusted with high school. I thought about joining the Navy. I wasn't doing well and was getting into fights when boys harassed me. My dad's a World War II vet. I've always felt so proud of him." He paused to pull the strands snug, and then told of how he grew up thinking that serving in the military was his responsibility. "I had no idea that my dad couldn't bear the idea of my going to Vietnam. This school was his last-ditch plan to keep me from enlisting. I love sailing, so I couldn't pass it up." I looked at his earnest face. He was dressed in a clean T-shirt and khaki shorts. Not everybody here was a hippie. And I wasn't the only one whose dad had sent them here.

An awkward, shy guy, Bruce, said, "My dad gave me a choice. He'd pay for one year of school, college or whatever. It was up to me to choose. But I don't know what I want to study. Then he saw *the article*." A chuckle went around the circle.

We passed around ropes and tools, as our fingers worked the strands, and we admired our rising pile of ratlines. I'd never hung out with a group of guys working together. I liked being included, and how we were quiet, until someone told a story, and then we were quiet again as we worked.

Harry, with thick black hair, spoke slowly and softly, with a singing cadence that I figured out was a Canadian and a First Nation accent. "My sister Rose works for the Chiefs of the Six Nations in Ottawa. She met Stephanie when Rose gave a talk about the need to get our youth off the Reserve. Stephanie told her about this sailing high school. Rose spoke about me and my brother, Freddie. We wrote long letters to Stephanie, and she gave us full scholarships."

At the office I'd read their letters written in very uniform cursive. I asked, "Where'd you grow up?"

"By the Driftpile River in Alberta on my great grandfather's land. We are Métis, meaning half-French, and half-Cree and Sioux." As he talked, his ancestors were so alive for him. He spoke of generations back, fur traders, translators, and gold prospectors. At the end he said with distinct pride, "We belong to the Queen. We are British subjects. We made our treaty with Queen Victoria who came to visit our reserves." Listening to Harry, I realized how limited my view of the world was.

Harry said, "We've never seen the ocean before! We are so grateful to Stephanie. This is the greatest thing that could have ever happened in our lives." His adoration and gratitude to Stephanie sounded even stronger than mine.

We worked, sometimes stretching our arms, circling our necks and shoulders when our muscles tightened. The rope was rough on my fingers, leaving raw skin and blisters, but over the days ahead, I would develop calluses from pulling the strands tight.

Zip walked over and crouched down to admire our pile of spliced ratlines. "I'd love to work in the rigging, but they need me back in the engine room."

I was so curious about him. "How's a farm boy like you so good in the engine room?"

Zip grinned. "I worked all summer on a cattle ranch forty miles from town, so we had to fix everything. Engines, pumps, tractors, irrigation equipment. So here, I'm up for whatever job they throw at me. Get salt out of the electrical boards? Sure! Water pumps working? OK! Lights on? Winches working? Let's do it!" He laughed as he stood up to leave. "It's my idea of a good time."

As we cleaned up before dinner, I collected our rigging tools and put them in a wooden box. As I'd spliced, I'd felt calm and hadn't worried about sounding smart or sarcastic. I liked working with these quiet guys and listening to their stories. Here I was, wearing blue jean overalls for the first time, with my hair in a braid to keep it out of my face—feeling content.

David chose a select crew of riggers who would climb the rigging to cut and replace ratlines as they went—the ones I knew were Rick, Pogo, and tall, lanky, super-shy Grant, who loved heights; they'd work with a few paid crew members. They practiced the knots they'd need aloft: half-hitches, clove hitch, lashings. Ted rated the rigging team "Seriously Salty." Kim walked up to David. Her face was determined and I knew how badly she wanted to join their ranks, but David shook his head. "Only a few experienced sailors are allowed aloft for now." She scowled and rushed off.

Stephanie talked with David and inspected our splices. Then she walked over to a cluster of teachers who didn't look happy, arms crossed or hands on their hips. I picked up the last tools slowly so I could listen. The math teacher complained. "How can we teach classes with our students working all day?" I found a broom to sweep the deck and moved closer.

Stephanie said, "This rigging work was unexpected. We'll never get out of here until it's done. Once at sea, we'll have more time for classes. For now, everyone," she paused to look at each of them, "will work most of the day. Schedule your classes close to dinner. Splice with your students and discuss issues of history or politics as you work, or the math involved in the rig. Get to know the students better." They nodded sullenly and walked away toward the galley for dinner. When Steph saw me noticeably close by, she winked, and I grinned back.

The next morning at muster, Stephanie sounded chipper and determined. "I'm flying back to New York to fundraise for miles of rope. I'll write to your parents to say what a great job you are doing." Afterward, students clustered around her, and her face lit up as she talked to each one, touched them on the shoulder, or patted them on the back. Kim threw her arm over my shoulder, and I let myself lean against her. "I admire her so much," she said. "She had an idea and is making it happen."

"When I arrived, I missed working with Stephanie." I glanced at Kim. "But now the ship is where I want to be." I watched Stephanie. "Look how she loves all of us. I want this crazy school to work so badly."

Kim gushed. "I love her so much." I nodded to agree. We were Stephanie's girls.

Before Steph left, she checked her list, gave last messages to teachers and crew. When she turned to me, all she said was, "Library and Richie." I gave her a grin and a mock salute.

That night, when I made my weekly collect call home from the payphone on the dock, Dad wanted to hear everything about the ship. I was afraid he'd worry about the rotten rigging.

His voice boomed with excitement. "Frankly, I'm jealous. I'd give anything to be down there working on the rigging. This is what I hoped for you and Woodie, good hard work." I told him I was good at splicing, and didn't cringe when he said he was proud of me. I relaxed my protective guard with him.

I told him about my struggle with the library. "I can't find any place to put it. There aren't any bulkheads where we can set up bookshelves. Stephanie's depending on me."

Ever the architect, he said, "You're going to have to think outside the box. Find a place with good access for the students, so the books are part of their daily life." I was pleased. I'd become one of his architectural students, with a puzzle to figure out.

When Mom came on the phone, she told me how busy she was with her college classes and tutoring Hubbard; then her voice lowered, "... and dealing with your dad." When I mentioned the ship, she had to put dinner on the table. She didn't even want to hear about it.

•

I woke up slowly, opening my eyes for a quick glance around. It was still dark. I remembered as if through a fog. I was in our VW bus with my mom. She was driving and we were going over a river on a bridge with no sides. I was afraid we'd fall off. My mind said, "This is a dream. I have to write the dream before it fades." I wanted to stay asleep, but I'd promised myself I'd write it down. But it was so short and nothing really happened. Should I wait for a longer, bigger, more exciting dream? I wanted to go back to asleep, but Mike had said don't judge it. Write whatever you remember.

I sat up and fished around under my pillow for the journal. I pulled on my glasses and wrote. The VW with my mom, where were we going? We were driving on a bridge over a slow muddy river. What kind of bridge? A metal grid with no sides. I was afraid we would slide off into the water. I stashed the pen between the pages, curled on my side and slipped back into sleep.

I woke up again at dawn. Kim sat on her covers and scrawled in her journal. I whispered, "A dream?" She nodded without looking up. I stayed silent, not wanting her to lose her dream. I pulled out my journal and opened the page. There it was. The first dream I'd written down. I read the words, closed my eyes, and I was back in the dream. My mom shifted gears, her hands on the wheel, and I looked out the window at the slippery bridge. I closed the pages, like I'd caught something precious and I didn't want it to get away.

•

That evening after dinner, we brought our dream books to class, and settled around the circular table in the Smoking Room. I told Mike I'd written down my first dream. "But it's really short and kind of stupid. I almost didn't write it down. But you told us to, so I did."

Mike leaned forward. "I am so glad. You are letting your inner self know that you are listening." He turned to the ones who hadn't written down a dream yet and encouraged them to keep asking themselves to remember a dream before they went to sleep.

"But what do I do now that I wrote it down?"

Mike leaned back and brushed his bangs to the side. "Jung believed that our dreams are windows into our inner world, showing how our psyche is hard at work. We are trying to understand our life and grow while we are asleep, and the images in the dream help us see what is going on."

"But how does a little dream about me and my mom in a car mean anything?"

"Tell us the dream."

I read the dream from my journal, as he nodded and jotted down notes. "Explore this like a puzzle. All the parts of the dream are you. You are traveling, and the parent in you is driving the vehicle of your life."

I groaned. "I'm still a kid getting driven around by my mom. Oh, God, that's so embarrassing!"

"But in the dream, you are also the mother driving the car. You are also the bridge. Describe your bridge." He looked at me intently.

I'd never had a class or a teacher that paid this much attention to what I thought, let alone what I dreamed. But I was confused. How could I be a bridge? "It's a narrow metal grid, a 'singing' bridge like we have in Ohio, and it's crossing a little river. It doesn't have any sides and I can slide off the bridge."

"Bridges take you from one place to another in your life. You are certainly on a bridge time in your life. But you don't feel safe."

I felt the fear from the dream. "I feel so scared that I could slide into the muddy river, but nothing bad is happening. Yet." This little scrap of a dream said so much about me.

He nodded, closed his eyes for a moment and then looked out the porthole as he pulled his thoughts together. "Don't waste your time worrying about what might happen." Then he grinned. "It's better to deal with scary events when they actually happen. We can't even imagine what they will be!" I wrote his words as fast as I could in my journal.

•

Doing so much splicing work, I didn't know when to tutor Richie. The next day when I saw him at lunch, we were both holding our plates of food. "Let's go up on deck and have lunch." He tried to scoot away, but I smiled my charming smile and said, "Stephanie's orders."

He hung his head. "OK," he said, in mock misery.

We sat in the shade on a deck bench with a view of the Coast Guard station. "What do you like to read?"

He stuffed his mouth with a sandwich and chewed a long time before sighing. "I don't like to read books. I do like my mom's letters, but I'm allergic to her perfume and I can't read cursive. So Harry reads them to me. He's in the bunk below me."

Maybe Richie was dyslexic. "Have you heard of *The Hobbit?*"

"Yeah, but I'm waiting for the movie."

I wondered if Richie had trouble reading and did everything he could to hide it. "Pogo and my brother say I have to read it. How about we pass it back and forth and read it out loud?"

"Let's flip a coin to see who reads first?" He pulled a handful of coins out of his pocket and handed me a silver dollar. "Heads wins."

I got heads, and read first. *In a hole in the ground there lived a hobbit. Not a nasty, dirty wet hole, . . . it was a hobbit hole, and that means comfort.*

He smiled and stretched out on the deck bench. "I love being read to. You're good at this." I flushed, and kept going, caught up in the story, forgetting that we were supposed to trade off reading. Then I noticed his even, slow breath, his closed eyes. What a joke on me—he'd fallen asleep. I left him there and rejoined my splicing team. At dinner, when I saw Richie, he grinned at me. Had he been pretending or was he really sleeping? Was this Richie: 2, Me: 0? I didn't know.

Afterwards Richie showed up with his sleeping bag at the fantail in the evening when I was writing in my journal before I went to sleep. "Read to me?" he would ask. He'd found a copy of *The Hobbit* and handed it over. Sometimes I said yes and read. We'd talk about which characters we liked and he'd beg me to keep going if we were in an exciting place. Sometimes I said I had too much to write. Either way, he climbed into his sleeping bag and fell asleep, curled up next to me. I patted his head good night, feeling like Wendy with my own Lost Boy. I was also relieved that I could tell Stephanie that we were having a literature class together.

•

I'd been on the ship about ten days when someone woke me up by shaking my shoulder. "It's 4 a.m. Your watch." I jolted awake to see an indigo night sky. I tiptoed around the sleeping figures on deck, dumped my bedding on my bunk, put on a clean shirt, and took my post at the gangway. It was a quiet night except for the clanging echoing from the engine room door.

Each hour, I went on fire watch, moving along all the decks and hallways quickly. I worried about leaving the gangway unguarded. Rats or bad guys could sneak on board.

At 7 a.m., I circled the decks, rang the bell, and forced myself to yell, "Morning!" I hated being loud. When a workman signed in the log and wrote the date, I realized it was my eighteenth birthday. I decided to keep it a secret because people didn't really know me yet, and I didn't want anyone to make a big deal about how I could go drinking now. Getting drunk sounded so disgusting and stupid anyway.

A huge yellow truck backed toward our ship's bow, positioning a crane on the concrete dock. The bowsprit was going to be installed. A team of students and crew had removed the tangled cables, then had scraped and painted the bowsprit with red lead paint to prevent rusting. When I watched the burly engineers stand around the thirty-foot long tapered steel pipe on the dock, I decided this was the best birthday present ever. Having a bowsprit meant that our ship would sail.

When my watch ended at 8 a.m., I ran into Pogo. "Let's watch them install the bowsprit." We hurried down the gangway toward the crane. At the ship's bow was our figurehead, a huge carved golden eagle. I wrinkled my nose. "He looks so mean with his hooked beak. I wish we had a mermaid."

"I see bald eagles a lot in Maine. They are majestic and powerful. They crash into the water and fly off with fish in their claws." Pogo looked toward the harbor. "The sea can be brutal. I think it's good to have a fierce figurehead to guide us through storms."

"Do you think we'll ever be in a real storm?" I shivered even imagining it.

"Chances are..." He shrugged in his cute bashful way. "We better get back to work if we ever want to get out of here!" His warmth diffused my fear.

After lunch, I pulled Kim down the gangway to watch from the dock. A welder with a metal helmet and face guard sat astride the bowsprit, which was now fastened to the ship. His legs clamped around the belly of the metal shaft as he leaned forward.

Kim snorted. "Looks like he's bareback on a big mare, with his heels in her flanks ready to go on a run." We both dashed away from the shower of sparks from the welding torch. We made sure we didn't look toward the blinding-white flame..

In the afternoon, as I stood on the dock with the Salty Dogs—Ted, Rick, Pogo, and David the rigger. I saw something that made me gasp. "There's someone all the way up at the top of the mast, attaching cables!"

Ted said, "That's where a triangular jib will fly between the mast and the bowsprit. Wish that was me up there!"

Rick glanced down from the bowsprit to where the ship meets the water. "You know that dolphins will leap in the bow wave when we sail?"

"I can't wait!"

•

After dinner, as a bunch of us talked at the fantail, the sky darkened, the wind picked up, and suddenly it was pouring. We ran under the porch roof, and most of us huddled along the back wall. But I stepped to the edge where a wall of water poured off the roof in sheets. I extended my arm through the silvery rain. It felt magical, like I was standing behind a waterfall.

Kim dove into the tumult of rain on the back deck and danced. Water sheeted down her face and body, her blond curls were glued to her neck, her eyes closed, and her face turned up to the sky like she was in love. I'd never seen anyone look so alive except in the Woodstock movie. Kim just did things. She didn't think about it or wait. She jumped in.

Watching Kim in the rain, I was jealous. She was so clearly a wild girl, the opposite of me. I wasn't brave enough; I didn't fight when frightened. I'd learned too well to stay quiet, to hide. Some things never leave a person. I was convinced a huge blinking neon arrow pointed down from the sky at me, making it clear that I was not—say it: *not*—a wild girl. I felt awash in a wave of sadness.

Do wild girls think the rest of us are wimps? Did Kim glance around impatiently and wish someone would dance with her in the rain? Maybe she didn't even think about us because she was so immersed in her own wet, slippery self. She was more alive than us—than me.

I wished, with all my heart, that someday I'd dance in a downpour. That I would be brave and wild in my way. Then the rain stopped, the dark clouds blew out to sea, and Kim shook off water like a dog running out of a lake. She shouted to the sky. "I groove on flexibility! Rain is so flexible!" She sounded like a beat poet, like Alan Ginsberg or Jack Kerouac, or like she was stoned from the rain. She skipped past me, toward Zip and Lisa, who grasped her outstretched hands. Kim was inspired. "My philosophy of life is flexibility. I dig people who are flexible." They hooted like coyotes.

I knew that I was not a flexible person. I was not cool or groovy. How could my happiness in the rain have vanished so fast? Did I have any idea what my philosophy of life was? I was certain I was already behind because I didn't know what I believed.

Maybe the best thing for me was to go to my cabin and write and then I'd feel more alive. I loved the slippery way I felt as I put words together, flowing like a stream. Maybe writing was as magical as dancing in the rain. Maybe I had a secret, wild, flexible girl living inside of me, where no one watched. But maybe someday, someone would read what I wrote and see me, and know who I was.

•

A few days later, Mrs. Roberts, with her hair-sprayed grey curls, and glasses on a chain, rounded up the girls after lunch. Her voice was disdainful. "I am taking you below decks to explain your maid's duties for the care of the staterooms."

A chorus of us girls squawked. "Maids?!"

I hissed at Kim, "Be good."

She whispered back, "We have to stop splicing to be maids? Fuck this shit."

I smiled a frozen smile toward Mrs. Roberts, then hid behind a girl so I could speak quietly yet urgently to Kim. "This is for Stephanie's sake, so we can have donors visit to help raise money."

The boys on the mizzen deck watched with curiosity as the six girls were herded along. Mrs. Roberts pulled out her heavy collection of keys and opened a secret locked door in a mahogany-paneled bulkhead. We stepped out of the bright sunny deck and entered a dark wood-paneled room with a grid of beams overhead, and formal furnishings, a piano, and a fireplace.

Kim murmured, "A fucking fireplace on a ship!"

We passed through a grand dining room with chandeliers and paintings of ships before we descended a curving staircase into a dark hallway. Mrs. Roberts clicked on her flashlight and pointed out a line of paneled doors. She led us into Marjorie Merriweather Post's stateroom, all white and gold décor, four-poster bed, marble fireplace mantle, mirrors, and delicate lampshades. She fawned over the luxury details, but hissed at us not to sit on the chairs or touch anything.

Kim snarled, "She's making sure our dirty little paws don't sully anything." I glared at her as we moved through seven staterooms in the pale curtained light from the portholes. Ruffled canopy beds, matching coverlets, delicate furniture and stuffy air; I lost track of all the rooms.

Mrs. Roberts pulled back the curtains in the last two rooms. "You will be making up these beds with clean linens for our guests. I expect nurse's tucks on the corners."

Lisa gave her sweetest Minnesota smile. "My mother taught me."

I said, "I learned the nurse's tuck in Brownies."

Kim's head whipped in my direction. "You're shitting me!"

I whispered, "The Cub Scouts went camping and we Brownies learned to make beds."

Kim and I rolled our eyes and grinned at each other as we both said: "Pathetic."

Mrs. Rodgers ordered, "I want every surface dusted." She handed out feather dusters and cloths, and we wiped down end tables, mantles, chandeliers, and bedsteads. Then she herded us along to the last door, which she unlocked.

Sunlight poured down a steep stairway. We were back in our maid's quarters. So this was how the maids moved in and out of the staterooms. After Mrs. Rodgers locked the door, she sniffed disapprovingly at us and our messy rooms. Once we were sure she was out of earshot, we let loose, hooting with laughter.

A few afternoons later, before dinner, Kim blew into our narrow bunk room like a foul wind. I was writing in my journal. She growled, "Fuck," as she threw her dirty clothes off the bed. "Fuck," as she slammed a pillow behind her. "Fuck," as she kicked off her shoes, sank down, and leaned against the wall and glowered.

I finally asked. "What are you upset about?" I didn't tell her how rude I thought it was to say *that* word.

"I was down in the officer's mess stamping and sorting laundry *alone* instead of working on deck." Her upper lip curled. "I came to this ship to learn something, and it's not stamping stupid laundry." She scowled. "These male chauvinistic attitudes are killing me." She hit the bulkhead with her fist. "I know one fucking thing: I'm going to make the right connections. I'll show them. I will ignore their ridicule. I'm going to do such a good job on splicing, they can't ignore me. Then they won't be so damned cocky." She threw open her journal, and with a red Sharpie, she wrote rapidly. "I'll show them."

I glanced at my watch. "Gotta go. I'm on serving duty for dinner in the officer's mess." I sat up to brush my hair, and pulled it back with a barrette, before leaving.

Kim glared at me. "See where they're keeping us, belowdecks. Fuck the galley."

A strange thing happened to me when people were mad and swearing. I wanted to cry. It was like I was trapped at home and Dad was yelling at me again. But I was also ashamed that I wasn't fighting to make things better, like Kim. I tried to be upbeat. "I'm on duty with some nice guys. I'm not really ready to go up in the rig. Not yet, anyway."

Kim's eyes lit up. "That's what I'll do. Climb the rig on my own. That will be frigging amazing." She laced her shoes tightly and dashed out before I stood up from my bunk.

After dinner in the hot galley, as moths careened into the dangling light bulb, I wiped down the stainless steel sinks and counters. Kim snuck up behind me, threw her arms around my waist, and lifted me off the ground.

"Kim, let me down!"

Plopping my feet back down, she laughed. "I fucking did it!" Then she glanced around, "Any good leftovers?" She grabbed a dirty plate with food left on it.

"What!?"

Her blond curls were smashed under a bandana tied around her head. She talked as she chewed, radiant. "Man, I climbed the rig to the first platform. Alone!" Everyone had been below for dinner when she'd climbed up on the railing. "I pretended I was climbing a ladder to a roof. I didn't look down, I climbed." She extended her arms up as if reaching for the next hold. "I held on tight and kept going up!"

"But Kim, it's so high!" I felt almost dizzy thinking of her up there.

"It is so high! I finally looked out at the harbor. I had such a rush." She held out her quivering filthy hands. "I didn't freak out, but I hated climbing down."

She seized my hands and danced me around. "I can't wait until I fly free and loose up there, while the ship is sailing! Shit, I'm going to have to get so frigging brave!"

I gazed at her, with pride and envy. My eyes teared up. "You already are, Kim. You are so *fucking* brave." In that moment, I felt secretly brave, too. It was the first time I'd said *that* word out loud.

At muster our scuba teachers, Karl and Peter, asked, "Who can describe a barnacle?"

One of the smart-ass boys said, "It's those white things stuck to the dock and on shells."

A nerdy kid asked, "Is it a mollusk, like a mussel or clam?" Peter shook his head.

Pogo spoke up. "They are arthropods, in the family of Crustacea, the same family as lobsters and crabs." We looked at him, impressed. Pogo shrugged. "What can I say? I'm a scientist's kid who grew up on an island."

Karl followed up. "OK, so who's seen barnacles on the hulls of boats?" A lot of students raised their hands except for those of us who grew up inland. "What do you do with barnacles on a boat?"

Rick said, "You scrape them off every year when you prepare a boat for launching in the summer."

I wondered what was the big deal about barnacles.

Peter asked, "How thick do you think barnacles might get if a ship has sat in tropical waters for..." He paused. "For, let's say, four years?"

Ted ventured, "How about an inch a year?"

Peter said, "Yesterday we put on our scuba equipment and explored under our ship."

Yikes, this was not an academic or scientific conversation.

"The barnacles are at least a foot thick on this hull. Like a coral reef extending downward from the bottom of the ship."

Oh shit. That sounded bad.

Karl explained. "Barnacles this thick create a serious drag on the ship. It makes the engines work much harder to propel it." Stephanie had conferred with experts. The ship had to go to dry dock before we could sail. A dry dock was a large empty structure filled with water that the ship motored into. The door was closed, the water drained (hence the *dry* dock), the ship's hull was braced so it would stay on an even keel, and then it could be scraped, repaired, and painted. "Stephanie is working on what port can take our ship."

Oh, no. I was flooded with questions. Who would pay for it, the school or the owners? For us, "the owners" were a mystery. We would later learn that one man owned the boat, but he had hired a ship's representative to pretend to be the owner and to manage legal issues. We called these men we'd never met, who held so much control over our lives, "the owners." Would they pay for dry dock? None of us had any idea.

Karl explained how the scuba students were needed for a special job, before we could motor to dry dock. On the hull of the ship were large rectangular screens, the size and weight of subway grates, called sea chests. They had to be scraped to uncover salt water intake valves. These valves kept the ship's combined 6,000-horsepower engines cooled. If not enough water circulated, the engines could overheat and catch fire. I worried: A fire at sea? This was a speedy introduction to Danger at Sea 101. But when I glanced around at the kids on deck, no one looked scared. We were already used to so much danger, we didn't even notice. We were also teenagers. Immortals.

•

The next morning, standing at the railing, I watched the scuba team prepare on the dock. Once they'd pulled on their wetsuits, they looked professional as they fitted on masks and hooked up breathing tubes to air tanks on their backs. They put on weight belts and watches, then checked each other's gear and gauges before descending a wooden ladder and slipping underwater. I couldn't believe they weren't afraid to go into the dark water.

At lunch when the scuba team sat down with their plates, Kim and I joined them. She asked, "What's it like under the ship?"

Zip said, "It's amazing down there. Like a reef growing down instead of up."

Bruce added, "You wouldn't know it was a ship if you didn't see the propellers and rudder."

Zip enthused. "There are sponges, and anemones, and lobsters. It's crazy, crawling with life! I even saw a moray eel poking its head out of the reef, right on the other side of this metal hull." He banged the bulkhead with his hand.

●

A few days later when Karl and the scuba crew discussed the day's work scraping barnacles off the sea chests, Richie slipped in close. I nudged Kim and Pogo, nodding my head toward Richie. He wanted something. As Karl walked off to dinner with the teachers in the officer's mess, Richie followed him, tugging on his shirt to make him stop before he stepped into the teachers' sanctuary. Richie begged, "Please teach me to dive."

Karl looked at him. "You have got to be kidding, Richie. You don't do any work on the ship. Why should I take all that time to train you when we have this huge job to do?"

Richie pleaded. "Believe me, I'll work harder than anyone scraping barnacles."

Karl was curt. "You start doing your watch job. After you've done it every day for a week, then come talk to me. Not another word until then." He moved into the officer's mess and closed the door quickly.

●

We seven girls and three women teachers were surrounded by skin all day. Sixty boys and men with tan, dirty skin. There were torsos of all kinds: sweaty, scrawny, baby-fat, muscled, long, lean, solid-bellied, pudgy, and mostly bare-chested. From young teens to nearly seventy years old, our guys looked like the Dirty Dozen had showed up at Woodstock. The boys and men were a dirt-streaked palette—saw-dusted, rust-scraped, bruised, rope-burned, speckled with hemp dust from splicing, sweat-greased—from pallid oil-greyed, freckled sunburned white-boy tan to sun-deepened browns, beige to olive, red bronze to jet black skin. An international bunch: American, Canadian, Scandinavian, Mexican, Caribbean, First Nation, Japanese. Below decks, the engine room boys and oilers, who chain-smoked on breaks from their twelve-hour shifts, were ghostly pale. Most boys wore jeans or shorts, many riding too low on lean hip bones. And those jeans were ripped, torn, frayed at knees and thighs, ragged and tattered across their asses, revealing more than most of us girls wanted to see.

We girls watched bodies all day. Muscles pulled taut over rippled lines of ribs. Back bones protruded as boys leaned forward to cut rope or scrub decks. Their wing bones moved like curved blades under their skin as they reached out their shoulders to haul on lines. Belly-button hollows, deep or shallow. Outcroppings of short hairs on upper chests, low-belly curls surged upward from low-rider jeans. Blond, brown, and black hairs furred their legs and tops of toes. The boys stretched out on deck chairs, on the deck, in the rigging, like models in a life drawing class, their torsos were studies in light and shadow—sprawling, napping, resting, working. And we watched.

Did we girls have any idea how much they noticed us? Our long and short, thin and rounded, legs and arms, rosy, ruddy, tanned, freckled, some shaved, some not, washed and creamed, or grimy and callused, American white girls and one always-elegant French woman. They watched our manes of hair swish from chins to shoulders to waists—straight, curls, and waves. Some girls worked in bikini tops and short shorts or short dresses, but I kept my torso covered, in long sleeves and bell bottoms. I didn't want to be exposed or watched.

•

One Sunday off, the girls hung out in the maid's quarters hallway and the metal door at the top of the companionway was shut. We had to talk. We sprawled on the carpet, leaned against the walls, compared notes, complained, and admired.

Joyce stroked her long blond hair. "I think that Mark guy is hot."

The girl with freckles and long brown hair grimaced. "That boy Luke's a pig."

Kim said, "He's actually sweet when he's not coming off like a rapist."

Another girl frowned. "So many guys act like sex fiends. They stare at us all the time."

Kim wrinkled her nose with disgust. "Some guys sneak their hands on me when we wrestle. But their advances don't mean shit to me." She scoffed. "They're boys. I want a man."

I murmured, "No one makes advances at me."

Kim snorted. "Of course they don't. You're too couth!" She rolled on her belly, propped herself up on her elbows, and grinned at me.

I crossed my long legs, straightened my back, and protested haughtily. "Well, you are *uncouth*." But I knew what she meant. I'd always been this way. I couldn't have wrestled with boys if I'd tried. I'd always felt prim and proper.

What we really wanted to know was "Which boy do you like? Who has a crush?" But we didn't ask.

Kim said, "Zip is pretty amazing. Never met a Western farm boy superjock before." Did we all blush? Zip fascinated us. What would he do next? We wanted to hear his laugh, and we watched him move his muscled, lean body in low-rider jeans.

Kim said, "He's not a hick, even though he plays the part. He's actually very intellectual. Surprised the shit out of me."

I teased her. "So, Miss Perceptive missed something?" I'd written him off because of his belching, but now I paid closer attention.

Zip chatted with all the girls, but we could tell that he liked Lisa, and this embarrassed her. When people talked about Zip, we always eyed Lisa.

Then someone asked, "What are we going to do about sex?" We all tensed, on high alert, like an electrical charge had surged through the room.

Lisa blushed. "Because of my Christian faith, I feel good about being a virgin. I'm waiting until I get married."

I looked down at the carpet while I talked. "My mom always said you stay a virgin until you get married. But then last year she said, 'If you really love someone and you're going to get married, then it's OK.'" Had she been giving me permission to have sex with Alvin?

Kim was straightforward. "Before I made love last year, I felt inferior, like a little kid. I didn't feel whole or complete." She was sprawled and relaxed, lying on her back with her feet up against the wall. "Sex is really deep for me, almost sacred." She gazed at the ceiling. "But I have to love the guy and be into the same things."

Other girls talked about boyfriends at home, but they didn't reveal if they'd had sex.

I confessed. "I really loved my first boyfriend, but I was so scared about sex." I glanced around the room. "But now that I've done it, even if I just kiss a guy, they assume we'll have sex. I hate that. I get worried sick about whether I'm pregnant until my period starts. I want to go back to kissing."

We all nodded. Kissing wasn't so complicated and wouldn't ruin our lives. The girl who flirted talked about sex like it was a bargaining chip. How she promised the guy that they would have sex eventually, but not yet. "Otherwise, the guy wouldn't want to be with me." Kim and I caught each other's eyes. We hated flirting. We wanted only to be really ourselves with a guy we liked.

One girl asked, "But in case we do have sex. What do we do to be safe?"

One girl had brought a diaphragm, just in case. "Anybody else?" Everyone shook their heads. No. We didn't have anything for birth control.

Kim asked, "What about the pill? Does anyone want it?" We glanced around the room, uncertain and embarrassed. Even though the pill had been around for ten years, none of us had tried it.

The question "What do we do to be safe?" weighed on us.

•

That afternoon, I was unsettled after talking about sex. I holed up in my cabin, feeling disgusted by a memory I was trying to bury.

The day I flew into New York, Steph put me to work right away, folding and addressing the next mailing. She explained that her current student intern would be leaving the next day. She smiled and said, "You get the honors of the sleeping mat on the office floor starting tomorrow. I'll find you a place for tonight." She made a call and wrote out an address for me. At the end of the day, I stuffed my toothbrush and change of underwear into my macramé purse and headed for the elevator. "See you first thing," she called as the doors shut.

Early evening in the canyons of brownstones, people walked dogs, and doormen watered gardens at the bases of sycamores shading the street. A breeze off the river lifted the heat. I recited the order of the Avenues: 2nd, 3rd, is it Madison? Then Lexington, 5th, and then Park? Finally, I stood in front of a polished brass plaque etched with the correct number and street. My first night in New York at some fancy apartment.

I gave the doorman the name, and the elevator opened directly into an apartment that was the whole floor of a building. It felt like a mausoleum as I stood there on the tile floor.

"Mom's not home," said a thin guy who slouched into the entryway. He looked me over. "Hey, I like your outfit." I was going to tell him I'd made it, but he offered me a toke on his joint.

"No, thanks." I confessed that I was starving from working at Stephanie's all day. In the massive kitchen, he pulled out bagels, cream cheese, and lox. I thanked him and ate ravenously.

Something was so lifeless about him, so terminally bored, that my Ohio chatty gratitude fell flat. I was suddenly exhausted. I tried to wash my dishes, and he stopped me, embarrassed I didn't know I was to leave them for the maid. Somewhat awkwardly, I asked, "Where will I sleep?"

His response was, "Wanna ball?"

•

Lying on my bunk on the ship, I played this moment over and over. How could I have been so stupid, and not said, politely, "No thanks." After a month around Kim, I'd been building up enough attitude, where I might have said, 'Hell, no. I don't even know you.' And gone to sleep. But last summer, fresh from leaving home, I was still my father's obedient daughter, trained to submit. A fresh flush of shame sliced through me.

•

Ball? I'd never known anyone who used this expression before, but I guessed what it meant. I'd read hippie comics by Robert Crumb, where pencil-drawn ugly people with long noses and huge feet, walked along in a slouchy way saying "Keep on trucking." The cartoons used that word, "balling," for sex.

I didn't have what it took to say no to the boy in the fancy apartment. I shrugged. "I guess?"

In a formal bedroom with heavy curtains and ornate lifeless furniture, he pulled off his clothes to reveal a hairless boy body before he turned off the light. His kisses were quick and hard, his unshaved chin rubbed my chin raw. I turned my face away. He quickly ground his way into me. I lay passive and lifeless until his shudder.

After he left, I rushed to the bathroom to wash off his spasm of sperm. Terrified and cursing as I washed, "Oh shit, oh shit. What did I do?" I must be a bad person. I'd had sex with Alvin, but I'd loved him. This was different, and now I'd had sex with two people.

I fell asleep miserable. I woke to a dark room, a telephone ringing far away. A maid brought in the phone on a long cord. Stephanie's voice cut through the lifeless apartment. "It's nearly ten o'clock. Where are you?" I hurried back to the office, doing my best to hide that anything had happened. I kept rewinding it in my mind for days as I folded envelopes and ran errands, my body sullied.

•

A week later after dinner, Kim and I arrived early for our Mythology and Dreams class. Kim was secretive about a dream. I asked, "What's the matter?"

"I'm kind of creeped out," she confessed. "I had a sexual dream about someone on the ship. I'm kind of attracted to him, but it's not like I want to be with him. But the dream was so blatant." She looked vulnerable.

"Wow. Crazy." I was a little jealous of Kim having had such an intense dream.

Mike asked us, "Have any of you had dreams about the ship or with people on the ship?" Everyone shook their head except Kim, who nodded slightly. Mike added. "I'm fascinated with how long it takes our dreams to catch up to when we're in a new place. It means we are still more connected to home, old friends, and family. Watch to see when the ship shows up. And remember, it's not the real ship, it's how the world of the ship lives in you. You guys are doing great. Keep writing them down. More will come." He smiled mysteriously.

Kim lingered after class and I stayed with her. She confided in Mike. "In my dream, I had an intense sexual experience with someone on the ship. But I don't want to be in a relationship with this person." It was as if she was appealing for help.

Mike smiled. "Don't worry. When we're sexually drawn to someone in our dream, it's because we want to merge with the qualities that person embodies. Now don't say who this person is, but describe this person's qualities."

Kim narrowed her eyes. "This person is dynamic and positive, and gets recognition for all the work he does on the ship." She glowered. "Nobody will let me do those jobs. I'm desperate to get respected and be allowed to work in the rigging."

Mike nodded thoughtfully. "This makes so much sense. You desperately want to be like this guy, so in your dream you merge sexually with that energetic, skilled person."

Kim had been subdued during class, her brows drawn together, her mouth tight. But as she took in Mike's words, relief blossomed across her face. "Having sex in a dream is about merging with myself? This is crazy!" She grinned at me. We snagged our journals and headed outside to write.

A week after Richie first asked Karl to teach him to scuba, he reported to Karl: "I've done my watch every day for a week." My friends and I instantly grew silent and listened carefully from our table in the crew mess.

Karl was not overjoyed. "About time."

Richie talked fast. "We had a deal; you'd teach me to dive."

Karl scowled. "Not so fast. You have to keep doing your watch jobs. If you skip out on it, scuba classes are over. You understand?"

Richie clearly hoped he'd be off the hook to scrub pots and pans. "Yes, sir, I will."

Karl looked at him doubtfully. "How old are you now?"

"Fourteen, sir."

He shook his head. "You'll be the youngest I've ever taught, if, and I mean if, I take you on. You realize how serious an undertaking it is to dive underwater, and manage your equipment and gauges and pressures? Don't want to waste my time if you mess around and don't take it seriously."

My friends and I glanced at each other, amazed that Karl would agree to teach Richie.

Richie had none of his usual smirk or wheedling smile. He was as serious as we'd ever seen him. Was Karl going to take a chance on him, when most of us had already written him off? I still read him *The Hobbit* occasionally, but I'd stopped trying to tutor him since we now all worked on splicing. Richie said, "I promise I'll learn everything you teach me, Karl."

They made plans to get gear the next day, even though Karl looked up to the ceiling, as if asking, dear God, what foolishness am I risking. He turned to Richie for one last promise. "Now there's no joking around, no bugging me."

"I promise."

Richie's dirty little hand reached out to Karl's large brown hand, a firm shake.

•

A few days later, I was sitting on deck when I heard a squishy slippery sound. Kim was dripping wet, in her bathing suit, leaving a trail of water as she carried her snorkeling mask and fins. Her blond curls were hanging in wet corkscrews on her shoulders. "I wanted to see the reef under the ship."

As she dried off, I asked, "Is it scary below the ship?"

"I swam around the whole hull." She put her hands on her hips. "If I want to know what the fuck is going on around here, I have to go look." I followed her down the steps into the girls' quarters. She peeled off her bikini, tossing the wet top and bottom on the metal floor in our little bathroom, leaving them to mildew.

"Did you see the barnacles?"

She pulled on a clean pair of jeans, and a T-shirt, and looked at me with a strange excitement. "They're alive. They open and close their mouths. It's a living, breathing world down there. You can see seagrasses moving, and sponges. I can't wait to go snorkeling over a real reef." She pulled her journal out from under her pillow. "I have to write about it," she said, and her feet pounded up the steep stairs.

I lay down on my bunk and closed my eyes. I imagined putting on the mask without it fogging up.. I put the breathing tube in my mouth, and I slipped into the dark water beside the ship and swam along the hull. I saw the long white hull above me, the line of portholes, but suddenly a huge fear washed over me. I could hardly breathe.

The ship above me had rows and rows of portholes towering overhead. It was cold water, and the sea was full of bodies. A lifeboat hung askew on lines above me, then crashed down, spilling people into the water. I was surrounded by screams and crashing waves, and smoke billowing overhead from the massive smokestacks.

I remembered the front page of a faded newspaper, a full-page drawing of a sinking ship on May 7, 1915, when my mother's grandparents were lost at sea. The *Lusitania* was one of the finest passenger liners, setting sail from New York for England despite German warnings of being at war with Britain. My great grandparents sailed toward a continent in the agony of World War I, toward a submarine picking off ships near the coast of Ireland.

I imagined the mayhem after the torpedo and the roaring explosion, when everyone rushed, frantic to find their children, desperate to retrieve life jackets from cabins and fight their way to lifeboats as the ship listed rapidly. But what my great grandparents chose to do haunted me. They walked to their stateroom, closed the door, and were never seen again. The ship sank in eighteen minutes. I hadn't ever imagined what it was like on board the *Lusitania* until now, as I lay on my bunk in this tiny cabin, with a porthole on Miami harbor.

•

At muster Mrs. Roberts showed up with a tight smile, holding papers. She whispered to Ron, the teacher giving us our work assignments, and he stepped back.

We murmured around the foredeck. "She looks happy. Must be bad news for us suckers."

She took over with a smile of triumph. "I have orders from your new captain, Captain Johnson, who has been hired by the owners. First order, for your safety, all rigging work is stopped."

The outcry sputtered all over the deck from students and crew. "What do you mean? We've made such progress!"

Mrs. Roberts raised her hand. "All the rigging materials are locked below decks. They are out of bounds. Captain's orders. He wants you to polish the brass and begin varnish repair." Protests rumbled through the students. She raised her hand. "You haven't had a captain before, and it's about time that you learned a captain's orders are absolute onboard a ship. I have materials here for your jobs." She smiled with triumph as she silenced our protests.

Half of us were assigned to polishing duty, and the other half were to learn the steps involved in scraping, sanding, and varnishing mahogany, starting on deck boxes on the mizzen deck.

The students, teachers, and crew were incredulous, asking a flood of questions. "Varnishing and polishing brass? What the fuck?! Is this a museum? If all the rigging work is stopped, we'll never get out of here. Who is this stupid captain? Hush, someone's up on the bridge." Mrs. Roberts rounded us up and sent half of us off to polish brass in teams. A feeling of dread sank through me. It felt too much like home.

•

Kim was spitting mad as she scrubbed brass hinges on the radio officer's door. "Why the fuck did they load this ship with so much bloody brass?"

My hands were aching and it had only been an hour. "Brass is everywhere I look!" Door latches, handles, edges of portholes. I rubbed my rag, wet with Brasso, over and over on the nameplate saying Radio Office. No one had polished the brass for a long time, and it was stained green and brown and pitted with salt. I growled, "She's coming to check on us."

Mrs. Roberts marched up the starboard deck until she stood over us. She wore a shirtdress, belted at the waist, her grey hair tightly permed. "Keep moving your hands in a circular motion. Don't scratch the brass. You should be faster, there's a lot more to do." She ordered us around like Dad—we never did a good enough job, and he'd keep handing out more tasks. Dad had managed to send us to a school that worked us even harder than he did. She bustled off primly.

Kim's mood darkened. "This will never get us out to sea." She looked up into the rig. "I can't believe I'm forbidden to climb aloft."

I noticed brass railing braces bolted to the bulkheads of the cabins with ropes strung between them. "Kim. I never noticed these before."

"When there's a storm, you hold on to those ropes as you make your way down the deck."

Usually when I walked down the deck, I reached out to the wooden railing that edged the ship. "I guess if there are high seas, I wouldn't want to be close to the railing." But my mood sank. "*If* we ever get out to sea."

All over the ship, fifty teenagers grumbled. "Will we ever sail?" But underneath the discouragement were unspoken questions. Why didn't the owners want the ship to sail? Chick was off in Europe searching for crew and officers, Stephanie was in New York fundraising for materials, and suddenly the owners brought on this unseen Captain Johnson who stopped all necessary work? What the fuck was going on? This refrain would become our mantra for months.

•

A few days later at the end of October, news spread around the ship that the band Santana was playing for a couple of nights at the Hollywood Sportatorium. A lot of students and teachers had been going to concerts. Kim came back stoned from seeing Ike and Tina Turner and the Voices of Harlem. She danced around the fantail in the dark with her eyes closed, saying "Music turns me on so much." I didn't want to miss out on Santana. Sixteen of us signed up. Kim and I dressed up in miniskirts and joined the crowd of boys as we clomped down the gangway.

Eight kids climbed into the school's errand van with a teacher and took off ahead of us. The remaining eight of us squeezed into the school's station wagon, including a few who hid under blankets in the back. Our teacher Ron was driving. The bottom of the car grated over ruts in the driveway.

Ron whirled around as if the thought had just struck him. "Do any of you guys have pot on you?" Even though his black hair was in long ringlets, he was not a permissive hippie. Kim joked about how we were trying to loosen him up from being an uptight Harvard grad.

"Of course we do," a few said. "We're going to a concert."

Ron slammed on the brakes. "No way. Hand it over. We don't want anything in the car with us." A lot of the boys begged until he agreed to a deal. They climbed out of the car, passed joints around, took tokes and held their breath, until they climbed back in reeking of smoke and giggling. I coughed and ignored them. I thought getting stoned made people stupid. I didn't want to be stupid or boring.

The car took off on a highway heading south of Miami. We were squeezed in tight, with a kid lying across our laps in the middle seat. Kim complained. "Today I had to be a tour guide to three 'distinguished' guests for Stephanie. One was a photographer who wanted to put the ship on the cover of a magazine. We were walking down the deck when these engine room guys came running. We looked over the railing and the ship had sprung a fucking leak and diesel was glugging out down the hull. Jesus Christ! And good old Kim had to be up-beat and positive and take them down for a tour of the staterooms." She groaned.

Zip growled. "We got that leak patched up, but Captain Johnson is such an asshole. He's not letting us have the tools we need." I glanced at Zip. He'd cleaned up nicely for the concert, and he was growing long side-burns. He grinned. "Boy, am I ready to let loose and dance!"

Kim agreed. "Damn straight. Time to dance!"

Oh no! People dance at concerts? I thought we sat in seats and listened. I'd only been to one concert and that time only the people way up front danced. Ron turned on the car radio and of course Santana filled the airwaves. We cruised down the highway in the warm night as the drums beat the rhythm to "Oye Como Va." I shook my head to the music and decided to flow with it all.

Once we arrived, I was caught up in a river of people, carried along into an enormous amphitheater facing a tiny stage, where I could hardly see the drummers and guitars, but the music on loud speakers pounded. We stood together swaying in the narrow row, the Latin beat rumbled through my body, and I moved my head in time with intricate guitar riffs. Before I knew it, we were all crammed into the station wagon heading back to the ship.

The highway was jammed and slow, so Ron exited and took a two-lane road between orange orchards, miles and miles of trees, with billboards of enormous oranges and grapefruits. We were suddenly thirsty and so hungry. Some kids called out to Ron, "Look, orange trees! Stop. Let's go pick oranges!" They finally convinced him to pull over on the gravel shoulder. Ron called out, "Get one orange and come right back to the car."

We piled out of the car, scrambled through the weeds into the orchard, running and yelling for the fun of it, down the aisles of trees, in the dark, stumbling over lumpy soil, trying to reach into the trees for an orange. Laughing and goofing around.

Suddenly, a shout stunned us. "Police! Stop!"

We ran for it. Zip yelled, "Circle around back to the car." But I was lost in the dark rows of trees, heart pounding and confused. Where was our car? The police were shouting. Flashlights like spotlights zigzagged through the dark. I stumbled and tripped in ruts. Voices called out, "Which way's the road?"

The police were charging after us through the trees, cursing, "Damn kids." Barking followed, and a deep voice shouted loud and clear. "We'll set the dogs on you if you don't stop."

We stopped and they cornered us in a gully, growling dogs leaping and pulling on leashes. "You kids are damned lucky. When we saw you girls, we didn't let the dogs loose. Otherwise, we were gonna teach you boys a lesson." He pointed his flashlight over Kim and my bare legs in short skirts. I was shaking and panting. Those dogs would have ripped our legs open.

A kid whimpered. "We were hungry."

"Don't you know it's a federal crime to pick Florida oranges?" The loudest burly voice launched into a speech. "First of all you're trespassing, and secondly anyone caught stealing oranges can be charged with second- or third-degree misdemeanors. We should call your parents. Where are you from?"

"We're students at a school on a ship docked at MacArthur Causeway, sir." They ran the flashlights over our faces and we called out the names of home. "Ohio. Connecticut. California. Alberta, Canada, sir. New Jersey. Nebraska."

"Show your ID." The three policemen muttered. "More trouble than it's worth. Long-distance calls." One shone the light at us. "Empty your pockets." Their faces were in the dark, but the flashlights showed big hands, uniforms, glints of badges, and the dogs growled and yanked on leashes. The dark shadowy branches hulked overhead, the weeds crackled underfoot, the sound of trucks and cars whizzed by on the road. None of us had anything but a little money and ID. "How'd you get here?"

"Our car's over there, sir. We're on our way back to the ship, sir."

The loud-voiced man lectured. "We'll let you off this time, but if we ever find you in this orchard again, we'll let the dogs loose and then lock you up."

We walked back to the car down the gravel breakdown lane to where Ron waited, his head in his hands leaning on the steering wheel. He groaned as we opened the car doors. "How did I ever get caught up in something this stupid?" He didn't talk to us as we climbed in. He just turned the key, engaged the engine and pulled out on to the road slowly and very carefully.

I shook in the dark, but some giggled. "Those cops were real Florida crackers."

One kid pulled an orange out of his shirt, held it up in the headlights of a car behind us. "It's green and hard. You can't eat it."

"Shit, you actually stole an orange? After all that."

Zip shook his head. "We are so stupid. We didn't know they weren't even ripe now."

But as I calmed down, I was still glad that I'd come. I couldn't wait to write about it.

A couple of nights later, as I brushed my teeth before going to sleep, Kim charged into our room and looked at me intensely. I felt caught like a deer in the headlights.

"I've got to talk to you."

It was always a bad sign when someone said this.

"You're making enemies."

"Enemies? How could I make enemies?" Enemy was such an intense word. I didn't think I did anything wrong. Sure, I could get sarcastic sometimes but underneath it, wasn't I really wimpy?

"When you tell people your impressions that you've written in your journal, you're playing games with people's heads."

"Oh, that." Oh, shit. I'd been worrying about that.

•

Kim and I were known as the girls who wrote in journals, and we both planned to write what we thought about every kid on the ship. But Kim talked to people, worked, wrestled, raced with them. I watched everyone but only talked to a few of them. But because I had a journal, students I never talked to came up to me when I was writing.

One afternoon the flirtatious girl from out West pushed her long blond hair back with a flipping movement of her fingers. She asked, "What are you writing about?" She hung out with the older partying students.

"About the ship." I shrugged. "And trying to understand people."

"Did you write about me?" She sounded coy.

"Well." I hedged. "I write a little about everyone I can." People walked down the deck glancing at us. I closed my journal.

"Would you let me see what you wrote about me?"

"Are you sure you want to hear what I think?"

"Of course!" She smiled a winning grin.

I flipped through the pages until I found her name. "It's just what I think."

"I want to hear it."

So I read, *There's this girl with long blond hair who flirts, really flirts with the boys. Bats her eyelashes, flips her hair back, and laughs in a really silly way. She's like someone in a stupid teen movie. I wish she could talk to them like a regular person.* I stopped there and glanced up at her. Her face was cold. She stalked away, and never talked to me the rest of the year.

Oh shit, I probably shouldn't have said *stupid teen movie.* Was I cruel to read what I'd written? Some journal writers hid things in code, or wrote in tiny writing so they could tell the truth. I was determined to be as truthful as I could because I wrote for myself. But was I too critical?

When people told me to do something, I was trained to be compliant. Why couldn't I say *No?* I vowed to myself: From now on I was not going to tell people what I thought. It was private.

Right before dinner as I wrote in my journal, an older guy sauntered up, one of the partying friends, with thick matted curly hair pulled back with a kerchief, an imposing muscular chest. He demanded, "So what have you written about me?"

"I don't think I've written about you."

"I'm sure you have." He stood too close, and looked down on my pages.

So much for my resolve. I felt intimidated and flipped through my pages. Had I written about him? I found a single comment. Should I refuse? Or maybe it was a good thing to tell him what I thought? Served him right. I read: *There's this guy who is mean to the little kids, the 14- and 15-year-olds, like Richie and Woodie and his friend Jake. It makes them more negative and tougher. Not a good idea.*

He scowled. "Those little shits are so annoying. I have to put them in their place." He stalked off and never spoke to me again either. No loss. But two out of fifty people mad at me—I didn't want this to get worse.

After that I was determined; I wouldn't read from my journal again to anybody. Then I forgot about it, until Kim careened into our cabin talking about making enemies. I slumped on to my bunk and shoved the red leather journal under my pillow—the guilty object. I guessed that reading from my journal had been a really bad idea, even though Kim did it. I tried to defend myself, my voice shaking. "But don't people want to know what they're doing?"

"You're playing games with people's heads."

She stared at me. Then she pulled out her journal from under her pillow, plopped down on her bunk, hunted through the pages, and then read. *Elizabeth is telling people what she sees on the surface. But she hasn't delved into who they really are. She isn't getting to know them. She doesn't understand why they act like a jerk.* She looked at me, clearly disappointed. She was two years younger than me but I felt like the younger, clueless one.

I'd assumed that I was somehow wiser, that my journal writing was better, more descriptive and telling the story, while she poured out waves of feelings. But I was impressed by the word *delve*. The message of her words hit me. I lay down on the bunk and stared at the ceiling. Why didn't I want to get to know people?

My mom raised me to be critical of other people. We lived in a wealthy old village but we were the odd people who raised our own food and made our own clothes. Mom and I made sarcastic comments about country club ladies in their matching sweater sets and A-line skirts, and the men in bright yellow or green pants. We made our clothes because we couldn't afford to buy new stuff, and because clothes were a badge of being different. Even though we lived in a modern glass house and Dad drove a Jag and a BMW, he kept Mom on a tight budget to pay all the bills. I spent my babysitting cash on patterns, fabric, and thread. At school, my best friend and I shared a secret language of eye rolls and raised eyebrows. In our eyes, most people missed the mark. I wondered if anyone was good enough for me.

After Kim confronted me, I worried. Was I really a mean person? My eyes stung with tears. Then a thought hit me like a kick in the stomach. What if the most important thing to do at this crazy school was make friends?

Kim sat up, her finger holding a spot in her journal. I faced her, feeling hangdog sad and scared. She narrowed her eyes and studied me, before she read again. *The thing is, what she is saying is right,* and then she emphasized, *a lot.* She paused. I held my breath. She read the words slowly, like she was talking to my heart. *But it doesn't do them any good until you get to know them, and care about them. Only then will they hear you.*

I was blown away. It didn't matter that the words accurately described what was wrong with me. Kim had written the coolest thing about me. The words sank in. I had to get to know people. I had to care about people. It would take me years to realize how profoundly this early habit of being critical kept me closed off from caring about other people, kept me separate and isolated.

I'd been fighting to survive for so long, fighting my dad. I'd worked so hard to understand life, read important books, remember my dreams, and write. I was always running to keep up, always behind in my expectations of myself. I looked at people to analyze and judge who might be a smart, interesting friend. But I hadn't really thought about caring for other people. I thought about how Kim walked around ruffling the heads of the little boys. She cared about them. Or how she'd comforted the girl who was crying the other night. Could I do that? I looked over at Kim and she smiled and pushed her curls behind her ears.

The tension in my chest released. She didn't think I was a terrible person. Kim playfully kicked at my foot and I pretended to wrestle back with my foot. I was flooded with relief. We cracked open our journals and wrote furiously.

•

After a grinding week of polishing brass and sanding wood, I lay on my sleeping bag in the dark listening to the guitar players sing a song about an old honky-tonk guy in ragged clothes named Mr. Bojangles who'd danced for change. Strangely this poignant song became our ship's anthem overnight, matching our overall mood. Weary and sad. I lay on my side and rested my head on my tired hands to watch.

On the ship, nothing had been going right, but Steph was determined to boost our spirits. On the plane down from New York, she sat next to a young guitar player. He was between gigs, had an album coming out in the winter, and he said yes when she offered to pay him for a week giving classes on the ship. He sauntered up the gangway with a backpack and guitar and signed in with a name none of us knew yet—David Bromberg.

The guitar player kids clustered around this tall awkward guy like iron filings to a magnet. With his crooked-tooth grin, aviator glasses, and a halo of wild hair, he half-talked, half-sang with a quavering voice. Between songs he talked capos, finger picks, keys of G or B, about playing backup for Dylan and Jerry Jeff Walker, and composing a song with George Harrison. They watched as he fingerpicked his steel-stringed guitar or mandolin.

Every night, we sang along on the chorus to "Mr. Bojangles." The song somehow lifted me. David's last night on board, an older guy with a guitar strapped on his back strolled up the gangway and they played late into the night. I was so tired; I fell asleep early.

In the morning, Kim was bursting out of her skin with happiness at breakfast. "I sat in front of them playing last night. I dig the songs so much." She sighed. "I'll always remember the night when Jerry Jeff Walker played on the ship." She shivered with excitement. "I felt it all through my body."

I choked on my juice. A living legend sang on the deck, and I slept through it. I groaned inside. That was so typical. I missed out on the good stuff, even when I was right there, while Kim knew what was great and was in the center of it all.

•

A few nights later after Dreams class, Kim, Pogo, Ted, Jane, and Woodie were drinking beer, laughing, and talking. I was grumpy and tired from another week of scraping and sanding peeling varnish from cabin walls. I wanted to write about everything on my list. They decided to walk over to Miami Beach and go swimming, even though it was dark. "Come on, Elizabeth. Take a break from writing!"

"No, I need to catch up. Aren't you scared of swimming in the dark?"

"It will be great. You'll regret it!" Off they went in a parade of laughter.

I was relieved to have some quiet. I needed a break from people. I wrote until I was sleepy. They still weren't back. I wandered around the deck, feeling lonely and left behind. I fell asleep on my sleeping bag at the fantail.

A deep sound woke me up. It was dark and shadowy on deck and several voices were making a slow *ahhhhh* sound and then higher to a long *aummmmmm*. I jolted upright and looked around. They were back, hair wet, and sitting in a circle chanting this strange sound that reverberated through me. Their eyes were closed, mouths opened in a deep, long *Om*. Some kids walked by and watched, some joined in, while others joked, "Weirdos," and walked on. Slowly the chant quieted and stopped. Most of them stood up and headed off to sleep.

Afterward Kim sprawled on her back on the deck next to me and watched the sky. "It was all so beautiful."

"What did you do?"

"We skinny-dipped in the ocean. I felt awkward at first, but then it was amazing." She stirred her arms overhead in the darkness. "Have you ever heard of phosphorescence in the ocean?" I shook my head. "Pogo said it was plankton that was streaming silver through our fingers."

I imagined my friends, and even my little brother, naked in the water, moving thousands of minute silvery particles through the water. And dumb old me had been back here on the ship, writing.

Kim talked softly, her voice gentle in the dark. "When I was in the water I was flowing. Light was reflecting on people's faces." She sighed. "Something happened to me. All these realizations came together." She looked at me intently. "You know how I like to blow guys' minds when I cuss?" I nodded my head. "I want to do things that people don't expect. I react the opposite way from how I'm supposed to, because it pleases me. I like being perverse and contrary." I watch her, amazed. I had no idea she did that on purpose. But now, she gazed into the night sky, her face relaxed.

She wasn't screwing up her face with anger, or mad at the boys, or the ship, or the work, or at anyone. I'd never seen someone change like this. My envy eased. I waited for her to speak.

She stretched her arms and legs and sighed a big sigh. "In the ocean, in the dark, I stopped working so hard. I didn't have to think of something crazy to do. We were all doing this amazing chant. We were making it up as we went along."

She took my hand with the fool's gold ring and moved it through the pale light from the lights on the dock. "It was silvery, like this."

Her peacefulness spread through me. It was OK that I wasn't there. It was enough to listen to Kim. I knew with a strange certainty that someday I too would swim at night in the ocean and spin my arms in phosphorescence.

•

We'd all been up so late that we were really groggy when the morning bell slammed us awake. Under Captain Johnson's rule, it hardly seemed worth getting up. Even Kim and I had joined the complainers. "We'll never get anywhere at this rate," we grumbled as we pulled on our clothes and headed to the mess for another cold breakfast. There was still no power in the galley. We were still hauling food from the refrigerated truck on the dock. There was still no water in the water lines.

At muster, we slouched and answered with flat voices as Ron called the roll call. "Yeah, I'm here, barely." People didn't even laugh.

But then everything changed. Stephanie in a bright new blue and red flowered dress introduced a dynamic stocky man in a white uniform. "This is Mr. Neilson." The old captain was never mentioned again. Mr. Neilson took one look at us motley students and tore into us in a thick Danish accent. "You call yourselves cadets? Look at you! You call this muster. You are—" and the word he said sounded like *FIL-thee*. "The ship is filthy. You want to sail, but you are not fit to sail this ship." He shouted, "Stand up straight. Stand in straight lines."

We jolted into action and scurried to form lines. He roared, "Bosun, call muster!" A young sailor in white uniform with short blond hair blew a silver whistle. "Now we'll go down the line. Say 'Cadet' and your last name." He pointed at Jane at the end of the line and she spoke up quietly. "Cadet Hoste." "Louder," he demanded, "I need to hear you. You are declaring that you are a cadet on a great ship. Start acting like it."

Jane spoke up louder. "Cadet Hoste!" The lines of students and teachers and crew announced ourselves. I gulped and said the words, "Cadet Garber." My brother followed, "Cadet Garber, sir."

Mr. Neilson's voice charged into us. "This is no way to dress. Ragged like beggars. Where are your work clothes?" He leaned toward Stephanie, talking quickly.

"Do you all have blue work shirts and jeans?" she asked. Most shook their heads. There was more discussion. "Immediately after muster, tell me your shirt size and we will get you all matching shirts today."

Mr. Neilson barked orders. "Tomorrow, you will be clean. Hair brushed and pulled back. Work uniform, clean clothes. No rips. You will not *steeenk*. First call at six. Breakfast at seven. Muster at eight. We will have inspection of your quarters, bunks, lockers. Everything is to be clean and in order. Then we get this ship ready to sail. Dismissed."

We stood in shock. Probably no boy had washed his clothes in a month. Their bunk rooms in the fo'c'sle looked like a bomb had gone off. Kinda like Kim's side of our cabin.

Steph called orders. "Bring your duffels of clothes and sheets to the dock. We'll run carloads over and back to Miami Beach." She assigned a crew to wash the clothes at the laundromat. Kim grumbled. "Of course, we're on laundry duty." Other crews were assigned to scrub the heads, the galley, the mess. I said, "I prefer washing clothes to cleaning grease in the galley." Ron called out the rest of the plans for the day. Showers at the motel tonight. All classes were cancelled, even though classes had been quite sporadic.

Stephanie gestured me over. I realized that when we were polishing brass and sanding woodwork, I'd completely forgotten to figure out a place to organize the library. And I'd completely forgotten about tutoring Richie. Ahead of me in line to talk to Stephanie and Mr. Neilson was Karl, with Richie at his side. He was reporting on their work scraping barnacles off the sea chest grates for weeks. "Richie's the only student who has stayed working with me all along. I've never seen him work so hard." Karl said they'd stayed under the radar so the previous captain, who never left the bridge, wouldn't know what they were up to. He said, "I knew we had to get the job done if we ever want to get out of here."

Stephanie thanked him and ran her fingers through Richie's hair. He beamed a proud smile up at her. Then she looked at me, and I patted Richie on the shoulder. "We've been reading *The Hobbit* out loud." Richie nodded before running off. Then I grimaced. "But I still haven't figured out the library." She gave me the eye, meaning get moving on it. I nodded and raced off.

The station wagon was busy all day, ferrying laundry and students, and fetching matching blue work shirts for all students, teachers, and crew, which were passed out at dinner. Students hauled heavy-gauge brooms up the gangway.

No one hung around on deck that night, no guitar players strummed at the fantail, no students went over to the Coast Guard bar, no pot smoke wafted from shore where students hid behind shipping containers. Everyone organized their gear, made up their beds with clean sheets. The boys cursed as they brushed snarls out of their freshly washed hair. We crashed early.

When the bosun blew his silver whistle at 6 a.m., we rolled up our sleeping bags and ran below to place them neatly at the end of our bunks. Hair brushed, long-sleeve matching blue shirts buttoned, jeans pulled on, we raced for breakfast and stood in lines on deck by 8 a.m. sharp. We called muster, our voices crisp and strong, each of us declaring ourselves a Cadet. Mr. Neilson made an inspection of our quarters as we each stood next to our bunks. He lectured a few boys. "You can do better. I'll be back to check tomorrow."

We returned to deck for instructions. Mr. Neilson's deep voice commanded us. "Now that you are clean, you will clean the ship. You make this ship shipshape." His cadets brought out the heavy deck brushes, each made from a block of wood with rows of thick bristles across the bottom. They unrolled the canvas fire hoses, connected them with pumps to run salt water, and he shouted to us: "Take off your shoes! Roll up your pants! Divide up in teams!" The chilly salt water from the bay poured over my feet as I sprinkled soap down the deck. They showed us how to swing the heavy brushes to hit the deck to work the bristle into the grain of the teak. We rinsed off the scummy water with the hoses. My toes and feet had puckered by the time we'd made our way from the bow, along the entire length of the ship, all the way to the stern, all 360 feet.

We didn't stop there. Teams hauled hoses and soap and brushes up to the second level then scrubbed the walkways from the bridge down along the row of lifeboats and launches on each side of the bridge and the officer's cabins. We shouted, "Watch out below!" as dirty water poured down from the upper deck. We scrubbed and rinsed, beginning the huge task of cleaning four years of grease and dirt. We would do this every morning from then on.

•

Mr. Neilson now had the keys to the ship and opened all the locked doors of workshops and tool closets and set us to work. The previous captain had refused to give the blueprints to the engineers hired to repair the engines and water systems, but now the engineers could proceed.

He sent his cadets aloft wearing wooden clogs, and we watched a few ratlines give way as they flew up and down the rig for a full inspection. Mr. Neilson personally inspected and approved the few sections of the ratlines we'd replaced before we'd been stopped. "But why only this? The whole ship needs to be done." The rope and tools were brought back on deck, and huge rolls of rope were delivered for replacing the running rigging. Stephanie had raised enough money to keep the materials arriving and to pay the engineers to return.

•

As I looked down the deck at all of us, student and teachers, dressed in blue work clothes, pant legs rolled up, hair tied back, scrubbing the decks, I felt a flood of happiness. This was what Stephanie had said all along, a sail training experience changes students' lives. Ted smiled. "This definitely has a high salinity count."

•

Mr. Neilson made an announcement at muster. "Starting tomorrow, at 6 a.m. work begins. You are divided into two teams. My quartermasters will work with you. One will lead you to practice lifeboat drills while the other team will scrub the decks and polish the brass. Next week the teams will reverse. Then breakfast, muster, and job assignments for everyone." When some teachers murmured, he grew fierce. "All work must focus on the ship preparing to sail. All classes are canceled until the ship sails."

"I have another serious topic," he said. "You need to know there can be no illegal substances on the ship."

Some mumbled. "It's crazy that pot is illegal."

"I don't care what your philosophy on drugs is, but onboard a ship, if something illegal is found, the ship can be impounded, passengers and crew may be prosecuted, put in jail, or removed from the ship." His face was stern as he looked over each of our faces. "There is no discussion on this topic. Any substance must be removed from the ship by lunch today." He looked us up and down. "You must give me your word by saying, 'Yes, Sir.'"

A chorus of somber voices resonated across the forward deck.

He'd said at muster, "Any hardness I give you as we train is to help you. I'm trying to give you a chance to *survive*."

His spirit buoyed Kim. She was so moved by Mr. Neilson that when she ran into one of the negative boys, she lectured him. "He is a beautiful man. He's come here because he loves the program. He is working his ass off."

He sneered. "Working our asses off, more like it."

Kim was furious. "He is giving us all he can give! Can't you see, he's our only hope to ever get out of here? He will save our school." The kid walked off and shrugged, but most of us were caught up in the momentum. I worked steadily, propelled through the days, hopeful at last.

•

Kim rowed on lifeboat drills the first week while my team scrubbed the deck. By breakfast, I was weary from slamming the heavy brushes and hauling wet canvas hoses. But when Kim arrived for breakfast, she crashed onto the bench. "I'm wasted. That rowing! Hard-core shit." She shoved French toast into her mouth, chewing with her mouth open, while she explained that she was trying to row in time with the others. "But I fucked it up a lot. I couldn't always follow our quartermaster's calls. Some didn't even try to follow instructions."

Ted grinned. "We need Neilson to '*vip dem intu szhape*.'"

"You rowers looked so funny!" I confessed. We watched them from up on the deck. "Your oars looked like chopsticks sticking out every which way." Some teens could barely lift the heavy wooden oars, others plunged their oars too deep into the water and couldn't get them back out quickly enough. We watched the young Danish mate show them how to feather their oars. The lifeboats mostly jerked around in circles to the amusement of the Coast Guard guys on the opposite dock. How would I manage to row if Kim was exhausted?

•

A week later, in the grey light before dawn, I was barely awake and climbing down a rope ladder with wooden rungs hanging against the metal hull. My hands grasped the scratchy rope while my sneaker fished in air to find the next wooden slat.

Suddenly my foot slipped off a slat. Students above me were trying to climb down, and below me they clambered into the lifeboat, while I floundered in the middle. I lowered one hand at a time, while my feet slipped, jolted, and banged against the ship's beat-up hull. My arms shook from holding on, my legs wobbled like rubber, and all I'd done was get into the lifeboat without falling and embarrassing myself.

Once I'd clambered onto my rowing seat, the twelve-foot oar felt like iron instead of wood. The seven other teens could hardly lift their oars either. In broken English, the shy mate gestured how to hold our hands on the oar, how to lean back and lift the oar out of the water. But our oars fell askew. When I tried to budge my oar in the water, it stuck like a sword in stone. I was certainly not the chosen one who could pull it out.

The boat turned sideways on a morning breeze, gulls took off, circled, and cawed overhead. What if something happened when we're out in the middle of the ocean? This was our lifeboat. I was determined. We had to learn to row.

•

On our Sunday rest afternoon, Kim was restless even when she was lying on her back, her Indian-print short dress twisted around her. She sighed. "I'm so desperate to be touched and held. I can't wait all year to have sex, but it can't be with one of these..." she rolled her eyes to emphasize the word, "...*boys* on the ship. I want to be with a man who knows something."

I lay on my back, and my hands smoothed out the folds in my embroidered Mexican dress. I was simmering in confusion about having sex. I was only supposed to have sex with one person, the guy I married, but I'd already blown it.

Kim rolled over on her belly and gave me the eye. "Tell me about that older guy who used you last summer." In our ongoing conversations about sex, we'd already covered first boyfriends and losing our virginity. I hadn't dared tell her about the ridiculous first night in New York guy, but I had mentioned a mysterious weekend with an older man in New York. Her look pierced me. "I want the whole story. We've got all afternoon!"

Did this man take advantage of me? I wasn't sure about Kim's certainty. I told the story from the beginning.

Stephanie was going on one of her fundraising trips for the weekend and said she couldn't leave me at the office alone. She made some calls and told me to pack a change of clothes. "I'll introduce you to a friend of ours where you can stay. Wear your linen suit." Saturday morning, we took a cab to a brick apartment building and entered an old-fashioned elevator with metal-levered doors. "Push the button for the Penthouse." As the elevator chugged upward, I raised my eyebrows. She smiled. "Don't worry, it's not like our penthouse. By the way, his name is Carleton Lawrence. You'll find him interesting."

What I noticed first was the sheen of his beautifully tailored shirt, the pleated linen pants, before I looked into his clean-shaven face, his well-cut hair, his quiet eyes. How old was he, thirty or forty? He opened the door into a room filled with beautiful old and modern furniture, the walls covered by paintings and drawings and packed bookcases, its floor layered with thick woven rugs, like an apartment photograph from *Vogue*. I gravitated toward the glass coffee table and a bronze sculpture of a girl and a deer. I ran my finger over the deer's cold back. Stephanie and Carleton talked about people they knew and how the school was going, as I wandered around the room. I followed them through glass French doors to a rooftop garden, with a few trees in full leaf, tall grasses, and flowering shrubs. Lunch was set on a metal table. Stephanie drank a cup of coffee, then leapt up and kissed me on the cheek. "Have a good weekend," she said before rushing off to the airport.

In the wake of Stephanie's intense energy, the garden was still. I glanced at Carleton. He was slight, shorter than me, his movements graceful. He named the cheeses and poured us both a glass of chilled white wine. I tasted it carefully. "I like the weight of this, slightly sweet but with body." I'd learned to talk about wine from my dad and his wine cellar. Carleton split open ripe figs and set out slices of pears. He didn't treat me like I was seventeen. I felt elegant and knowledgeable in this beautiful garden.

He led me through his two-story apartment, taking me to each room, pointing out oil paintings, old books, antiques—an art history lesson that jumped from old to modern, from Europe to Asia, to family collections. I touched marble and carved wood, inlaid stones, all the time listening and watching his cultured face as he talked. I felt easy with him, and strangely comfortable even when he took me into his bedroom. "Let me take your jacket," he said.

He undressed me slowly and I offered no resistance, as if I was floating down a slow river. He led me to the bed and slipped off my top, talking to me as he had about art, appreciating my small breasts, my slender body, as he stroked me gently and slowly. He sent me to the bathroom to wash. Then I lay on the coverlet in a stream of sunlight amidst the silk-covered pillows while he found places that startled me, sensations that made me gasp, in this room of gold-framed paintings. On the beautiful soft sheets, he entered me gently, talking quietly as he stroked my breasts, my face, watching me as he moved his slight body over me. I observed myself with a calm detachment, feeling neutral, present, and curious, as if the art lesson was continuing.

Afterward he asked me if I'd ever had an orgasm. "I'm not sure." Without shyness, I explained that if I lay on my belly and tightened up inside, something released inside of me. "Is that an orgasm?"

He kept stroking me. "That's good. Someday you will learn to feel that release while making love."

He put on a kimono to go downstairs to make supper and directed me to take a shower, offering me a kimono as well, pale peach with delicate embroidery. I felt beautiful, enchanted, and confused.

But then a thought came to me like a shock, while in his shower. *Oh shit, I've had sex again.* Was I a terrible person to have had sex, now with, oh God, now it was three people. What was I doing?

My thoughts quieted again as I dried off in the peaceful marble bathroom. Almost hypnotized, I enjoyed our dinner of scallops and asparagus with another white wine. I slept deeply and woke to the beautiful room. In the morning, he directed me to shave under my arms because he said my sweat was unpleasant. I followed his instructions.

After breakfast, an elegantly dressed willowy woman arrived; she was polished, made up perfectly, with silky hair. She kissed him on both cheeks. "Oh Carleton, who's your young friend?"

I felt like a country girl, naïve, rough, watching the grownups chat. He introduced me, saying a friend had asked him to put me up for the weekend. After she left, I compared myself to her. He said, "She can never compete with you, because you are young. Your skin is so fresh. Your breasts are perfect." He cradled them through the fabric of my dress. "Nothing compares to a young body."

Was I valued only because I was young, and once I grew older I wouldn't have value? I felt claustrophobic. He took me upstairs again. He directed me to undress and lie on my belly on top of him as he stroked my back, my buttocks, slid his fingers inside me, rocking me on top of him. I watched the light through the windows, as I tried to pay attention to my body, to a glimmer, a hint of sensation deep inside. I felt grateful for his patience and encouragement.

I stopped the story here to tell Kim, "I think he was helping me learn about sex. I don't think he was using me. But let me finish."

I was in the shower, when the phone ring. He called to me. "It's Stephanie. She says it's time for you to come home." He kissed me goodbye in a friendly way and invited me back.

I rushed down, circling round and round the elevator cage. Once I was back on to the street, I breathed in the dirty street, bus exhaust, honking taxis, and I loved it all. I'd left a place like the Land of the Lotus Eaters in the *Odyssey*. I'd felt almost drugged, but I was sure something important had happened to me in the beautiful apartment. A secret smile radiated through me as I walked uptown back to Stephanie.

She looked up from her desk and her open checkbook. There was a pile of paid bills. She asked casually, "How was the weekend?"

I answered neutrally, "Interesting. Nice," like I was commenting on dinner. And we spoke nothing more about it.

Back in our smelly bunk room, Kim was impatient. "How old do you think he was?"

"Maybe thirty or forty?"

Kim squinted suspiciously. "What's his name? There's something familiar about his apartment."

I said, "Carleton," and as I said the first letter of his last name, she bolted up abruptly and we both said his last name together: "Lawrence the Third!"

We howled with laughter, saying the words at the same time. *"You know Carleton!"*

We laughed so hard, our eyes teared and snot came out of our noses.

"Oh, I know Carleton!" Kim crowed. "In all of New York, there is only one. Lovely hard-up dude. Money spender who doesn't have any, lover of many lands, and film producer. Need I say more?"

I stared at her. "This is too crazy!"

Kim snorted. "He sniffed after me when I was fifteen. He's a friend of my dad's and Chick. I guess a lot of these rich families help support the school. I didn't want anything to do with him." She added with a tough voice, "But I'm a Jersey girl."

I guess that meant she was a tough girl who wouldn't fall for a play like that. Should I have known this? But I'd been delivered to him. I trusted Stephanie, and it was a strange, amazing time in his apartment.

Kim growled. "That Carleton. He's part of my New York past I try to forget about." Kim had rarely mentioned her dad, who she said lived like he was rich but didn't help out her and her sisters who lived in the country. But he'd sent her to Stephanie.

I looked at Kim and asked what I hadn't dared think until then. "Do you think Stephanie knew what she was doing?"

It wasn't like I felt bad about the weekend. I'd felt special and learned things. It sure was better than *balling* with that scrawny boy.

"Who the fuck knows?" Then she said "Carleton" again and we laughed.

•

I'd known it was coming. We were to begin our sail training. Everyone—students, teachers, and crew—had to climb up and over the second platforms on the fore and main masts. The new rigging was complete now, all the way to the top, even though we were only climbing about half-way.

It had been crazy watching people work that high up. Some students worked in the rig for weeks, cutting out the rotten "rungs" and replacing them with freshly spliced ratlines, lashing them securely to the cables or shrouds, which reached from the deck to the masts high above. These students leaned against the shrouds, secure despite the wind and the gentle rocking of the ship. Kim had finally been accepted as a rigger, and she loved it up there; her hands grew rough and callused, and smelled smoky from the waxy lashing line.

When the day's work was done, a few riggers climbed even higher, compelled to touch their hand to the cap on the top of the main mast, called the truck, 180 feet above the water. I was not around when my brother stationed a friend on deck to take photographs of him as he climbed to the top. He found me later, when I was writing in my journal in one of my hiding places. He punched my arm. "Hey, I did it." When I looked confused, he was sarcastic. "So sorry to interrupt you, but I slid down the royal back stay." I still looked confused and he rolled his eyes.

"Follow me, I have to show you." He took me to the base of the main mast. "You do know that there are metal stays that keep the mast steady?" I shrugged, sure, I sort of knew that. He pointed out a series of heavy metal cables painted with white lead paint that sloped forward at a mild downward angle from the mast towering over us.

"So which one did you come down?" He pointed to a cable that attached to the top of the mast and came down behind it at a very steep angle, all the way down to the deck. I couldn't believe I'd never seen it before. "Holy shit, Woodie, you came down that?"

"Yep, I did it," he drawled, "just like they did in the *Hornblower* books." He rubbed his hands but grimaced. "I had my hands on the cable to lower myself down slowly, but my hands heated up." He'd crossed his ankles around the cable but he didn't want to hold on too tight and scar them. "I was going too fast and had to grab the metal with my thighs to slow down and the cable burned a hole in my favorite shorts. But I made it." I stared at him and up at the cable. He glanced around before he leaned in closer. "Mr. Neilson met me on deck at the bottom of the cable. He must have seen me from the bridge and *flew* down here. He said, 'We are *never* going to do that again.'"

"Was he mad at you?" I didn't want Mr. Neilson mad at me. He wasn't the Captain; we still didn't have one, but he was our highest ranking officer. I adored him but also stayed out of his way, keeping a low profile.

"No, Mr. Neilson was very serious and he spoke to me sailor to sailor. And that's why I know I'll never do it again. I've learned."

Of course, I'd studied the chart of the masts, the yards, and the sails to learn their names. I loved saying the nautical terms. *Topgallants* and *flying skysails* were my favorites. They sounded so literary, right out of *Moby Dick*. But I'd never gotten straight about all the lines that came down to the railing on the ship, which controlled the raising and lowering of sails, or moved the yardarms sideways to catch a better wind. I was ready to join a line of students to pull any rope they told me from the safety of the deck, but I was certainly in no hurry to climb.

But the day came when Chief Mate Neilson had one of his young Danish mates blow the silver whistle and we lined up on deck. We were divided into groups of students, teachers, and crew, assigned to one of the two forward masts. I was in the group assigned to the main mast. Our rigger, a young guy with blond hair that fell in his face, reviewed how to climb, where to grasp, how to look up. He said, "If you get scared, don't look down."

I drifted to the end of the line, so I could watch. One by one, students mounted the starboard rail, grabbed the shrouds, and climbed in a long angle until they reached the first platform. Then they kept going, this time straight up, climbing the ratlines parallel to the mast up to the second platform. They clambered onto the second platform, moved carefully around to the other side, and descended back to the first platform, and then down to the railing where they'd jump down onto the deck. It didn't look impossible. In the future we would move out on the yardarms and eventually bend on the sails.

It was one thing to watch them climb but another thing to realize I was going to the second platform. My hands shook. I was light-headed. *I can't do this.* But the line was moving forward, fewer and fewer students were still on deck, while the early climbers had returned to the deck already. I stood at the end of the line, inched toward the railing, only a few students ahead of me. My hands were numb and cold as I stepped forward; two students were left ahead of me. One climbed up and over the rail. The rigger gave him a hand, made sure his feet were secure before he commenced to climb.

It was like a dream I couldn't escape. I wasn't a sailor, I was the librarian. But we all had to go aloft, and I was next. I stepped up and pulled myself around the rail and grasped the cables. The rigger said, "Enjoy the climb. I'm following you up." The metal rung dug across the width of my sneakered feet. Glancing up to the web of lines, I panted, my hands shook, but I grabbed on and climbed, trembling as I mounted the long triangle.

I made it to the first platform. I sat on the metal platform bolted to the mast, and took a big breath. I'd made it this far, but I was too afraid to look around. The rigger said, "Good job. Time to keep going. I'll be right behind you."

I put my foot in the first rung, and then the next, climbing the straight ladder of ropes parallel with the massive main mast. These rungs were short and sagged a little with each step. My weight was held by lines that I might have spliced and that others had lashed into place. I chanted aloud to myself, "I can do this. I can do this." I climbed steadily until the second platform. A crewman above leaned over the edge and gave directions. "Reach your hands up one at a time, hold onto these shrouds and pull yourself up onto the platform." That's when I realized I had to lean my whole body out over wide-open empty space, holding on only with my hands. I froze and whimpered, "I can't do this."

The rigger on the rungs below me called up. "You OK? Climb up and over. You can do it."

I cried. "I can't." No one could save me. My dad's words pummeled me. *You are weak.*

The crew member above looked down over the platform and asked pleasantly, "Want a hand up?"

I looked up at his weathered face, and my voice shook. "I can't do this."

He reached out his hand and said, "Put your hand right here" with such certainty that my hand rose and grasped on. His strong, warm voice compelled my other hand to reach for the next handhold. His voice willed me upward. The rigger below guided my feet to each new foothold until I pulled myself up onto the second platform, over one hundred feet above the deck. I clamped my arms around the mast, sickened by its slow sway. I couldn't stop shaking. I was convinced I couldn't get down, that no one could save me.

My dad's voice was relentless. The same old chorus of insults. You never learned to work. His voice ripped into me. *You don't apply yourself.* I glanced up at the kind crewman who was staying with me. He talked to me gently, but I could hardly hear what he said. My breathing was tight, my frantic thoughts quieted to despair.

They conferred about me. The older man promised me the two of them would stay with me until I was ready to descend. I glanced down. Students on the deck moved toward the foredeck for dinner. Late afternoon light over the harbor turned pink, then lavender out over the sea, a winter sunset. I breathed more fully. "We will get you down safely," they promised. They sounded so calm, but fear choked me. It was impossible for me to get over that platform. The kind man reassured me. "One of us will climb down ahead of you and one of us after you. We will guide your hands and feet. We are right here."

Trembling, I peeled my hands off the mast to stand. I grasped on to the metal shrouds. My mind said, I can't, I can't, but I was supported by these two crewmen who contained my fear with their certainty. One said, "I am going down ahead of you." The other said, "I will follow you." They were so kind to me.

I extended my foot over the void. Nothing except one hundred feet of air under my foot. Then a hand guided my foot to a rung, and held my foot there. I sent my other foot down over the void, but my hands were screaming, I can't hold on, I can't do this, I'm weak, but the kind man's voice said, "I am holding your hands, I will guide them to the next handhold."

My body shook but he guided me. I went down rung by rung, holding on to the metal shrouds, one man above and one below. I descended until I reached the first platform. I stood there, my legs shook a little, but I breathed, and then I kept going, down from the first platform to the ladder of metal bars. I was closer and closer to the deck with every step. The rigger moved ahead and I climbed the rest of the way on my own.

When I finally reached the deck, my legs wobbled, and I leaned on the railing. Almost no one was left on deck except my brother, who walked over to me. "You OK?"

"Did you see me up there?"

He nodded. He'd waited the whole time for me. Then he turned and left.

The older crewman climbed down on deck and patted me on the back. "Good job. Get some dinner. You'll feel better."

I slipped into the crew mess, ladled a bowl of stew, and slid onto a bench. No one had noticed I was missing. A celebratory high energy was spinning through everyone. They were talking about sail training exercises and learning to walk out on the yardarms. They were miming how to reach down over the yards to haul up a sail.

One boy said, "You're standing on a cable that's moving back and forth out at sea, and you have to reach over a yardarm and clutch the sail. Yeah, sure!"

Another kid said, "They say 'one hand for the ship and one hand for yourself' but if you need both hands for the sail, what happens to you?" And everyone thought this was so funny.

The teacher Ron talked about his fear of heights. "I'm the only one who seized up. Mr. Neilson called to me, 'Come down slowly, and don't shit on the deck.'" Everyone was laughing.

I'd never felt so invisible. No one seemed to have noticed what I'd experienced, except my brother. I scanned the room until I saw him. He gave me a thumbs-up, like he was proud of me.

I left quickly and hurried down the deck without looking up into the masts and rig hovering overhead. I felt such relief going below, closing the metal door, lying on my bunk in the silent girls' quarters. I didn't even write in my journal. I fell deeply asleep.

•

We guessed it was Stephanie's idea, but no one asked who organized our trip. All we knew was that Simone, the French teacher, rounded up us girls after lunch a few days later. She spoke quietly, her accent lilting. "Girls, meet me at the gangway in fifteen minutes."

We were confused. "Why?"

"I'll tell you later. Clean up a little."

We signed out and followed her down the gangway. We seven girls in clean skirts and blouses, hair brushed, were suddenly the focus of great curiosity around the ship. "Where are the girls going? Hey, what's happening?" Boys lined the ship's railing. "How come they get out of work?" Some of us ignored them, while others waved back gaily, as if they knew what our secret mission was.

Once we'd all climbed into the old wood-paneled station wagon, she said "I'm taking you to a clinic so you can all get the pill. Stephanie decided."

We blushed and giggled, clearly embarrassed but also kind of pleased that Stephanie thought of us and had taken matters into her own hands. Strangely, we didn't think to ask if our parents had given permission or to say whether we even wanted to go on the pill. Of course, we'd read about the pill in *TIME* or *Seventeen*. Some of us had found our mother's circular dial of pills by accident hidden in a drawer. We glanced out the windows nervously as the car crossed the causeway toward the towers of Miami. Some of us were certain that we wouldn't need the pill. We were nice girls. We were careful. We didn't have boyfriends. Well, not yet. It was all so confusing, but Stephanie had decided, and we were all going on the pill.

Simone explained. "We'll be living at sea a long time, and Stephanie wants to make sure there aren't any problems while we're out of the country."

Strangely, going on the pill seemed like following orders to climb the rigging or practice rowing. It was what was expected of us. Stephanie took on our sex ed with a seriousness that was as nontraditional as our school. We didn't know yet that she'd give the boys their own sex lecture consisting of one sentence: "Get condoms and use them." Like an order.

In a doctor's office, we filled out papers, each of us putting down what we were told before arriving—that we were eighteen, whether we actually were or not—implying that we were old enough to make this choice on our own. Ushered one by one into small exam rooms, we changed into white gowns, and lay on exam tables.

When the nurse placed my feet in the cold metal stirrups, I shivered. I struggled to answer a few cursory questions. "Have you ever used birth control before?"

"A diaphragm."

"Have you been sexually active recently?"

I blushed. "Kind of, this summer."

"What month?"

"July, I guess." Was I a bad person to say yes? She murmured to the doctor when he entered the exam room. He slid a cold, hard speculum into me and pressed hard on my belly. He nodded to the nurse as he left, like he was telling a secret I was not supposed to hear. Had I passed the test? Was I Okay? I guessed that he was making sure no one was pregnant before dispensing the pills.

An hour later we emerged, awkward and embarrassed, into Miami's November heat. We climbed back into the car, our bare legs sticking to the burning hot vinyl seats. Each of us grasped a bulky white paper bag with a nine-month supply of pills. I looked around at the other girls with a grimace. A strange weight hung over us. We were all in on a secret we couldn't tell our parents. Should we be doing this? Was this OK?

I felt almost sick holding this bag. Would I use them? The girls in the station wagon glanced at each other, wondering the same unspoken question. *Will you?*

I wavered back and forth as the car jolted through the city. Should I save them until I decided I wanted to use them? But how long did it take before it worked? Did the doctor say it would take a month or more? Already I couldn't remember.

One of the girls giggled. "What are we going to tell the boys when we get back?" One of the girls demanded we all swear to not say a word about where we had been, but by nightfall the story about the pill field trip was all over the ship.

Someone turned on the radio as the car headed back down the highway toward MacArthur Causeway, as the hot wind flung our long hair around our faces. Then Melanie's number one song, "Brand New Key," came on the radio, a girl's flirty song teasing a boy to come skate with her because she needed his brand-new key. We sang along with the chorus, buoyed by the tune, and suddenly I felt racy and almost a little wild. Was this song really about sex and the pill, and I'd never known?

·

It was late on deck. I'd hidden myself in a nook near the radio officer's cabin with enough light to write. It was a good place to hear secrets.

One of the grease monkey boys was annoyed with someone. "Where've you been? We had a pump burn out and we needed you, man." He drew hard on a cigarette.

I peeked around the corner and caught a glimpse of red hair. Zip was on the bench, shoveling leftovers into his mouth. He paused. "Something crazy happened. You can't tell anyone." He glanced around and I drew back into my alcove. "I was so tired of the engine room. I needed a break. I went for a dive off the boat before dinner."

The kid mumbled, "I hear you, man."

"I've been practicing relaxing underwater to stretch out my air longer."

The kid grunted.

"But I must have fallen asleep, 'cause the next thing I heard was a huge *Kaboom, Kaboom*. I jolted awake into pitch dark water."

"Where the fuck were you?"

"I didn't know where I was or even which way was up. There it was again. *Kaboom, Kaboom!*"

"Pistons, man. Right, from a ship?"

"Yup, must have been a freighter. I was floating below the surface out in the Miami shipping channel."

"Shit, man." The kid took another puff. Around the corner, in the dark, I held my breath. Zip was out there, floating in pitch black water near cargo ships. I shivered.

Zip took a bite. "Damn, I was terrified of getting sucked up by a propeller, but I didn't even know which way was up. I had to chill, calm down and then I remembered to feel around my face for bubbles rising to the surface." He took another bite. "I broke through the surface. I was way out in the channel. Thank God the ship was not as close as I thought."

He swam to the closest land, the south coast of Miami Beach. It was a tough swim, and he was exhausted when he climbed ashore in someone's backyard. "I pulled off my gear and crept out barefoot between houses. It was so weird. Through the picture window, I saw Walter Cronkite talking about Nixon increasing troops in Vietnam. And then I walked back."

The scrawny kid laughed. "Well, you got your nap. Time for the night shift. A shitload of work to do." He put out his cigarette in a can and strolled off. Zip finished his dinner and stared off toward the Coast Guard Station. I held my breath and stayed still, even though I was dying to write all this down.

When he stood up to leave, he walked over to where he could see me in the shadows and flashed his grin. "Not a word about this to anyone. Karl wouldn't let me dive alone if he found out."

I held my finger over my mouth and blushed. "My lips are sealed."

•

Kim and I lay on our bellies at the fantail, watching boat traffic, cargo ships, and sleek gleaming yachts, but what caught our eye was a small sailboat in the main channel.

I pointed. "That little boat looks like it's right out of *Moby Dick*." Wooden, rounded heavy hull, a single mast, two sails.

Pogo joined us. "You're right. It's a wooden double-ended rowing boat, like they used for whaling." Under his Panama hat, his eyes squinted into the late afternoon light. In high school back in Maine, Pogo had built a wooden rowboat.

As other boys appeared, I grinned at Kim. "The Salty Dogs are here." But she didn't take her eyes off the boat. The sailboat turned abruptly and steered toward us. A couple of boys climbed down from the rigging and joined us. I put the camera to my eye, and captured the boat's arrival. There were two people aboard—one lowered the mainsail and the other stood tall at the tiller, aiming the coasting boat for the dock behind us.

Pogo asked, "What's on the outside of the hull?" He pointed at a series of brightly painted round discs.

Rick wondered, "Are those Viking shields?"

The group of boys agreed. "We've got to check out this Viking ship!"

I focused the lens and clicked again, on two guys—one blond and the other dark-haired. Kim leapt up and dashed along the deck, leading a procession of boys down the gangway, to catch the lines and tie this boat to our dock.

At dinner in the crew mess an hour later, I studied the newly arrived sailors at the next table surrounded by students who told them about our ship. They were brothers; the older, dark-haired one, a serious-looking guy with a beard, was Jakob, and Emil, with messy blond hair and a quick grin, was a teenager. Jakob had just graduated from a merchant marine academy and they'd sailed down the East Coast living on their boat.

Pogo was excited. "He's either a ship's engineer or a deck officer." Our ship was desperate for officers before we could sail. Chick was searching for officers all over Europe who were coming off tourist cruising schedules, and here an officer had just sailed up to us.

Most of the girls circled the table, joking with the cute blond brother and eyeing the serious older brother. The girls were flushed and animated, but Kim looked fierce and intent, like a cat hunting, her body taut, ready to pounce. She set her eye on Jakob, who wore a khaki shirt and shorts, had rough-cut hair, a trimmed beard that followed his jawline, and an expression that was austere.

Soon Mr. Neilson walked through the group of students and introduced himself to Jakob and Emil, inviting them into the officer's mess. Kim returned to our table disappointed. "This would be the perfect night to be on mess duty. I want to be a fly on the wall!"

"You could beg the cooks to let you serve."

"Nah, I don't want them to think I'm just some girl serving dinner. I want him to know I work hard on this ship."

At muster the next day, we were introduced to our newly hired Second Mate, Jakob, and crewman Emil. It was quite an accomplishment for a recent grad to get a full-time job on a square-rigged ship. He took the work seriously. In less than a month he would be named First mate, and without him we would have never made it out of Miami.

At muster, I watched Kim, who was grinning, until she noticed me. Her face went neutral, hiding her intention. In the weeks ahead, I studied her actions for clues every time Jakob was present. I knew he was just what she was looking for, a man who could really do things, not one of the boys. But could a gritty sixteen-year-old girl capture a twenty-four-year-old officer's attention?

It had been two months since we left home, and on my weekly call home, Dad was excited to hear updates about the ship. He'd always been the coolest guy when he was full of enthusiasm, whether it was about his architectural jobs or about modern sculpture and art. Now we talked about the ship, the progress on the rigging, sail training exercises (I didn't tell him I'd frozen up in the rigging), and my endless search for where to put the library. Our conversations brought out the best in him. I was convinced I'd gotten my fun dad back, and my strange ever-hopeful amnesia seemed once again to wipe away the bad stuff that had happened with my dad.

"Dad, Mrs. Roberts finally agreed that the library could go in the crew quarters somewhere." That's when my dad offered to build the library. I just had to get Stephanie's approval.

I presented the plan to Stephanie. "I finally have a solution for the library. We could build bookshelves on the crew mess walls. Then the books would be near the kids to use all the time!"

Her face creased with worry. "We don't have money for wood for shelves or a carpenter.'"

I bubbled with excitement. "Stephanie, don't worry! My dad said he can come down and build the shelves—he has the wood, and it wouldn't cost the school a dime."

I called him that night from the payphone. "Dad, you wouldn't believe how relieved she looked. So, when can you come?"

"I'll load up the VW bus with what I need, and leave right after Thanksgiving. I can't wait."

"Me too. This is so exciting."

When I ran into my brother on deck, I told him the plan. He stared at me. "Are you nuts?" He looked at me like I was an idiot.

"It will be great, Woodie. He's going to build the school a library. And this ship is everything he's always wanted to experience. This will make him happy."

Woodie shook his head slowly, looking at me with sadness and bitterness. "You have no clue."

I wanted to reassure him; it would be different this time. But he walked away swearing under his breath, his hands in fists, his shoulders suddenly hunched. "That goddamn mother—." Perhaps I doubted my idea for a moment, but I'd convinced myself, the great dad I'd loved as a child was coming to the ship.

And it seemed to go well, at first. Dad left Ohio and drove all night in our VW bus loaded with a table saw, tools, and wood. I was elated when I ran down the gangway to hug him. He was larger than life, tall and barrel-chested, in a plaid shirt and khaki pants, already wiping the sweat off his bald head in the muggy heat. His voice boomed, "Hey, Sugar, show me around this ship."

I took him on a grand tour and explained everything we'd done. We ended in the crew mess studying the bulkhead walls. He calculated the curve of the wall and how much of a lip the shelves needed and where to put hooks for cords to hold the books snugly so they wouldn't fly off in a bad storm. My brother made himself invisible as much as he could, scowling if he had to talk to Dad. And Dad let him be, because he was having a great time getting to know my friends at dinner and on his work crew.

At muster the next day, a small crew signed on to work with Dad. After a planning session, his table saw whined through fresh pine boards at his impromptu shop on the dock. He hit it off with Pogo and they talked about architecture whenever they took a break. Dad called out to me over and over, "Hey Sugar, we need you to help install these bookcases." He wouldn't hear that I was a needed member of the splicing crew. I started to feel trapped. I convinced our rigger to say emphatically that I had to stay on the rope-splicing team to keep up with the demand for ratlines so we could finish rerigging the mizzen mast.

Woodie was working with Kim and the rigging crew on the installation team, going higher and higher up the masts, replacing the ratlines all the way to the very top sections. I'd never seen my brother so beaming with life. Until Dad arrived. After that, my brother shut down again, his eyes wary, his voice negative and sarcastic.

•

Within a week, I realized the honeymoon with Dad was over. He nabbed me as I emerged on deck after lunch. My brother was standing with him, looking dejected. Dad might have sounded upbeat to someone walking by, but to my brother and my practiced ears we could hear he was winding up. "We're leaving right now to get your foul-weather gear at the marine supply store. And we need to have a talk."

This was how he was at home. Ordering us around. After two months on the ship, I didn't want to go along with his orders anymore. But he'd trapped me. I needed the gear. It was expensive, and I had hardly any babysitting money left. I felt horrible leaving the team preparing for a party on deck that night. I protested, even though I knew it would be useless. I glanced at my brother to see if I could catch his eye. But he was too shut down to reach. He glared at the deck. I hoped he wasn't mad at me. I'd gotten us into this pickle.

"Sorry Dad, I can't. I'm part of the party prep team. I promised. I just need a size medium. I tried on someone else's stuff."

His voice amped up, louder and demanding. "You go with me, or to hell with gear for you. You can't sail without it." People turned to look and then glanced away. We were all teenagers. We all knew what grownups did when they got wigged out.

Woodie and I followed Dad obediently down the gangway. I felt like such a jerk when I called out to Kim, "Have to go with Dad. Will be back as soon as I can." Her arms were loaded with grocery bags. She was our dance party general for that night, making sure everything happened. She nodded and raced up the gangway.

The VW bus was emptied of tools, and Dad had set up the middle seat. I climbed in the passenger seat and Woodie slumped in the back.

A vise tightened around my chest. I was trapped in Dad's world again. I glanced at my brother, and we rolled our eyes and glared at our hands in our laps. Dad drove through the maze of shipping containers and turned off the dock onto the causeway toward Miami Beach. He tossed me the map, shouted a street name and number. "Find it."

I didn't know where we were. All I knew in Miami Beach was where the laundromat was and the quickest way to the beach on foot. I unfolded the old map as Dad's frustration increased. I tried to read the small print names of the streets but couldn't find the one he told me. I was so furious at myself. I'd let this happen. My brother had known. How could I have been so stupid?

Dad slammed on the brakes at an unexpected stop sign as some old people crossed the road. My brother and I threw our hands forward to brace ourselves. We knew the drill, the escalation, the anger rising. The danger. Dad called to someone on the street, in his big jovial voice, and asked where the marine supply store was.

A guy with a thick New York accent yelled back directions. "Turn right. Just down that road. Can't miss it."

Dad accused me. "Why didn't you tell me it was so close?"

At the store, he talked to the clerk about sailing while my brother and I tried on heavyweight yellow Norwegian sailing gear. Woodie and I discussed our options. I chose overalls to keep sea water from soaking me at the waist in a storm. Woodie decided on rain pants with suspenders. We had to roll up the cuffs. Dad said, "Put it all on. Let me see you guys." We followed his instructions, even putting on the sou'wester hats. We rolled our eyes and hoped no one came in. Dad kept going on and on to the clerk about the *Antarna* and how we were setting sail soon. He sounded like the greatest dad ever, getting his teens geared up for a year at sea. When the clerk rang up the order, Dad glared at us. "Neither of you appreciates how fortunate you are." Then he looked at me. "You look fat. Don't let yourself go to pot like girls do when they go away to school."

His words felt like a slap. I protested. "I have all these layers on." But he stalked off to sign the receipt.

Back in the car, we were trapped. I tried speaking up. "I've got to get back. There's work to do for dinner prep."

But he was just getting going. His face distorted and reddened as he lectured. "I am deeply disappointed in the two of you. You are not living up to my expectations."

It was a variation of the same lecture he'd given since we were little when we brought home our report cards. Even though I had good grades, my brothers didn't; because of dyslexia they struggled to read. We all got lectured for not doing our best, not working hard enough, and the lectures stretched on longer and longer over the years. As he heated up, we knew what would be coming—the litany of our sins. He'd been watching and keeping track of all the ways we fell short.

His bald head was sweating in the stuffy car as he zeroed in on me. "You aren't getting strong enough. You aren't working hard enough." It wasn't even worth defending myself. I knew Stephanie and the teachers said I was doing a great job. I was skillful at splicing lines. Sure, I was still a scaredy-cat with heights and heavy lifting. But I would learn to climb aloft. I wasn't the only wimp on the ship.

I defended myself under my breath. *I am getting braver every day.*

When he turned to look at my brother, he said the same old stuff. "Your attitude is terrible."

Without even thinking, I interrupted him. In the past, my father's voice would slam me into silence, and I'd give up. But not now. "That's not true. Woodie's been doing a great job up in the rig all day. Our rigger complimented his work and that *really means something.*" I spoke forcefully, punching words back at him.

Dad ignored me and shifted to a new tack, glaring at my brother. "Well, it's terrible that you boys are drinking at the Coast Guard bar."

I had to force down a smile. Yeah, it was crazy that fourteen- and fifteen-year-old boys were drinking there and no one had done anything about it, but Woodie wasn't alone.

Dad started up the VW bus and it was a quick ride back to the docks to the ship, where the lecture was cut short.

As we climbed out of the VW, he saw Pogo, his favorite assistant, prepping the long grill on the dock for steaks. Had Pogo watched for our return? Dad joined my friend and by the time he looked for us again, we'd disappeared.

•

That night, once our party was underway, after a great dinner with steaks cooked on the grill, everyone was drinking sangria. This was a party for us kids, finally. Not another formal reception event, when we had to work for two days to clean up the ship and stand around at attention in our clean work clothes reciting our possible itinerary to impress big-money donors to the school. Our fanciest event had been for the Panamanian consul, his wife, and their staff, since our ship was registered in Panama and flew their flag. He was so impressed with our school that in his speech he promised us free passage through the Panama Canal.

Dad threw his arm around my shoulders while he talked to Stephanie, as if everything was great between us. Her eyes sparkled and her red dress glowed in the Christmas lights and crepe paper we'd strung from the mast. She raved about the new library shelves in the crew mess, and praised me. "I admire Elizabeth's perseverance. She found a place to put the library, and enlisted your help."

I flushed. My determination had paid off, even though she had no idea the cost of my dad's visit for me and my brother.

Dad beamed. "I've finished the bunks you asked for in the crew quarters. I've had some great students to work with. What's next?"

"You've been a godsend. We could keep you busy for quite a while."

I shuddered. *Oh, no.* I hope this didn't go to his head. As they talked about the ship, I excused myself, ducking out from under his arm, and slipped away.

I was snagged into playing a game called Thumper, not knowing it was a drinking game. A big circle of students and teachers clustered on deck. Each person chose a personal signal, like scratching their head or pinching their nose. My signal was pulling on my ear. The game was fast. We had to keep track of everyone's signs and repeat them in the right order. If you messed up, you had to drink half a glass of punch—fast!— which was really weird if your dad was standing right behind you, like a chaperone.

I totally messed up the hand signals. Someone handed me a glass of punch, but first they poured in one of those little bottles of vodka. Yikes. I'd never had vodka, but I drank it fast as everyone cheered me on. After-wards I couldn't keep track of the hand signals at all. I ended up laughing along with everyone else until Kim decided it was time to dance. Someone plugged in the portable record player with little box speakers and played records. People started dancing.

I retreated up to the top of the ship's ladder above the mizzen deck to watch. Each song was better than the last. I recognized Motown; this was Marvin Gaye singing "I Heard It Through the Grapevine." I shook my head, my body moving back and forth, my toes tapping. But I couldn't let myself feel the joy of the song. I was trapped in agony because I couldn't dance. So many students and teachers were dancing, arms flowing, bod-ies turning, long hair flying, their upturned faces laughing. My friends called up to me, "Elizabeth, come dance!" They said it in a nice way, but I couldn't. I'd never been able to dance to rock and roll. It was like I was standing on the end of the high diving board, absolutely terrified of jump-ing, and I was dying inside, frozen with fear. I couldn't jump.

But the worst was that my dad was standing right below me, chatting it up with some of the teachers. He said to me, "I don't see why you don't go out there and dance, if you call that dancing—*he, he, he.*" I put my head in my hands, my frustration welling into tears. I wiped them furiously. Oh, God, let me die a million deaths. I could never climb down these steps and walk past my father and dance with him watching me. I couldn't. It was impossible. I was going to be miserable for the rest of my life because I couldn't dance.

But then he called up to me, "Night, Missy, I'm turning in. See you tomorrow." And he was gone to where he slept on the foredeck.

Everything didn't change at once. A tiny crack opened. Peter, one of the teachers, was a fantastic dancer, and he called to me to come down. I did come down and stood near the dancers. But I was too self-conscious to move. Then shy, tipsy Emil pulled my hand to dance in a gentle way. When he said, "This is the first time I've ever danced too," I knew I had to try.

Slowly, I started to move with the music, moving my head and torso and arms, and almost immediately, I felt good. It was the weirdest feeling. As soon as I got into it, it was like all the years of agony over not dancing vanished in an instant. All that time I'd been making myself miserable, and this freedom to move was just a second away. Holy shit. This was amazing.

Carole King pounded out her song on the piano, and—there on the mizzen deck of the ship, under the masts and our goofy tangle of crepe paper, lights, and balloons—her song "I Feel the Earth Move" undulated through me. I threw my arms out, and the words rose from her piano and transmitted right through me, lighting me up until I twirled giddy and wobbly, until I landed on the deck. I leaned back and closed my eyes and belted out the chorus, again and again.

As soon as the first song was over, I couldn't wait for the next. I kept dancing with Pogo, and Kim, and everyone. And my dad didn't see me. This was my world, and he couldn't invade it or see me thriving here. I was safe in this circle.

When someone put on Sly and the Family Stone from the Woodstock album, we started chanting "I Want to Take You Higher" as we formed a circle holding hands. All of us rocked our bodies to the beat, the crazy harmonica, the drums propelling us upward, our bodies rising and flying until the beat pulverized us, our heads shaking, sweat streaking down our faces, the words pouring out of all of us, dancing like we were in that crowd at Woodstock. We danced until we couldn't move anymore. I crept away at last to fall asleep on my sleeping bag on deck, feeling so alive, before I dissolved into sleep. Ecstatic. The last thought before sleep. I'd danced!

•

The next morning was Sunday, and the ship was quieter than usual. I stayed in our cabin to write about the dance. Kim was restless. She mumbled that she had something to do, brushed her hair, and put on a fresh blouse. I didn't say a word but these were definitely unusual preparations for her to make before going up on deck. She left and didn't return. I grinned to myself, Something's happening with Kim! I wrote, and napped, and read, meaning I essentially hid for the day, so Dad couldn't find me. But then *bam*, he caught both me and my brother as we headed toward the mess hall for early dinner.

"I have to talk to you two." His voice was forceful.

I stared at him suspiciously. He was strangely ebullient, as he steered us away from the gangway crowd to the quiet side of the ship for privacy.

We followed, knowing something was brewing. When Dad pointed to the deck bench, Woodie and I sat next to each other, obediently, in the shadow cast by the ship's ladder that led up to the bridge and officers' cabins. I was trapped in my old teenage misery, like at home when I stared at the dinner table as he lectured us for hours. But that wasn't me anymore. I forced myself to sit up straight and look Dad in the eye. Woodie slumped into his old miserable posture, staring at the floor. Late afternoon light reflected on the harbor and flickered across our faces.

It was clear Dad had planned this meeting. He sat on a chair to face us and lifted up a yellow legal pad to show us pages filled in his big script with lots of cross-outs and underlines. "Stephanie asked me to write a school letter about how things are going. She thought the families would appreciate hearing a parent's point of view."

He radiated pride in his effort. He'd worked on the letter all day and had handed her a final copy. Then he launched into a rehearsed speech. My chest tightened. I didn't know what was coming.

"Stephanie's made it pretty clear that I have a lot to offer to the school." He looked around at the ship, at the ropes looped around the rail at belaying pins, out to the Miami harbor and distant boat traffic. "You know, I've wanted to spend a year at sea my whole life." He looked at us, his eyes framed by his thick black glasses.

We nodded, warily. "Yes, we know this."

He leaned toward us, placing his hands on his knees while he built his argument like a legal case. "When I saw the article about this school, I thought, I would give this gift to my children." His tone was magnanimous.

Woodie and I both looked down and mumbled like an obedient chorus. "Yes, this is a great opportunity." But we also knew we were his "problem" children that he'd sent away.

Dad's voice took on a sharp edge. "Sit up straight when I'm talking to you!"

We jolted up on the seat like puppets, eyes tensed as our jaws tightened. I tried to push myself back away from my father, but the square, hard bench bolted to the deck wouldn't allow it. He laid into us. "This is the chance of a lifetime and you bloody well better appreciate it."

Woodie and I answered in chorus. "Of course, we do. We love it on the ship."

A few people walked by; an officer climbed down the ladder from the bridge. Dad paused and joked with him. I'm sure Dad thought no one could see through this charade, that he was having a fatherly chat with his children. I glanced around and saw Kim skulking behind a blocked-open doorway to the engine room. Other students strolled by. When they passed behind our dad's head, a few mouthed to us silently, "Are you OK?" When Dad looked away, Woodie and I shrugged, before Dad resumed his speech.

He stood now and moved the chair aside, walking back and forth, before stopping. He announced: "I've decided I will stay on board for the rest of the year. Stephanie says I have a lot to offer to the school."

Woodie and I jolted to our feet. One word welled up with heat. *"No."* Woodie glowered at Dad. "You will *not* stay on the ship."

We were instantly, absolutely unified. We said the same words, echoing each other, not knowing who said them first. "You can't stay. This is our school year. You have to leave."

Our father was stunned, his face clenched like a fist. "What do you mean, you ungrateful children?" His words pounded us. "Don't you know I've done everything in my life for you and your mother?" His body was big and heavy, his words punched us. "This is what I want to do more than anything in my life." His face accused us. "You mean to deny me my dream?" His face was red and sweating, his words lashed us.

But something had grown stronger in me. Somehow all the work—climbing the rig, splicing rope, scrubbing, rowing at dawn, even discovering that I could dance—had made me stronger. I spoke and Woodie echoed my words, both of us standing together, facing our father. "You can't stay. We'll leave if you stay."

Dad looked at us, his face contorted with anger, and he almost tripped backward. I could tell he was trapped and couldn't move in his argument. Woodie and I had stopped him. I felt a surge of power.

Then elation lit up Dad's face. Oh, shit. He had a plan. Like an unexpected chess move, he was sure he had us. He spat the words: "You are no children of mine." He was inspired, his voice electric. "As of this moment, I disown you both."

He gained momentum. "I will have nothing to do with you for the rest of your lives." He piled on the specifics. "You won't get another red cent from me." He paced in front of us, peppering us with his final lines. "Don't think you can ever *ever ever* come home again." He finished with the last punch, his final pronouncement: "You have no home!" His burly chest heaved, sweat sprayed from his head as he turned and stalked off.

Woodie kicked the bench, murmuring "that bastard" before sliding down beside me. My mind was blank. I stared at the thicket of lines, made fast to the railing. A Coast Guard boat's engine rumbled into life, startling me. I rubbed my hands over my face and through my hair.

Woodie shrugged his shoulders, leaned forward on his elbows, and rested his chin on his fists. "Shit, what happened?" He glanced at me. "Is he gone?"

I shrugged. We looked at each other. Woodie was fifteen. I was eighteen. Our father had disowned us and told us we could never go home.

A few friends who'd been hovering nearby crept toward us, looking around to make sure he wasn't coming back. "Are you guys OK?"

I could hardly speak, but I nodded.

I asked my brother, "Are you OK?" Woodie uncurled his fists. I looked him in the eye. "We stood up for ourselves!" I laughed with relief. "That was crazy!"

Woodie grinned. "Hell, yeah. This is *our* ship."

"Damn straight. This is *our* fucking school."

"Right on!" he laughed, and our friends joined in. We didn't have to figure out where we'd go until the end of the year.

"Hey." I took a breath and stood up. "We're going to be OK."

•

At dinner, I wasn't hungry. I left and tiptoed out onto the foredeck, afraid Dad would suddenly appear and yell at me. I climbed the ladder to the second level, passed the officers' cabins, and crawled under the port lifeboat where I could peer down on Dad's shop area. He'd loaded the VW bus with the table saw and hand tools. A few were helping him. After big handshakes and hearty life-of-the-party claps on the back for Pogo and a few others, he drove away, without a look or a word for my brother or me. All that was left were streaks of sawdust on the dock.

Later, I was so disoriented that Woodie convinced me to go to the Coast Guard bar where a lot of the students drank 3.2 beer. As we left the ship, he teased me. "Your birthday was almost two months ago. You're legal, so time to buy yourself a beer." He laughed like this was funny, since he was fifteen and had been drinking there for months. I'd never been to a bar.

After a few sips of watery beer in the dark smoky room where guys played pool, I became bored. I gasped with a sudden thought, and leaned toward my brother. "Woodie, I have to call Mom."

He smiled and raised his second beer in my direction, a tipsy, lazy grin. "Yeah. I guess you better."

I made my way back along the shadowy dock toward the brightly lit phone booth. Moths spiraled and crashed into the glass walls. In the shadows, I saw little flashes like fireflies, where people were smoking behind the metal shipping containers. I looked at my watch. "Oh, no, it's nearly 9 p.m." I was afraid she'd be asleep. I had to reach her before he returned home.

The operator's loud nasal voice asked her, "Will you accept a collect call from Elizabeth?"

Mom sounded tired, but awake. "Yes."

"Hey, Mommy. Hope I didn't call too late."

"No," she said. "I'm working on a term paper. I wish I could spell. I look up words constantly. The other day I forgot how to spell *how*. I couldn't even remember what letter it started with."

I stepped automatically into my role, the good daughter who listened and asked questions about her life. She had no idea I was standing in a glass box surrounded by darkness, cockroaches scooting around the metal floor, about to deliver terrible news.

Finally she asked, "So, how are you guys and your dad doing?"

"Uh, not so great. Dad left. Before dinner, I guess."

"Hmmm, that's unexpected. He was having such a fun time. I wondered if he'd ever come home."

"Well," I gulped. I said it fast. "He disowned Woodie and me and he left."

"He what?"

Now I had her attention. "Disowned us." Then I wondered out loud, "Can a parent do that to his children?"

"What did he say?"

I repeated his words as I traced the scratches in the glass. "That he'd never pay a single red cent for our goddamn education." I'd learned to repeat his threats and lectures in a flat voice, like a badly recited poem, to keep the words from hurting me. Like they were something that didn't touch me, that I only repeated to shock people. I'd done this in high school. I saved up the worst quotes from the weekend's lectures and repeated them Monday morning to my boyfriend in front of our lockers. It took some of the sting out.

"Hmmm. Sounds like your dad. How did this happen?"

I explained how Dad was all wound up. "He announced to Woodie and me that he was going to stay on the ship and sail the whole year with us."

I paused and Mom didn't say anything, so I kept going. "Woodie and I both told him, 'This is *our* school. If you stay on the ship, we'll leave.'" I didn't tell her how he yelled at us. "That's when he said he disowned us. Then he packed up and left."

"He's on his way home, right now?"

"Yup." A long sigh on her side of the phone. "I thought I'd warn you."

She sounded tired and wistful. "That's a shame. Your brother Hubbard and I have been having such a nice time. Hopefully, he'll calm down on the drive back to Ohio."

"Mom, he disowned us. He said we couldn't ever come home again." I crushed cockroaches on the metal floor with my heel. "I don't know if he'll get over it and change his mind."

She tried to reassure me. "You know I'll always let you come home."

My voice rose as I emphasized my words. "But would he *let* you have your children come home again? He forbade us from ever walking in the door again."

I caught myself before I raised my voice again. My brothers and I had an unspoken pact. We didn't get mad at Mom. I might grow impatient or annoyed with things she did, but I mostly didn't allow myself to get angry. She stood between us and Dad. This was one way we tried to protect her.

Mom said brightly, "We'll cross that bridge when we come to it." She paused. "So, how's everything else on the ship?"

I rolled my eyes. She was trying to change the topic and emphasize the positive. I gave her the news. "We're getting a lot of projects done. More engines are working. The ship might actually sail pretty soon."

Her voice caught. "Is it safe to sail? I mean, if it really doesn't feel safe, you come home."

"But Mom, Dad disowned us." My anger rose. "What the fuck does that word mean anyway? Dis-*owned*. I don't want anyone to own me, especially him."

She reacted, her voice stern. "Elizabeth, I don't want you using that word."

I'd never said fuck to her before. Kim's influence! I tried to explain, "Sometimes it's the only word that makes sense." My anger faded as fast as it rose. It was a short skirmish. We couldn't hurt each other.

She breathed a long sigh. "We'll work things out. Don't worry." She was back to reassurance.

"Yeah. OK, Mom."

"Love you," she said, weary.

"Love you too." Exhausted, I hung up the phone and leaned my head against the glass.

Some people walked back to the ship with a drunken sway. One of them called out to me in the glowing glass booth. "Hey, beam me up, Scotty." They laughed as they stumbled up the gangway.

I walked back to the ship. Would my mother ever stand up to my father and break away?

I slipped down to our cabin for my sleeping bag. Usually, Kim would be up on deck by now, but she was writing in her journal and glanced up when I came in. "You OK?"

"I don't know. I guess so." I sat down and leaned against the wall. "You heard everything he said?"

"Yeah, a lot of it."

"Who disowns teenagers? I used to love him so much but then he turned into a monster."

Kim closed her eyes, nodded her head, then she said slowly, "I know what it's like. My stepdad was amazing. Everyone loved him, and then, well, that guy disappeared."

"What happened?"

"The doctors said he had a full psychotic break. I was a kid, what did I know? They gave him meds and shock treatments."

"My dad had shock treatments, too. Before I was born."

"Glad you missed it. He'd forget everything that happened, like it never existed. Then one morning, I found him trying to shave with an axe. It was terrifying."

"Oh, God. What happened?"

There was a long pause. I didn't move, not wanting to break a spell.

"He killed himself." She sighed. "It's almost two years now. I was fourteen. I was the one who found him."

"Oh, God. I'm so sorry, Kim." My heart rushed and I trembled. How could Kim have survived this?

"We still live in his house. But Mom doesn't know how much longer she can hold on to it. I hope it's still there when I go home."

I took a long, deep breath, and released it slowly. We leaned back in silence on our bunks, watching the moths flick and singe on the hot ceiling light. Even though my dad had his rages, he was still there. My home was still *there*. I didn't have to carry his big dramatic gesture as a dead weight on my shoulders. We had this whole year ahead of us on our ship before I had to worry about going home. A lot could happen before then.

A guy came running down the deck, shouting like a town crier. "Hey, the water's working! They want us to take showers. Run the water first before you get in!"

I climbed down the ship's ladder backward fast, and of course Kim slid down and jumped right after me. Girls were cheering in their rooms over water, real water, running in showers.

I shouted out, "How's the water?"

One girl yelled, "It stinks." Another girl said, "It's sputtering." Cheers came from a third girl, "Can't wait to wash my hair!"

Kim called to me, "Who's first dibs?"

"I have to find my shampoo."

"I have it." She stripped and tossed her clothes on the floor before climbing into the tiny stall. The water chortled and spat. "Look at all this rust." She soaped her limbs and then hair.

I stripped down so I would be ready and found a towel. She emerged flinging her blond curls around.

"Don't get me wet!"

"You're about to get in the shower, ninny."

"I'm not a ninny!" When I climbed in, I gasped. "Holy shit, Kim, it's cold! No wonder you took such a fast shower!" I soaped and rinsed as fast as I could.

As I was drying off, I groaned, "My dad is obsessed with cold showers. He always says, 'Good for closing your pores.' He turns the water ice cold at the end of our showers and stands there so we can't change it."

Kim stared out the porthole. "Last year I was visiting my dad at his apartment in New York. He's always leering at girls. I didn't want to get undressed at his house, ever." She sat up and stabbed her legs into a pair of shorts, and pulled on a T-shirt. "But that day he ordered me to take a shower, and I said no. He grabbed me, and ripped some of my clothes off, and pushed me in the shower. He yelled, 'You will be naked in my house!'"

She shook her head, her pale blue eyes piercing. "Fuck that shit. I am so done with dads."

"Yeah, me too."

•

A few nights later after dinner, I watched Kim play chess with Emil on deck. People played chess a lot, but for this game a circle of boys stood around chuckling over each move. I didn't know the moves, but I could tell more than chess was going on. Emil was pissed that Kim was beating him. He complained to his older brother, Jakob, the serious new second mate, who lingered nearby, watching. "Make her play correctly!" Kim glanced at Jakob for just a moment, but I could feel a spark of electricity pass between them.

Jakob shook his head with a wry smile. "You're on your own. She's a maverick player, but she is playing the pieces correctly." He was tall and lean in his khaki uniform as he walked away and climbed the ladder to the bridge.

I stalked off in the opposite direction, grumbling. "'Maverick player.' I bet she loved that." I carried my journal even though I didn't feel like writing. The mood on board was so much better, but I felt cast adrift. My friend Kim was disappearing.

•

Even though we lived in relatively close quarters for fifty students, ten teachers, and ten crew and officers, we were a layered society. The adults lived, slept, and hung out in places unknown to us students. Even though most of the teachers had just graduated from college, some only three or four years older than me, and even though I had graduated from high school, I still felt like one of the kids. But I'd been having interesting conversations with Drew, a new science teacher, since we'd danced. He was tall and kind of cute, but I didn't have a crush on him or anything.

One evening when a bunch of us finished up our mess duties, we sat down with some teachers and crew in the officer's mess to eat watermelon.

Kim ate wedges and the juice smeared and dripped down her cheeks. She glanced at me, as I took careful bites, and roared with laughter. "Oh my God, Elizabeth, you're eating like you're having tea with the queen. Your pinkies are sticking out!" She was putting me down.

I glanced at my hands and blushed. "I never noticed that. At least I'm not eating watermelon with a knife and fork, like my father taught us."

"You're fucking with me, right? Knife and fork?" Everyone else around the table laughed.

"Doesn't anyone else do that?" I grimaced. "I don't like to get my hands sticky." I glanced at Drew, blushing.

Kim insisted, "It's finger food! Get your hands in it!"

I ended up clearing the table and washed the last dishes in the galley sink. When I returned to the officer's mess, no one was there except Drew. He said, "I have to show you something." I followed him through a bulkhead door down a shadowy hall until he opened a watertight door and we stepped into a dark room piled high with mounds of white canvas bags.

I guessed what they were. "Wow, these must be the hand-sewn sails from Sweden. Did you know they're made from flax grown in Belgium and woven in Dundee, Scotland?"

He laughed at me as he slipped his arms around me. "How did you know all that?"

"In New York, Stephanie raved about them. They're so valuable. I bet that's why the owners don't want us to lash on the sails. Or 'bend' on the sails, if you're really salty!" I talked faster because I was confused about his arms around me.

He asked, "How will we ever sail the ship if they don't let us bend on the sails?"

"Exactly! That's the—" Before I finished, he kissed me.

I was confused. Kissing was fun but this was unexpected. He paused to close the door, leaving only a crack of light. I asked nervously, "We can't get locked in, right?"

He tested the latch on the heavy metal door. "I won't close it all the way. To be safe." It was hot in the dark and he guided us to sit down on the mound of sails.

I was confused. I liked that he liked me, but this was completely unexpected. He kissed me with more gusto and suddenly we were lying down on the canvas bags. What was going on? How did this happen?

Everything was suddenly complicated. I went along with it, the sliding up and down of clothing, but before I knew what was happening he was moving on top of me with great enthusiasm, hot and sweaty. And I disappeared, waiting for it to be over—I had no choice but to endure, and wait—something to get through.

I'd had fun talking to Drew, but had I been flirting? Why did it turn into sex? And then it was all over. I tucked in my clothes before we snuck back down the hallway and left in different directions.

I slipped down the stairs into our room, where I planned on washing and not saying a word about what had happened, but Kim was journaling on her bunk. I couldn't hide from her piercing look.

She studied me carefully, with a little smile. "What happened to you?"

"I'm not sure." I closed the door and latched it. I spoke quietly, telling her how I had fun talking to Drew, and maybe we flirted a little, but suddenly something happened. Then it hit me, "Oh shit, now I've had sex with four people. Oh God! I must be a terrible person."

"But hey, did you like it?"

"I like him, but not that way. It was too sweaty and athletic for me." I searched for clean clothes, soap, and a towel.

She leaned back, stroking her chin thoughtfully. "That's interesting. I really like sweaty athletic sex." As if she was making a decision: "Like riding horseback. Maybe I don't have to absolutely love someone if I'm having a good time. Maybe that's what's good for me, at this point in my life." She was pleased. She'd decided something.

I sat down to think. What did I really like? "I like long, slow touching, on a beautiful morning with light coming in a window, and a lot of talking. And someone I really love. We would take a long time before we made love." I'd decided something, too. Maybe I could finally stand up for myself, and say no, until the conditions were what I wanted, rather than going along with someone else's ideas for me. "I want to enjoy it, rather than waiting for it to be over."

"Damn straight!" agreed Kim.

Then I gasped. "Oh shit, how long does it take for the pill to work? I started two weeks ago."

Kim grimaced. "A couple of months?"

"I am so stupid."

"Did you use any protection?"

"Noooo!" I slapped my head. "What an idiot I am. I forgot. I didn't say anything. It was so unexpected I didn't even think of it."

"Did he ask?"

"Noooo." I was getting irritated. I counted on my fingers how many days until my period should come. Due on Christmas. I prayed my period would show up on time. "Do you think all the guys on the ship know the girls got the pill?"

"Definitely."

Suddenly I worried about the rumor mill. Last month the flirty girl and one of the older guys were found getting it on, up on the upper deck. The word spread around the ship and people said terrible things about her. Not about him. Like high school.

"Do you think anyone will find out about this?"

"Are you sure nobody saw you?"

"Really sure. I have to tell him this can't happen again." But could I actually say to Drew that this wasn't right for me? I sat down with my hands gripped over my head. "I just want to have friends, and forget about sex. It's too confusing."

Kim urged, "Do what's right for you." But then she chuckled. "I'm kind of liking this sweaty athletic idea myself."

I wondered if she was thinking about the Second Mate she was going after. Playfully, I punched her on my way to the shower. "You can have it!"

•

First Mate Mr. Neilson stood at attention in his white uniform, his voice bellowing. "Three students broke into a shipping container on the dock last night." We jolted to attention, shocked out of our lethargy. He'd called Stephanie in New York. One student was going home. Everyone glanced around. Who was missing? *Oh, that kid*, we figured out. Who were the others? We were never sure. Neilson bellowed again, breaking through the whispers. "How can anyone trust us if there is this behavior? The dock owners nearly banned all students from the dock."

In November we had flown on the dynamic infusion of Mr. Neilson's leadership, but in mid-December, discouragement was running us down again. After nearly three months, it was hard to believe the ship would ever leave. We stood at attention, sober and serious, except some of the sarcastic boys, who taunted Mr. Neilson with their laughter. This was a battle for the soul of the school. Mr. Neilson stood stone-faced. "Why do you shit on my nose?" he roared. "I am more committed to you than you are to yourselves. I refused to be paid for my time here, just to let you know how much I believe in this school and ship." I was shocked. He wasn't getting paid?

A tall boy in the back snarled. "We aren't getting paid either. Our parents paid through the nose for us to work on this fiasco of a ship." A few snickers peppered the crowd.

The rest of us were caught in a horrible tension.

A student yelled, "The ship isn't going anywhere."

Another called out, "All we do is work. I'm supposed to be getting school credits so I can get into college."

Another retorted, "What a baby, why don't you go home so you can go to school?"

"Stop!" Kim had stepped forward and shouted. "This disrespect is killing us. These men have decades of sea experience and you treat them like shit." She cried. "I cringe every time someone insults Mr. Neilson." She was sobbing and angry at the same time. No one had ever seen her cry. "If you drive them away, how will we ever sail? You are destroying our only hope!" She turned and stomped away. Some followed her but she cried out, "Give me space!" as she ran down the deck.

The rest of us stood stunned, silent.

Zip spoke up. "We're the problem. I was shit-faced last night. I'm part of the problem." He glared at us. "We have to get our shit together. Let's get back to work so we can get out of here." The whistle was blown. Muster was over and we dispersed silently to our jobs on deck.

•

A few days later, at lunch in the crew mess, a group of us clustered around Kim and Zip. We'd heard that Neilson and his cadets were going back to Denmark. Kim's eyes were red. "I thought we had a chance."

Neilson's positive energy had lifted Kim, and helped carry the burden Stephanie had laid on her sixteen-year-old shoulders, to support the energy of the students. I'd felt like I could be more like Kim, but in the mirror that morning I still looked like a scared, moody girl. I'd thought I was becoming one of the helpful people, but maybe I was still one of the sad lost ones.

Ted mused. "Part of the problem is we're more like an alternative school, like Summerhill, instead of a formal sail training program. Maybe Neilson's expecting too much from us."

Zip had talked to the Danish cadets. "Neilson loves us and wants to sail the ship, but he's so frustrated! Stephanie keeps interrupting the work to get the students and the ship all gussied up for her fundraising events."

One of the serious students mused. "I think Chick and Stephanie are a big problem. They always promise us the impossible, and then it doesn't happen."

Kim and I were torn by our loyalty to Stephanie. Kim rubbed her eyes with her fists, "Maybe I have to be more realistic." It hurt to question my loyalty, but maybe Stephanie was creating a great illusion. When we spoke to her, we bared our souls. She was like our young, hip mother superior. What would happen if we lost faith in her?

•

That afternoon a piano was to be moved off the ship. The mysterious owners we'd never seen wanted the piano removed from the paneled living room on the main deck. Did they think the ship might actually sail and they wanted the piano off it? Who knew what they thought? A few crew and students moved the piano on a wheeled rig along the deck toward the foredeck. Neilson sent his Danish cadets up into the new rigging to the first yardarm. Ropes were lowered to secure the piano before it was lifted off the deck. The rigger was ready to wrap the piano in moving blankets when something happened.

Burly Mr. Neilson, in his khaki uniform, walked to the piano, carrying a chair. He sat down in front of the piano on the deck in the midst of a busy dockyard. His big hands stretched over the keys, and he played. I don't remember what the music was but the memory of it felt like he'd played Beethoven, perhaps the "Moonlight Sonata." He leaned in over the keyboard, his strong fingers reaching for the notes, his face serious and intent. Deep chords repeated and built and rose into the rig. Kim draped her arms around me. Tears streaked our cheeks.

When the piece was over, the noise of the docks crashed back, engines rumbled, and deep horns sounded in Miami harbor. The piano was wrapped, strapped, and lifted by the ropes, and a line of crew and students hauled the line, as we held our breath. The piano was gently lowered and brought to rest on the dock, where it was loaded onto a truck.

We lingered. Ted watched the crew members set the rigging back in place. Because of Neilson, Ted had cut off his long tangle of curls. Now his face was lean and tanned, his hair short like a cadet. He spoke without his usual joking irony. "Neilson could have used a crane to lift the piano, but it's a code of sailing ships to use what you have on hand. We used the rig and we did it together." He stared down at his hands. "I would do anything for that man."

The next morning at muster, Mr. Neilson and his quartermasters in white uniforms stood before us. He spoke to us thoughtfully. "You are following the journey of a cadet. You have come together as a team, to work and live and learn together. You are developing a sense of duty to your mates. This commitment to each other will make the difference between life and death at sea and in the rig." He paused and studied our faces down the line. "You will remember this time for the rest of your lives." They heaved their duffels on their shoulders and headed down the gangway. We knew Mr. Neilson wouldn't return.

•

Even though the Danish officers had left, a momentum was set into motion, and in the last weeks of December the endless lists of repairs were nearly completed. Soon Stephanie said the ship would be ready to motor to dry dock. We believed her. Stephanie and Chick hired a captain who was hard at work on the bridge, getting our papers ready to sail, dealing with port authorities, and overseeing the updates from the chief engineer and deck officers. We never saw him but we heard stories about him. He was a Swede, close to retiring, had been at sea his whole life, and was one of the few captains in the world still licensed for both sail and motor ships. His name was Stig Floden, which Ted jokingly translated to mean Stick Floating, which he thought was a "salty" name for our captain. We believed the rumors that we'd set sail after Christmas.

•

My period started on Christmas. All month I'd punched each day's pill through the foil disc like a prayer. Every time I took the pill, I was wracked with confusion. Taking the pill meant I didn't have to be afraid of getting pregnant. But I didn't want to have sex until I loved someone. But I couldn't trust that I was brave enough to say no when I didn't want to have sex. I didn't want to take the pill like a stupid crutch because I was a wimp who got stuck in awkward situations, because I couldn't speak up.

On that tropical Christmas morning, I made a decision. In our little bathroom, I whispered a strong, silent "No" as I packed away my stash of circular discs. Kim's circle of pills rested on the sink as her yes, so she wouldn't forget to take them. She was getting ready, and I was shutting a door. Kim and I, who had talked about everything, now had something she didn't bring up, and I didn't ask.

•

I was on gangway duty after lunch as waves of people charged off to the beach. A boy snickered at me, "Only losers serve their watches on Christmas." I ignored him but made sure he signed off in the log. I leaned back on my chair and kept reading *The Story of O*, which was totally creeping me out. Drew decided I needed to loosen up sexually, and he thought this book, about a woman treated as a sex slave by wealthy men, should do the trick. But the book helped me get clear about what I needed to do.

When Drew showed up with some other teachers in bathing suits heading for the beach, he asked, "How's your reading?" and gave me a friendly wink.

I answered with a false cheerfulness. "Very interesting." But I gestured for him to walk a few steps with me down the deck. I spoke quietly, nervous but determined. "Our getting close isn't working for me. I just want to be friends."

He smiled in a friendly way, and we both acted like it was no big deal. I handed him the book. "It's not for me." As he and the teachers walked away, talking about diving, I was relieved.

The ship was mostly empty on this strange muggy Christmas. My remaining problem was that I had an infected big toe. I'd run down the stairs in the girls' quarter a few days earlier and felt a piercing pain in it. I'd thought that was weird, saw nothing on my toe, and kept on going. Every so often if I stepped wrong, I'd feel that pain again. My toe reddened, then it got hot and swollen. Lots of us had cuts, blisters, bruises, rope burns, bad sun burns, or strains and sprains. Stephanie told us we'd get a medical officer on board before we sailed, but for now one of the teachers rummaged around in the first aid kit. When one of the girls complained she'd lost her needle for hand sewing, I knew what had stuck into my big toe. It now hurt with every step. One of the teachers promised to take me to the emergency room the day after Christmas.

If it weren't for the toe I'd be leaving the ship along with the other teachers and students. The engineers were sure we were only days away from motoring out of Miami harbor. The day after Christmas, three groups of students and teachers were going to fly to Grand Bahama Island to camp for a week until the ship arrived to pick them up. It was a legal issue. The American students had to board the ship outside of U.S. waters because we were sailing under the Panamanian flag. A small group of students would stay on board to prepare the ship for departure and, because of my infected toe, I had to stay too.

When my watch ended, I felt lost. As I limped down the deck, Pogo showed up, with sun-reddened shoulders and wearing cutoff shorts. "What's wrong with your foot?"

I was mortified when I started crying. "My big toe's infected and I'm hot and it's Christmas and I'm miserable." I didn't breathe a word about the breakup.

Pogo put his hand under my elbow and helped me hobble to a shady spot on the starboard deck. "Sit right here. I'll be back in a minute." He returned with my sleeping bag, pillow, and *Winnie-the-Pooh* from my cabin. He spread out the covers and I lay on the deck with my foot elevated. Pogo read aloud from my worn childhood book. His voice was comforting, like a cup of warm milk at bedtime. He gave distinctive voices to Christopher Robin, to sensitive Pooh, insecure Piglet, and bossy Rabbit.

After a while, I took the book and read aloud about Eeyore gazing into the river. *"Nobody cares. Pathetic, that's what it is."*

Pogo read Pooh perfectly, kindly and a little bumbling. "'*Good morning, Eeyore,*' said Pooh."

I recited Eeyore with a playful mournfulness, knowing his words by heart. "*If it is a good morning. Which I doubt.*" I lay back and watched Pogo's kind face and new feathery beard as he read. Contentment spread through me.

Pogo glanced up from the book. "I've never seen you really smile before."

I jolted up to sit facing him. "What do you mean?" I ricocheted from defensiveness to confusion to the verge of tears. Had I been looking sad all this time? I knew he didn't say sad, but I was sure that was what he meant. With no mirrors on this ship, I'd forgotten about the sad girl who stared back at me from mirrors at home. I felt betrayed by my own face.

•

I suddenly remembered a day that summer in New York, when I'd emerged from the passport photo shop at Grand Central, holding my envelope of black-and-white photographs. I was wearing my Stephanie dress with the puckered bodice and short skirt, and my round tortoiseshell frames with brownish lenses. I was looking for the subway, when a man asked, "Why are you so sad?" He was older, elegant in a suit, with thoughtful eyes.

Was I sad? The question had startled me. A moment before I'd thought I was happy in my Jones of New York dress. His question pierced me and sadness rose like a wave of nausea, tears almost surfacing. Did I carry sadness like a billboard? But I knew what his question meant. He would ask me to lunch and inevitably invite me to bed. Why does everything lead to sex now? It could be anything, my dress or my ring or looking in a shop window, any one thing drew a man's attention to make a comment that was designed to lead to sex. They approached like an imaginary drawbridge had opened, giving permission to ask a devastating question to a girl who was hungry to be known.

I hurried away, saying no to lunch (yes, he did ask), so politely. Only after I found the subway entrance, raced down sticky steps, and finally sank into a seat on a subway going uptown did I open the envelope to see captured on small square passport photos a pouty, soft-faced girl whose eyes ventured out under a weight of sadness.

•

Pogo reached out to touch my arm, his face concerned. "I didn't mean to upset you." He added gently, "I just wanted to say it's so nice to see you smile." Pogo was different than those men.

I was faced with a choice: I could sink back into the old sadness or I could bring myself back to this afternoon on deck and grasp the peacefulness I was feeling. I picked up the book and read a line from Piglet in a cute, little voice. *"We'll be friends forever, won't we, Pooh?"*

Pogo answered without needing the book, *"'Even longer,' Pooh answered."*

I leaned back on the pillows, beaming at Pogo.

Soon after, Kim returned from the beach and plopped down next to me, scattering sand. She leaned over to hug me. "I was looking for you." I smiled up at her. She said, "As I walked back, I was thinking about all of us." She wiggled my good foot fondly. "How long have I known these people? It seems a very long time already!" We nodded. Kim said, "Because of this trip we've become family. We all have something to give."

At the fantail, I could hear the guitar players warming up, and hoots of laughter from the gangway as everyone signed back in. Footsteps rushed up and down ship's ladders and down the deck. After the months of work to rescue the ship, it was our last evening in Miami.

My dad in full architect mode at our dining room table.

The annual family Christmas photo the year before we left for the ship.

The week before I left for the ship with my favorite books above me.

Woodie with his beloved camera before it got stolen.

Pogo sitting in front of the Grand Dining Room that we never entered.

Zip. Note the book library behind him.

Stephanie, Ron and Mike.

Am I ready to climb the rigging yet? I don't think so.

Did you ever have a best friend that's the life of the party, and you're the quiet turtle sitting behind her? That's me and Kim.

Harry from Driftpile, Alberta loved his first time at sea.

Richie Meeker, always ready for trouble.

Our photography teacher, Karl.

Rick, our best rigger, making a cargo net.

Splicing team at work.

Before Mr. Nielsen arrived, we were a pretty funky scene.

Grease Monkeys hanging out on the dock with Alfonso.

Kim is ready for adventures and I'm ready to write.

Pogo and Jane celebrate after the crew finish coating the water tanks with cement paint.

First mate Jakob.

Chick and Mr. Nielsen describe the work done on the ship that flies under the Panamanian flag.

We climb the rigging up to the second platform to show we're ready to go to sea.

We finally get better at lifeboat drills.

The official reception with the Panamanian Consul in Miami, when he promises us free passage through the Panama Canal.

We get ready to set sail from Miami.

Our new Swedish captain Stig Floden takes command as we leave Miami.

A Navy nuclear sub watches our approach to Key West.

Hauling lines in Key West.

Dry dock in Veracruz.

Our heavenly two weeks at sea from Veracruz to Panama for our sail training, finally.

Sailing from Veracruz to Panama.

Lashing the sails on a yardarm in Panama.

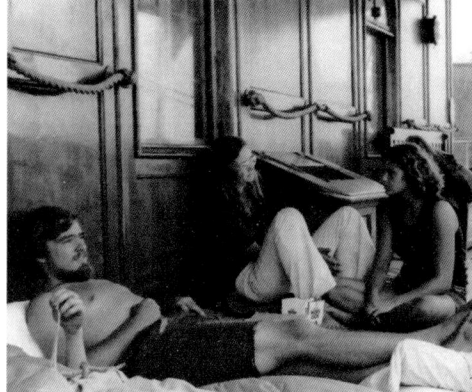

Pogo, Elizabeth, and Kim during the long wait while being held hostage in Panama.

Leaving the ship on the last day in Panama.

The last view of the ship.

Celebrating our mom
graduating from college
at age thirty-nine with
a degree in Criminal
Justice.

Woodie and me with our little brother
Hubbard the summer after the ship.

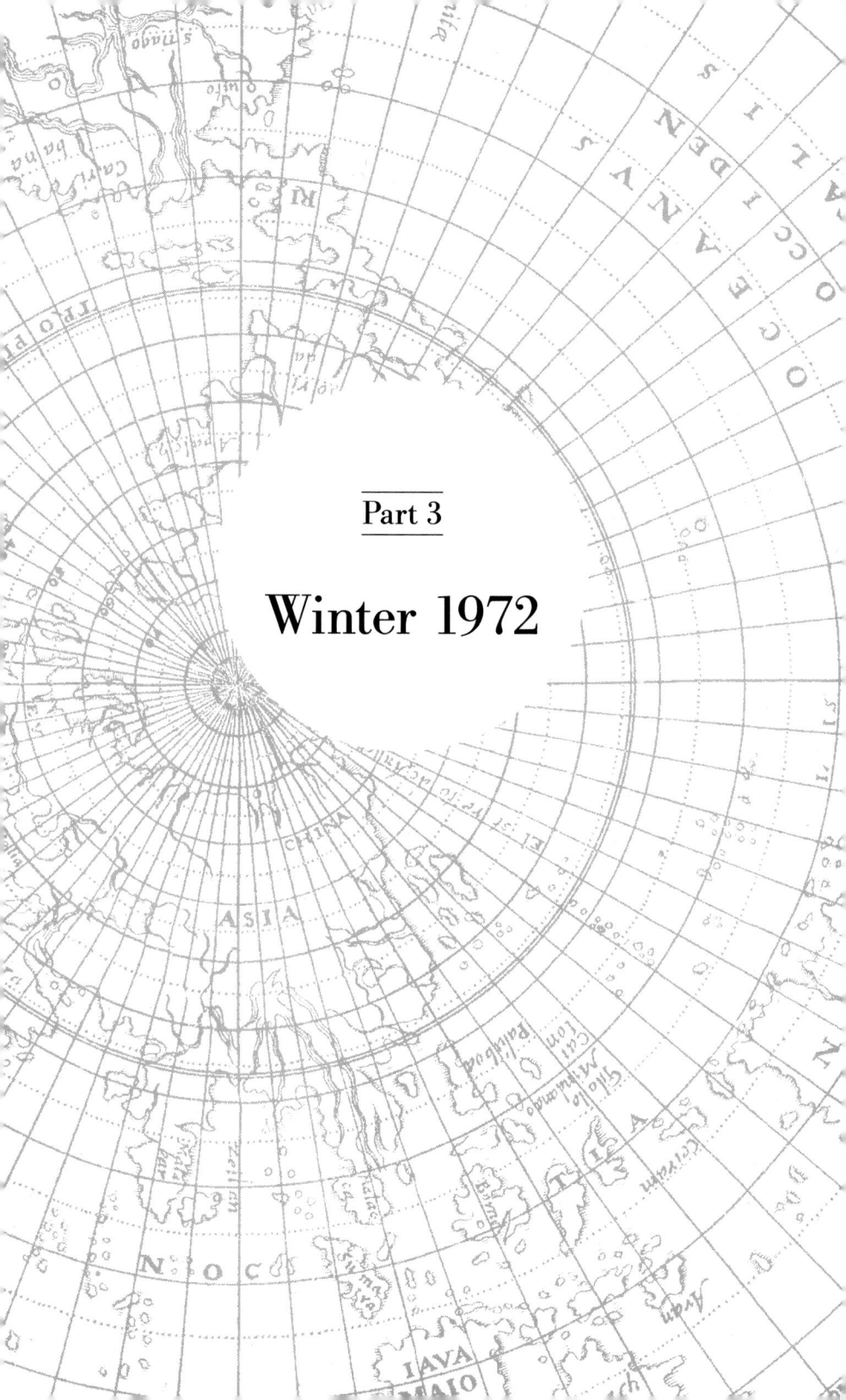

Part 3

Winter 1972

At Sea

The world is not in your books and maps. It is out there.
—J. R. R. Tolkien, *The Hobbit*

Early on January 1, engines rumbled below decks like a dragon. Zip, in his greasy jumpsuit, stared up at the stack spewing smoke, glanced at my worried face, and flashed a reassuring grin. "Accumulation of soot. We're flushing out old diesel fuel. Hot damn, the engines are working!"

I asked him, "Don't you have to fly with us to the Bahamas?"

He stage-whispered. "Stephanie made me Third Engineer, so I'm paid crew. They need all of us in the engine room to get this rust bucket out of here." He disappeared into the engine room. Trucks jammed the dock as engineers, electricians, and plumbers finished last inspections. New crew rushed up the ship's ladder to the bridge. A crochety radio operator swore as he struggled to bring ancient equipment to life. A pretty ship's doctor organized the medical clinic. A new hire, Nina, with a black ponytail and bangs, who would be the hostess for stateroom guests, hauled aboard her scuba equipment. I had to remember to tell Kim there was finally a girl diver aboard.

Stephanie hugged each of us students goodbye before we climbed into the station wagon, catching our quick flight to Grand Bahama Island. Wearing her blue dress with white anchors, she gave us our instructions. "Find the harbor and meet up with the camping teams. You'll see the ship when she arrives." It seemed pretty easy. We each carried a knapsack, a canteen, a bag lunch, and our passports.

We were a mismatched group: Reggie the liar, Joyce the flirt, quiet Ben, me and my journal, and Ted, who seemed dull without his guitar or his girlfriend, Jane. Did we even imagine the *Antarna* might not arrive? The engines, turbines, and pumps had never been tested together. There had been no sea trials. The ship had not moved from the dock in nearly four years, and yet we believed she would motor out of Miami, cross 112 miles to Grand Bahama Island, and arrive at Freeport Harbor. All we had to do was find the harbor, find the other students who had camped there for a week, and wait for the ship.

When we arrived at the airfield, Bahama Island Customs stamped our passports, writing "One Day" to clear us until we met our ship. When the five of us emerged from the tiny airport into the sun-bleached light, Ted called out, "Alright, we're on a mission to find the harbor."

Under a glaring sky, the concrete road passed for miles between rocky fields bordered by palms. We hoped this road would take us to Freeport Harbor.

After walking an hour, we dropped onto the curb to sip from our canteens. One kid whined. "How will we find the others?" The ocean shimmered in the distance.

Ted, like a newly wise man, said, "They will find us."

A pickup passed us. In the back a pile of filthy kids sat on packs, but they started to cheer and wave at us before they disappeared down the road. We leapt up, and Ted called out in his dry funny voice, "Follow that truck!"

We renewed our trudge down the road. Soon an empty pickup stopped for us and in a few miles dropped us at a scrubby field near the harbor where a group had gathered. This was a good place to watch for the ship. Other trucks and rusty vans dropped off more students, teachers, piles of packs, and scuba gear.

We ran around hugging each other, laughing. The camping kids were sunburned, and grimy, with hollows in their cheeks. Kim threw her arms around me. "Hey you! I'm starving. Anything to eat in your pack?"

I pulled out my sandwich and apple and handed them over. The newly arrived students passed around canteens and food to share.

Everyone wanted to know. "When's the ship arriving?" We searched the horizon beyond the harbor. No sign yet. Ted said, "I wonder how long will it take to motor a hundred miles? No one told us."

"They better be cooking a big dinner for us!"

A chorus shouted, "They better!"

I stood around with Kim and Bruce, and asked, "Didn't you have money for food?"

"Nope," Kim said. "We weren't given any money for the week. It was Chick's idea for us to survive off the land and the ocean. Some had money so we bought cheap food at first, cold cereal and milk, and fished for conch shells and grouper. But we never had enough food."

Sunburned Bruce pointed with confidence to his spear gun. "Peter and I swam a long way and speared four fish. He tied them to a long line to drag them far behind us, in case sharks came, so they'd snatch the fish and not us. We ended up with several five-foot sharks following us." He mimed how they'd faced the sharks, waved their arms, and tried to look as big as possible to scare them away. "But they kept coming after the fish. We finally made it to shore and roasted the fish. So delicious." Despite the grime, the bashful Bruce was stronger, leaner and more confident.

Richie ran up and hugged me, his freckles hidden under smeared dirt. "I dove, too." I patted him on the back and ruffled his hair, happy to see him. He was enthusiastic. "We built lean-to shelters. I helped lash them together. I found a conch to eat and kept one of the shells." We sat down in a large circle and the different groups of students compared notes on how they'd built beach huts with banana or palm leaves.

I asked Kim, "So what'd you do about food?"

She was deeply browned, with a ripped T-shirt over her bathing suit. She shrugged. "We did what we had to do. When we hitched into the town, the people that picked me up happened to be friends from my school, here on vacation." She rolled her eyes. "I couldn't tell them we were starving. They dropped us off and we walked through a huge grocery store. We ate while we shopped around, leaving empty containers on shelves behind full ones. We paid for some things while shoplifting other stuff in my clothes. We ran around the corner and stuffed our faces with all that we could eat, before we hitched back."

I stared at her. How hungry would I have to get before I stole food? Did I still envy their week on the beach? I was relieved I'd stayed behind waiting for my toe to heal.

First Nation Harry and Beck, a rich California kid, were dropped off, and walked over to sit down and join us. Harry brushed his dark bangs out of his eyes. I liked how he spoke in a formal way. "Beck and I made friends with Native Bahamians. They were happy to welcome an Indian from Canada. A tall elder invited the two of us to camp at his house. People from surrounding islands showed us how to spear fish, but not the poison fish. We smoked ganja out of a coconut bong with wine." He paused and spoke with feeling. "They are good people."

Beck, his shoulder-length hair in golden-brown tight curls, patted his belly. "We had feasts every day, pots of fish, rice, and beans."

Usually extremely quiet Phil, sunburned and freckled, talked animatedly about scuba diving on the reef. "I was diving when a cloud of small colorful fish swam within ten feet of me. I tapped the tank on my back and the fish turned and changed color. I tapped again, and their color changed again and again. It was awesome."

A little later, a taxi dropped off Pogo, who stood out as the only clean student. When he tried to slip in to sit next to Kim and me in the circle, we teased him about his nice clothes. He confessed that his girlfriend back in Bar Harbor had begged Stephanie to let her join him on the island. "After a couple of nights, she got tired of camping on the beach with no hot water to wash her hair." He was clearly embarrassed. "She took me to a hotel in town for the rest of the week, and bought me these clothes so they'd let me in the place."

His camping friends eyed him. "OK, so what did you eat when we were drinking fish broth?"

He confessed, "Well, one night, I ate Chateaubriand and drank a remarkable St. Emilion 1969."

My head whiplashed, and I stared at him. Was he teasing? How did my friend Pogo, who grew up in a little town in Maine, know about really good wines? Pogo had never said much about his twenty-five-year-old girl-friend, who had been his French teacher.

He whispered, "She likes to buy very expensive wine." Later I over-heard him murmuring to Ted. "I'm so relieved to be back. I finally convinced her that I was breaking up. I want to be eighteen and really live this time of my life. I didn't want to settle down with her."

Ted laughed. "Welcome back to the madness!" They gestured at the barren field and the motley collection of people. "Ain't this the life!"

As the afternoon faded, the sun set in the west over Florida a hundred miles away. People asked again, "When is the ship getting here?"

Pogo and Ted calculated how fast the ship might travel, taking into consideration that it hadn't sailed for four years and had a foot of barnacles on the bottom. If the ship could make ten knots (about eleven miles) an hour, it would take them about eleven hours to cover the distance of 110 miles to the island. And that was in the best of circumstances.

"Even if the ship left at noon," Ted said, "and all went well, it would arrive close to midnight. We better set up camp for the night."

We assessed the rocky, dry field and palm trees along the shore. Richie said the obvious. "I'm starving."

People called out, "Who's got any money left?" We were all hungry and thirsty. Everyone pooled the remaining cash. A group headed down to a store at the harbor for food and water for all of us. Kim spread out her sleeping bag and said I could share with her. After bread, cheese, and water, we sat up late in small groups before we fell asleep in the field. None of the fifty of us let ourselves imagine *what if the ship doesn't arrive?*

In the morning, early, someone yelled, "The ship! Holy shit, she's here!" We ran down to the edge of the rocky shore and shielded our eyes from the glare of morning light on the water. Out beyond the harbor at anchor was the *Antarna*. Amazingly, astoundingly, she was there. Luminous, white-hulled, four-masted, a mirage of perfection and beauty at this distance. We hugged and cheered and jumped up and down, our excitement contagious. "She made it! I can't believe it! She made it! Oh my God, I'm starving!"

Everyone hauled camping supplies and scuba gear in a long ragtag parade toward the docks. Had I ever doubted the ship would arrive? It was the culmination of Stephanie's vision and all our hard work, that we could sail this ship. A miracle really, and Stephanie's fundraising to pay the bills. It all came together. A feeling that expanded in my chest seemed to flow between all of us. Like pride and exhilaration. Almost like a chant we all shared. *We did it. We fucking did it.*

•

The water was rough with whitecaps, and our twenty-five-foot launch slammed on the waves. I'd never been out on the intense real ocean before. The launch was loaded with teens and gear, taking us out to the ship in batches. I held onto the bench and railing and braced my feet as the loaded boat rocked and plunged, spray drenching us. I couldn't stop looking at the *Antarna* as we approached, the hull and masts looming above us.

The launch bucked and jolted as I tried to stand. We formed a line to shove each bag across the gap of waves to the crew member who stood at the bottom of the gangway. Gear moved hand to hand up the gangway onto the deck, before we leapt across the gap to the gangway. As I faltered at the railing, a sailor reached down, grasped my forearm, and hauled me across the narrow chasm onto the gangway landing, and I scrambled up to the deck.

Our ship swayed, and all of us new arrivals lurched down the deck like we were clowns or tipsy until we discovered a way to swagger that propelled us to walk in nearly a straight line down the deck.

I climbed to the bridge to look out at the open ocean and then at the ship, which was completely different. It was like a homecoming. I was crazy in love with the ship. She didn't look like a disaster anymore. The teak decks were clean and sun-bleached from our two months of scrubbing them. The mahogany cabin walls were varnished and glossy in the glare of the Bahamian sun. The brass, all the ridiculous brass, glowed. I studied the students. Even the annoying little boys were suddenly adorable and dear to me. The sarcastic losers I usually ignored sat around laughing, and were actually funny and kind of cute. Everyone was bathed in sparkling light and I couldn't stop smiling.

I found the Salty Dogs—Pogo, Ted and serious Rick—waiting for lunch. Ted reported, "They found an octopus in the engines when they left Miami."

"That's crazy. How'd they figure that out?"

Rick added specifics. "The ship was steaming out of Miami harbor when it hit a headwind that strained the engines. A big black cloud of oily smoke started pouring out of the stack. The four massive diesel engines were overheating. The engine room was engulfed in steam."

"The ship almost didn't make it out of Miami? What happened?"

"They found an octopus in the cooling system, blocking water from getting to the engines. It must have swum in when it was a baby and grown inside the water pipes. But they couldn't get it out whole."

"That's sad. But were the engines OK after that?"

"They stopped billowing smoke."

Zip dashed by and I called out to him. "How was the trip over?"

His grin was wider than ever. "Crazy! The engines, generators, and pumps actually worked together!" He ran his hands through his red hair, streaking it with engine grease. "Once we were underway, I came up on deck and leaned over the railing. Turbulence churned the water from the reef on the bottom. Once it gets scraped off in dry dock, we'll move! Gotta go!" He raced up to the bridge.

Pogo asked us, "Heard about the pirate flag?"

"A pirate flag?"

Kim caught the question as she arrived. She glanced around and lowered her voice, and we leaned in. She knew the official story from her officer "friend" on the bridge. "Those creeps, the owners sat on the ship's papers and wouldn't let the ship leave Miami." She explained how there was an agreement: Because Stephanie had paid all their bills, the school could lease the ship for a few years. But once the ship had been ready, the owners had said they wouldn't agree to that. They'd trapped Stephanie into signing away all the money she'd put into the ship, over $300,000, because she was not going to let them hold up the school and us students any longer. Stephanie and the captain had organized the papers for the ship to be cleared to leave port. But someone said the very last shipyard bills weren't paid. Kim told us, "Supposedly our new Swedish captain said, 'Let the owners bloody well pay them!' Stephanie and the captain could be charged with piracy for not having the right papers, but the captain laughed about it. Jill, the art teacher, swiped one of the bed sheets and painted a skull and crossbones on it to make a flag. The captain loved it and let them fly it on the foredeck."

Ted was impressed. "This is seriously salty."

The bosun's whistle blew for lunch. From all over the ship, everyone ran for the mess.

•

After lunch, everyone was called to the mizzen deck. Captain Floden greeted us all warmly and waved to us to sit down. "We have begun our journey. Everything changes now that we are a sailing vessel." He formally introduced the crew, many who'd come aboard in the last days before departure. They stood shoulder to shoulder along one side of the deck— first, second, and third deck officers, deckhands, riggers, first, second, and third engineers (including Zip), telegraph operator, doctor, Nina, and the cooks—and explained their duties.

I nudged Kim. "Where's Stephanie?"

"She never sails. Afraid of the ocean or something."

The captain turned to us. "I want all the students and teachers to stand." He faced us, looking down the line, taking each of us in for the first time. "We would not be here without you. Because of your hard work in the rigging, in the engine room, and countless other tasks, this ship was ready to sail . . . And some of you were tireless in scraping barnacles." Richie beamed with pride. "I am honored to be your captain, and it is our time to honor you."

He clapped, and the crew joined in, and we smiled almost bashfully, taking in their recognition. The era of waiting on a ship that seemed unable to function was over. We'd loved Mr. Neilson, who had been like a tiger roaring at us to get us to work. But now that we were at sea with this older skilled captain a different kind of energy was palpable. The chaos and confusion we'd lived with was over. We had a captain who'd established order and who appreciated us.

He turned the meeting over to the First mate, the angular, solemn Jakob, who explained that we would be assigned to sea watches. "Four hours on, four hours off, two times a day. Bells will ring the change of watch." In his dour way, Jakob gave an example: "First watch is 8 to 12 p.m., and you'll be on again at 8 a.m. You are on your watch duties eight hours, and the remaining sixteen hours are for sleep, meals, ship's tasks, and to resume your classes."

The students groaned. "Classes?"

Jakob spoke sternly. "This is a school, and you need to meet your requirements." We would operate on the nautical twenty-four-hour clock, like military time. "Starting after noon, instead of 1 p.m., it will be 1300 hours, 1400 hours, and so on until midnight. All times recorded in the gangway log, on the bridge, and all watches, will be assigned in twenty-four-hour clock time. You'll get used to it."

Kim watched him intently. What did she see in him? He was so rigid and serious. He passed out papers that listed our watch assignments.

The captain stepped to the front again, warm yet professional. "This afternoon is for unpacking, and washing clothes, which look in great need." He smiled at us. "Inspection tomorrow at 700 hours and then we set the sails in the rigging." We erupted into cheers, as if we'd almost forgotten what we were here to do.

I threw my arms around Kim. "We'll be sailing! Just like you said."

•

First thing after breakfast the next morning, I joined the line of students and teachers that stretched from the sail locker along the narrow passage-way and up the ladder to the deck, as we moved out a few sails each day. Down the line came the call, a long *heave* and then a short *ho* and pause. With each *heave*, a long sail was passed a few feet at a time down the line, then we rested and held it on the *ho*. The heavy sail would slide out of my grip, until the next *heave* moved it along. The memory of lying with Drew on the mounds of bagged sails seemed a world away. With the next *heave*, I shoved away the memory, my attention absorbed in the work.

Once on deck, the sail was sent to the base of the correct mast. One at a time, each heavy sail was unwound and examined for rips. Pogo joined the sail repair crew, outfitted with a leather tool that fitted over his palm, a sail awl with a wooden handle, threaded needles, and waxed thread. Like a fairy-tale tailor, he sat cross-legged, bent over his work on the heavy sail.

•

Once the sail was ready, it was hoisted using a rope around its middle, which was passed around a brass winch, and then a long line of students pulled together as we called, "Humph, rise, humph, rise," and the heavy sail surged up the mast until it arrived at the correct yardarm. Up in the rigging, crew and skilled students spread out along the yardarm, standing on cables. I watched them lean at the waist over the wooden yard to haul the bound sail along to the end of the yard. I suddenly realized my brother was up there, leaning on the yard and hauling along the sail. I was proud of him. On deck, we watched them attach, or bend on, the sail.

Then Emil, Jakob's younger brother, called to me. "You're joining the bowsprit team. We're starting on the staysails." I looked toward the bow-sprit spearing the air ahead of the ship. "I'm attaching a sail out there?" Oh, shit. Why hadn't I signed up for sail repair?

Emil showed his small crew how we would bend on sails. He pointed to the lines that angled up from the middle and the end of the bowsprit to the foremast towering high above us. He held up the end of a long triangular sail and instructed us on how to attach a metal shackle through the grommet hole on the sail, around the rope stay, and how to secure it with a cotter pin. He grinned. "It's a piece of cake."

I groaned. "Yeah, right. All I have to do is get to the end of the bowsprit." But I had been getting more adventurous and agile. "Here I go." I sat on the edge of the deck and lowered myself onto the bowsprit, straddling my legs around the heavy metal pipe to scoot forward. Below me was the bowsprit net, ready to catch me, and maybe fifteen feet below that was the glistening ocean, calm and smooth today. I gained confidence as I moved out to the end, and soon I was absorbed in attaching the sail to the stay. A gentle breeze rippled the waves below me.

When I'd finished bending on the sail, Emil pulled the line around a winch and a few students hauled the long narrow triangle of canvas high above me. "Awesome!" I cheered—I was a girl who bent my sail onto the stay.

Emil gave me a hand as I climbed with confidence onto the deck. "Good job." Then he added, like he was telling me a secret, "When we are under sail, make sure you climb into the bowsprit net and watch for the dolphins diving in the bow wave!" I tingled with anticipation.

•

Before dinner Pogo said, "Come see what I'm doing in the carpentry shop." I followed him down from the foredeck into a short, dark hallway to an open door. David, a blond muscular man, our ship's carpenter, worked at a massive bench, shaving curls of wood off foot-square blocks to form a sharp point on one side. The crowded space was stacked with about fifteen blocks. Pogo said, "We started these in Miami and are nearly done."

"What are they for?"

Pogo glanced at David, who shrugged. Pogo hesitated. "They're plugs, in case a sea chest springs a leak." The sea chests were the large metal grids Karl and Richie had spent weeks scraping clear of barnacles so the ship's engines had a steady inflow of sea water.

"How could our ship leak? Isn't the metal hull thick?"

"The opening where water comes into the ship is vulnerable, and our captain wants to be prepared for an emergency."

David left, saying, "I'll be down after dinner to finish up."

Pogo drew a two-handled blade across the wood. "It's a spokeshave. I love the wood curls." I picked up a handful. Pogo said, "The first time I was ever in a boat there was a hole in the hull."

"What happened?"

He slowly pulled the tool. "I was maybe four, when my dad bought an old sailboat, but I don't think he really knew how to sail." One summer day, Pogo and his two older sisters and his parents crammed into the little boat and headed out into the bay off Bar Harbor. They had enough breeze to get to the middle of the bay but then the wind died down.

Pogo glanced at me with a quirky smile. "Suddenly about four inches of water rose in the boat. Mom panicked but Dad said, 'Oh Jean, you worry too much.'" Pogo's eyes widened. "Then a *whoosh*, and the water gushed up to our knees. A puff of wind, and we ever so slowly capsized."

I gasped, imagining him as a little kid out in cold water far from shore. "Could you swim?"

He shook his head. "Fortunately, my life vest worked and I bobbed about. But I panicked." Luckily, his dad was a strong swimmer who pushed him up on the upside-down boat. It wasn't too long before a lobsterman arrived, brought the family aboard, and wrapped them in blankets. "He attached a line to the sloop, gunned the engine, and the sailboat slowly righted herself. I've been afraid of swimming in deep water ever since."

"I'm afraid of deep water, and I've never been on a sinking ship!"

I sat on a stool and watched Pogo work as he told the story. He and his dad went to the boatyard and discovered a leather patch over a gaping hole in the hull of their boat. "Even though I was only four, I learned with my dad how to fix the hull and caulk the boat."

He walked around the carpentry shop. "We used a tarred hemp caulking strand. Here, smell it." He stuck a variety of objects and cans under my nose as he described the work they did on that sloop. Linseed oil putty. Nautical paints. He grinned. "When I was little, the smells were intoxicating. Whenever I sniff these smells now, I'm transported back." The whistle called us to dinner.

•

As darkness settled over the ship, wall lamps along the deck created circles of light where students or crew or teachers clustered. No longer was there a highway beyond the bow, no longer spotlights on shipping containers on the docks and a noisy harbor. The ship was darker and quieter under the stars. I wandered the deck after dinner, not sure where to settle.

The engine room's metal door was bolted open, releasing hot oily exhaust. Some of the pale grease monkeys, in blue jumpsuits, leaned on the rail for a smoke.

I climbed down to the crew mess and glanced through the open water-tight doors into the boys' quarters. A number of them lay on their bunks reading books or comic books, writing letters, or sleeping. Eighteen-year-old Harry lay on the lower bunk reading to Richie. It must have been a letter from his mom; I could smell her perfume even from the doorway.

The team on galley duty mopped floors and wiped down the tables and benches. The cooks had left out plates of cookies and a bowl of fruit. I munched on a cookie and admired the packed wooden book shelves running the length of the bulkhead. While my toe had healed in Miami, I'd hobbled around piles of books and loaded and organized the shelves. I'd gotten them ready for sea, with stretchy cords hooked onto either side of the shelf, to hold them steady no matter how rough the waves. My library was doing great after the first few days at sea. I picked up a few books scattered on the table and slid them back onto the right shelves before heading up to cooler evening air on deck.

On the starboard deck near the radio office, the Salty Dogs—Ted and the Exeter boys, shy Jane, and some others—clustered around Dave, the rigger. They sipped beers and compared notes on tall ships, arrangements of sails, and how they dreamed of signing on as crew.

Ted asked me, "Hey, you're into words, do you know what 'crossing the bar' means?"

"No idea. Getting off a sandbar or something."

"No, it's from a poem by Tennyson. For a sailor it means that you're dying."

"Oh, great, I'll keep that in mind in case that expression comes in handy."

When I asked, "Where's Pogo?" Ted pointed up the ladder toward the bridge. "Celestial navigation class tonight."

"Oh right, I forgot." I tiptoed up the stairs, slipped along the deck, climbed up the ladder to the roof of the bridge, and lay on my belly to spy on the class. Kim stood with a cluster of guys—including Rick, Zip, Pogo, and the scuba teacher, Karl—who stood around Jakob, who held a heavy brass sextant. It was a heavy metal triangle, with an eyepiece with glass lenses, which glided on a curving piece marked with numbers. He explained: "You make measurements between celestial bodies and the visible horizon to determine your position at sea, both at night or during the day with the sun. Next time, we'll meet at noon for more light for doing the math calculations." Kim grimaced, she was bad at math. As they passed the sextant around, I slipped down the ladder.

On the mizzen deck, most of the girls and a few guys sat in a circle making Turk's head bracelets, a white cotton braided knot, like a snug infinity circle, around their wrists. They stretched out long lengths of cord and discussed how long they should cut it.

"How big is my wrist?" they asked each other. They leaned over their outstretched hands with focused intent, as they wound and wove the cord around their fingers.

"How much did your bracelet shrink when you went swimming?" "Is it too tight or just right?" Some tried different thicknesses of cord. First attempts were messy and irregular. One of the younger boys begged someone to make one. Soon nearly everyone on board would sport a Turk's head bracelet.

Down in the maid's quarters, I picked up my sleeping bag from my bunk and grabbed a book. At the fantail, a solitary guitarist plucked the chorus of Iron Butterfly's "In-A-Gadda-Da-Vida". I knew I'd be in for an endless repetition until he got it right, so I left to find a deck bench half-way down the ship.

Sitting under a wall light, I opened *The Teachings of Don Juan*, which my brother had handed me at lunch. "You have to read Carlos Castaneda," Woodie said. "I know you're writing your dreams, but Castaneda teaches how to be consciously present in your dream."

I was confused. "How do I do that?"

"You watch for your hands in the dream. Eventually you'll be able to actively change your dream." I stared at him doubtfully. This was my little brother, who used to brag about how his getting paddled thirty-eight times in eighth grade beat the school record, and he was now serious about dreaming! He said, "This is about the path to becoming a warrior."

"OK," I agreed. "I'll check it out."

•

I jolted awake a few hours later when a group of boys ran by yelling, their flashlight beams zipping around me. Were they playing Capture the Flag in the middle of the night? Then I saw the silhouette of a large man in scuba gear climb over the railing onto the deck. What was happening? When the diver pulled off his mask, it was Karl, grumbling to himself. "So much for those boys on shark watch for me."

"They ran off. They're wound up about something."

When he saw me, he reported with excitement, "I did it! I got the mattress positioned over the leak." Then he noticed my confusion. "You don't know what's going on, right?"

"Not a clue."

He pulled off his tanks and set them on deck. "A couple of hours ago, one of the engine room kids barged into my room. 'Get your scuba gear! We have a leak in one of the sea chests.'" He glanced over at me to make sure I understood. "Remember when Richie and I scraped the barnacles off the sea chests?"

When I nodded, Karl explained. "Last night, an intake valve gave way, meaning there's a hole in the hull with water pouring in." He fussed with his scuba valve. "When I got on deck, two students had hauled a single mattress out on deck. I asked, 'What the hell are you kids doing?' One explained, 'You need to swim down to the sea chest screen with this mattress. We think the suction from the hole in the hull will suck in the mattress and stop the leak." Karl sat down on the deck and took off his flippers. "It sounded crazy."

I stared at him. "There's a hole in the hull, and you had to cover it with a mattress?" It sounded like a joke.

"Yep. When I was ready to go in the water, a bunch of kids leaned over the railing with flashlights. I asked, 'What are you guys doing?' 'Watching for sharks.'" He grimaced. "Not exactly comforting. And then I worried the lights would actually attract sharks." Thinking of sharks in the water sent a wave of fear through me.

Karl peeled off his wetsuit while he talked. "Once I was in the water, they tossed the mattress down to me. When I swam near the hole, the mattress was sucked right up against the sea chest."

"Amazing. A giant Band-Aid." We laughed.

Karl poured fresh water from a bucket to wash his gear as Jakob arrived to give new orders. "Now that they've plugged the hole in the engine room, you have to finish the job. Attach this canvas patch to protect the sea chest while we're underway." Jakob held out a layered canvas rectangle with cords for lashing it into place.

Karl asked, "Can't this wait 'til morning? It might help to see what I'm doing."

"This needs to be secured before we sail in the morning." Then Jakob hurried back up to the bridge. Karl shook his head as he pulled his gear back on, adjusted the mask and breathing apparatus, and climbed over the rail and down the ladder. He was so calm in an emergency that I fell back asleep.

I slept through the sunrise and missed Karl's second return onto the deck. I finally woke in full sunlight when Pogo arrived and sat on the deck next to my bench. He seemed strangely goofy. "I saw the most beautiful sunrise over Grand Bahama this morning."

"Sorry I missed it. Hey, did you hear about a leak last night? Karl put a mattress over it."

Pogo laughed. "Yeah, I know. A boy shook me awake on deck last night, saying, 'We've got a leak. Get one of the sea chest plugs down to the engine room right away!' Did I run! By the time I raced down the ladders in the engine room, water was surging around their feet."

I gasped. "What did you do?"

Pogo shrugged in his humble way. "Because Chief Engineer Alfonso is a big guy, and I'm scrawny, he sent me crawling in where the water was gushing. I pushed the wooden plug as hard as I could, but the pressure from the leak kept shooting the plug back at me. We were desperate, and I was soaked and cold. But suddenly the water slowed to a trickle."

"That must have been when Karl shoved the mattress against the sea chest."

"Exactly, but we still had to fasten the plug into place. Finally, Alfonso whaled at it with a sledgehammer and whacked that plug into the hole, which stopped most of the water. Alfonso ordered the bilges to keep pumping full tilt and full time, until we get to dry dock. What a night!"

"Were you scared?"

"I didn't get scared until afterward. Thank God the plug worked." Then he gave a shy grin. "David and I celebrated with a bottle of rum at the bow as we watched the sunrise. I'm a bit looped. I'm off to sleep."

I glanced at my watch. "Yikes, I'm on duty at eight." As I gathered up my sleeping bag, the engines rumbled to life below deck. On the bridge, an officer called orders: "Prepare to raise anchor." I dropped my stuff below decks and rushed back to the crew mess for breakfast.

Kim plopped onto the bench next to me. "Scoot over. I'm tired." She lowered her voice and spoke with urgency. "Don't say anything, 'cause they want to keep quiet about a leak in the hull last night."

I tried to look concerned. "Really?"

"I worked with Jakob and the rigger in the sail locker in the middle of the night. We used an old sail to fashion a canvas patch for a leak in the hull. But in case we hit rough water, we can't heel the boat to the port side."

I quietly crowed with pleasure. "I know all about it! Pogo and Karl told me, and they were there!" I'd actually known secrets Kim didn't know!

But I was completely clueless about the dangers of motoring along the coast of Florida, in water a mile deep, with a makeshift canvas patch that a sixteen-year-old had helped make, over a slowly leaking hole in the hull. What if we went through a storm?

•

That night was our first night underway, and the dusk dissolved like silvery fog into deep indigo. The last moments of sunset painted an edge of light along the masts and the miles of rigging above me. Kim and I reported for our four-hour deck watch at 2000 hours, which included fire watch rounds, man overboard watch, and finally bridge watch. I still had to do mental math to take 8 p.m. and add 12 to make 2000 hours. I hadn't seen Kim much lately, and she seemed aloof and serious on duty. I was glad to split up as we each circled the deck, moved through the passageways, watched for fire or danger, and finally stared out over the dark surface of the water in case someone had gone overboard. A sobering task.

When Kim and I entered the bridge at 2200 hours, Captain Floden spoke to us quietly with the touch of an accent. "I'm going to teach you girls how to steer the ship." He was the father of five daughters, and a grandfather. I was pleased, but when I glanced at Kim, she scowled. I bet she was hoping her first mate would teach us.

It was my first time on the bridge, a mahogany-paneled room, where I expected a huge wheel to steer the ship. Instead, a small brass-trimmed wooden wheel faced the bow in front of the row of windows. The captain explained the function of each instrument, machines with dials, a large compass, and a pedestal crowned with a handle to turn the engines to full, half, slow, stop, or stand by. The room was shadowy with a few green lights and reading lights.

"It's as quiet as a library," I said.

The captain smiled. "It's different when something serious is going on."

I wanted to ask, *Like last night?* but I didn't. I found the captain's calm comforting. He stood at the wheel. "Stand with your feet astride to balance. Lightly hold the spokes of the wheel." Then he nodded for me to try it. Kim left for the bridge deck to scan for ships.

I touched the wheel and it was almost too easy to move, considering how huge a ship we were steering. He said, "Focus on the compass to track our path and use the wheel to hold steady." A grid with a tiny needle floated over moving paper, marking an inked track of our course.

I was determined to stay close to the compass direction the captain gave me, but the thin wavering ink line tracked the erratic path I steered. Even a tiny move set the ship swinging off course one way; and when I compensated, the ship swung the other way. The little line zigged and zagged on the page, showing my mistakes in glaring relief. I stared so intently at the thin line of ink and the compass that I forgot I was steering a 360-foot ship. By the end of my hour at the wheel I rarely wavered far from the centerline.

When Kim spelled me at the helm, I lingered in the low-light calm of the bridge and traced my finger over the charts of the curving line of the Florida Keys and our first destination, Key West.

After watch when I lay down on deck after midnight at the fantail, I was surrounded by the sounds of the ship moving through water. The masts and yardarms sounded alive as we moved, like something breathing in a forest of massive trees. The steel hull ached from the pressures of masts and decks bearing down and of water pressing in. Kim's voice startled me when she dropped her sleeping bag down near me and grumbled, "Man overboard watch is a brain and eye buster."

I sat up. "I can't bear imagining someone in the water. How long would we take to turn around?" When I thought about standing at the wheel on the bridge, I gushed. "I loved steering and the captain is so cool."

Kim scrunched up her nose. "I don't know what I think of the captain yet. I didn't feel comfortable with my stern Swedish grandfather." She snorted with frustration. "Most men in my life have been a real letdown." She stared at the stars. "I love standing outside on the bridge wing deck. It feels like traveling on the back of a whale."

My happiness sank. For Kim, steering the ship was like riding on a whale, while I was totally focused on a line of ink on graph paper. I wanted to stop comparing myself to Kim, but she always seemed to be deeper than me.

•

The ship motored for two nights and two days, following the shipping lanes along the coast of Florida, where the cities glowed like a line of jewels on a golden chain.

At breakfast after our second night of motoring, Zip walked by a group of us girls as we ate breakfast. He flashed his freckled, irresistible grin. "The word around the ship is that Jane and Elizabeth are the best at steering a close course." He gave a thumbs-up. Wow, I blushed, a rush of pride. Maybe it was OK that I focused so hard on the thin black line.

After breakfast, as I reached the foredeck, the captain called orders on the bridge. "Turn to starboard. Starboard engine half speed."

Students and teachers lined the railings as we motored past white sand beaches and an old fort before a slow turn right toward the channel into Key West harbor. The crew prepared lines to throw ashore as the old town and dockyards came into sight far ahead. Teams of crew members and students stood ready to haul heavy braided lines, called hawsers, around winches to pull secure as we tied up at the docks.

A boy yelled and pointed toward the channel. "What's that?" A pair of tall, thin poles rose out of the water, then a wide horizontal blade surged upward, like a rigid whale's tail. A submarine breached in the channel ahead of us. I gasped. "That's crazy!"

A watertight door on their deck opened; sailors poured out and formed a line down the rounded wet deck and some climbed onto the tail. Wearing white caps and blue uniforms, they pointed their cameras at us, hippie kids on a four-masted sailing ship, motoring toward them.

Karl said, "I think it's a Navy fast-attack nuclear sub."

On the bridge, our captain called an order, "Engines dead slow," as we moved closer and closer to the sub in the narrow channel. We realized the sub was in our way when the captain called "Reverse engines." Our engines rumbled and the ship shuddered as the space between us and the sub shrank. All of us watched, frozen now, as our ship struggled to slow. Finally, Captain Floden called, "Hard to port," and our ship made a sharp turn to the left to miss the sub. Then a long, hard jolt, and we stopped stock still. Our ship was lodged on a sandbar.

As kids, teachers, and crew ran to the port railing, everyone asked questions. "Why did they get so close to us? How will we get off?"

I slid in next to Ted. "Does this count as 'crossing the bar'?" He grinned, while I was pleased. I'd made a joke.

I hovered near the stairs to the bridge catching voices sputtering over the radio. The Navy captain acknowledged he was responsible. Our officers and crew and the sub officers debated strategies for dislodging the ship. They studied the tide charts; in Florida the tides varied between six and eighteen inches of water.

Pogo was incredulous. "In Maine, we can have twelve-foot tides. That tide would lift a ship off a sandbar easy."

A plan was made. The Navy would send a tug to pull us off the sandbar at high tide that afternoon. We waited on our strangely unmoving ship in the channel. I grabbed my journal to write while we waited for rescue.

After lunch, someone shouted out: "The Navy tug's here!" We ran to the port railing as it pulled alongside our bow. A Navy sailor tossed a thin line attached to a weighted monkey fist, a heavy knotted rope, to our crew at the bow.

Ted laughed. "This is seriously salty!" After waiting for hours, this was prime nautical entertainment. Everyone lined the railing to watch. Our crew hauled on the thin line to bring aboard the tug's heavy towing rope. They wrapped it around our massive bow winch and secured it. Karl snapped photos of the thousand-ton tug as it churned the water to build up engine power before it began to haul the towing line connected to our ship. It pulled and pulled, but nothing moved.

Suddenly their tug swung wildly as they lost control of the steering. Some kids laughed and pointed as the tug danced sideways, before anyone sensed the danger. The tug crew attempted to loosen their end of the line, with no success. Karl watched through his camera lens as a sailor ran toward the towing line with an axe, as the rope smoked.

Karl saw the danger and shouted, "Everyone, run! That line can blow. Leave this side of the deck." Some kids moved quickly, but others were glued to the rail and didn't move. Karl yelled, "Move it! Hustle! Clear the decks. Run! Now!"

My body unfroze and I joined the crowd hurtling down the deck, running breakneck toward the stern. Some raced up a ship's ladder to watch from above. Then a sharp crack, like the retort of a gun, as the tow rope snapped. The line recoiled and ricocheted down our deck, crackling and snapping, before smashing against our teak gangway on the side of the hull. Momentum propelled the rope across the deck—where moments before we'd all been standing. The rope hurtled up, busted a hole through the hull of our launch where it hung on a divot on the upper deck. Only then did the line collapse, limp and frayed.

Students, teachers, and crew emerged. "Oh my God, did you see that?!" "What happened?" I was both shaken and strangely excited, as was everyone else. We milled around, uncovering clues to re-create the path of destruction, like tracking the path of a tornado. Kids pointed out their discoveries with the excitement of detectives on a case. "Look at this gash in the metal."

"Oh no, our gangway is shattered." We rushed to the rail to see scraps of teak floating in the water. Our beautiful gangway.

Woodie came up to me, his face almost grey. He told me what he saw from the upper deck. His usually joking voice was flat. "I watched the line as water squeezed out. The rope thinned and smoked. Then it snapped." He stared at me. "That line could have decapitated people or sliced them in half." He walked away, shaking his head; my brother, who saw the truth sooner than the rest of us.

I remembered frustrating school meetings where a few students complained about having to follow orders on a ship. We were a generation famous for challenging authority. Who are *you* to tell *me* what to do? We'd been told the necessity of following orders at sea, and the rule of captain's orders. Those kids had rolled their eyes when the first mate admonished them, "Your lives could be at stake. You don't question orders. There might not be time."

"Yeah, sure, man. Sure." They'd said back then. The crowd on deck was sober now.

The next day, two tugs—one at the bow and one at the stern—at a higher tide, managed to extract us from the bar, and we finally arrived at the dock in Key West. The Navy said they'd be back to replace the gangway and repair the launch, but no one from the Navy ever came.

·

We had no idea why the ship landed in Key West. Was it a quick stop on our way to dry dock? But days stretched into a week.

Rumors abounded. Stephanie was negotiating with the owners about our destination for dry dock. Would it be New Orleans? Or Veracruz? The unseen power of the owners was insidious as they seemed to delay and prevent us from moving. Once again, we were stuck at a dock in Florida, waiting. Waiting for our trip to begin, waiting for the ship to sail, waiting for orders.

Kim disappeared a lot. Pogo and the Salty Dogs spent evenings at Sloppy Joe's bar, Hemingway's favorite. The teachers hung out at a Navy bar, and sailors on the sub told them they'd tracked us since we'd left Grand Bahama. Others got stoned, and I was one of the loners who holed up on deck reading.

Waiting to leave from Key West was dreadful. In Miami, the maze of shipping containers gave us a veil of invisibility. But in Key West, we were a spectacle, on display for the tourists. My sleeping spot near the fantail was now in full view of the docks, lights, curious eyes, and meandering drunks until late at night. I moved my sleeping bag to a spot on the port side upper deck, out of sight under a lifeboat.

We scrubbed the decks and polished the brass every morning to prepare for two hours of visitors. They asked the same questions. "How soon are you leaving?" "Where will you be sailing?"

We answered pleasantly with our memorized answers. "We hope to leave in three days" (as we growled to ourselves: *We don't have a clue*). We chanted the itinerary dutifully to every tourist's smile until their eyes glazed over: Panama, the Galápagos Islands, Ecuador, back through the canal, across the Atlantic, and on and on with the old story Stephanie had dreamed up. But even my faith had begun to fade.

We did have a few afternoons off. One afternoon, Zip returned sunburned and laughing, with large buckets filled to the brim with lobsters, their antennae waving. Pogo from Maine joked, "You sure those are lobster? Where are their big claws?" But we'd heard about these spiney Florida lobsters.

Zip laughed. "Always a wise guy! You just eat the tails. Give me a hand." He passed the buckets up to the kids surrounding the boat. "Tell the cooks to start boiling pots of water." How did Zip know how to make things happen and have a great time?

In the crew mess that night, as we feasted on lobster tails, Zip recounted how he'd rented a Boston whaler with an older kid with ID. "We took two cans of gas and went as far as we could and still get back." In thirty feet of water, they jumped in wearing their scuba gear and swam down to discover they were on top of a herd of lobsters on a sandy bottom. "We learned to grab them, two at a time, and not get our fingers pinched. We tossed them in the boat until the whole bottom of it was covered with lobsters. When we returned, the owner said, 'Don't tell anyone you did that. Fishermen would be furious.'" After dinner a lot of teens and teachers headed into town to go drinking, while I chose *The Bell Jar* and found a place to hide.

I knew that doldrums happened around the equator when the trade winds dropped. We weren't at the equator yet, we were still at dock, but I'd lost the wind in my sails. In Key West, I fell into my own doldrums.

Sylvia Plath's words pierced me. *"Wherever I sat—on the deck of a ship or at a street café in Paris or Bangkok—I would be sitting under the same glass bell jar, stewing in my own sour air."* I was stewing and wretched, but I didn't want to read the words of a woman who'd gassed herself in her kitchen oven. I was a sad girl who had lost her home and didn't know what to do.

I was afraid Pogo and Kim wouldn't want to have anything to do with their moody, miserable friend. The shadow of depression from home had crept on board. I'd thought I'd begun to climb out of my funks, to be someone who was adventurous, but I was sinking into the old slump.

A few days later, after that day's tourists were escorted off the ship,

Kim and Pogo found me. They'd each invited me to walk around town a few days before, but I'd put them off until they showed up at my hiding place, under the lifeboat. Today they seemed to have combined forces, their faces set and serious.

I asked, "What are you guys doing here?"

Kim dropped down beside me. "You have to come with us."

"I can't." I stared at the deck. "Nothing is ever going to change. We'll never get anywhere. My life will never happen. I'll be miserable and depressed my whole life." Then I said the scariest thought out loud. "And you guys are going to get tired of me and not want to be my friends anymore?" My eyes teared and the pages blurred.

Pogo asked, "What's the matter? We miss you." Kim nodded.

I pouted, and read aloud from *Winnie-the-Pooh*, in my best Eeyore voice: *"Nothing, Pooh Bear, nothing. We can't all, and some of us don't. That's all there is to it."*

Pogo took the book. *"Can't all WHAT?" said Pooh, rubbing his nose."*

I replied in Eeyore's flat, miserable voice, *"Gaiety. Song-and-dance. Here we go round the mulberry bush . . . I'm not complaining, but There It Is."* Reading aloud to them broke the logjam of misery.

Kim jumped up. "Time for some gaiety." She seized my hand to pull me up.

I grimaced. "Okay," I said as I pushed myself to standing. "Now what?"

"Let's go throw Pooh sticks," Pogo suggested. "There's a bridge over there. I'm sure we can find some palm leaves to float under it." They linked arms with me on either side. "Here we go!"

Stephanie's parent letter mailed on January 17, 1972:

This letter is to let you know the ship has set sail, leaving Key West at 10 a.m., after waiting a day for better weather.

I'm thrilled to announce we will motor five or six days to Veracruz, Mexico. The ship's agent working for the owner has flown to Veracruz to make all the arrangements. I can assure you; this is the perfect port for our going into dry dock.

•

A few days out of Key West, the ship rose on rough waves as Kim and I lurched toward the officers' table to deliver dinner. We stumbled back to the middle hallway, laughing and holding on like bronco riders, before the ship rose on the next wave and we pressed uphill to the galley for the next dishes to serve. Soon, the French chef shooed us away. *"Allons-y.* Get to your cabin and try to sleep." The shy Mexican cook smiled and waved. I called to them, *"Bonne nuit,"* and *"Hasta mañana."*

I was relieved Kim and I would brave the trek back to our cabin together. We hauled ourselves up the steep metal ladder to the forward deck and paused under cover before we dashed into the rain. I assumed we'd run the length of the port deck to our cabin near the stern. But she turned in the opposite direction and disappeared into the dark with a quick wave, heading for the officers' cabins on the starboard deck. She hadn't been around at night on the fantail deck, but I hadn't paid much attention. Now it was clear: she was sleeping with Jakob.

Her vanishing hit me like the cold rain. I felt cast off.

I held on to the wall railing as the ship rose and crashed. The roar of the sea and the wind tearing through the rig was enormous. I shook myself. "OK girl, you're going to do this."

When I finally took off down the deck, a wall of rain doused me. I staggered from the waves heaving the deck, and grabbed for the thick rope secured every few feet by a bolt anchored into the cabin wall. In seconds my glasses were streaked with water. The round wall lamps gave only a faint blurred light. I clutched my way along the wall, to stay away from the railing. The noise was deafening. Surging seas spilled foam across the deck. The rain soaked my legs and arms. Above me a forest of masts, yardarms, and lines creaked and swayed. Stepped through to the bottom of the hull, the masts sent wrenching pressures and groans that torqued through the ship.

When I reached the last rope railing, I gasped. The wide, open mizzen deck stretched ahead of me before the final cabin where the door to the maid's quarters offered refuge. I suddenly remembered how Laura Ingalls Wilder's books described blizzards on the prairie, when families attached ropes to the house so they could hold on as they walked blind into the storm. Then you wouldn't be lost forever, and you could haul yourself back. But no one had strung a storm line on the deck for the girls to cross to the last cabin. I had to make a run for it. The open deck was alive with rain pelting from different directions in heavy darkness. I was alone in a collision of winds.

Back in October when we'd hung out on the fantail, bullshitting about what we thought might happen this year on the ship, Ted launched his theory. "We won't really bond as a community until we have a storm at sea." We'd talked about movies of ships in storms, how wet guys in foul-weather gear shouted above the storm, held onto the wheel or ropes or a lifeboat, that saved or didn't save some people.

They'd all worked together in the storm. But I'd never felt so alone.

As the wind bashed against me, I tripped and fell onto my knee. I squinted into the wind and scrambled forward, aiming for the stern cabin. I was flooded with relief when my fingers grasped onto the large knot on the end of the railing rope. I stopped to catch my breath. The ship plunged and I was knocked against the wall but held tight, then pulled my way up the last steps to the stern deck, and finally reached the watertight door of the girls' quarters.

I twisted the metal door handle and slipped in between the surge of waves before the door slammed shut behind me. I grabbed on with both wet hands to descend our steep stairs backwards. The ship shoved me through the cabin door onto my bunk, and the door clicked shut with the next upsurge. I pulled off my sneakers and soaked clothes and fumbled in the dark for a towel to dry off as best I could between the lunging waves.

All this time I heard no voices nor saw any light or sign that anyone else was on the ship. It was as if all the students and crew had vanished. I knew that up on the bridge officers must be at the wheel, the engineers must be in the engine room and, below, students and teachers must be in their bunks, all of us getting through the night.

In the darkness of my bunk, I couldn't see the storm, but the jolting and plunging of our ship rumbled through my body and deafened me. When aching groans rose from the metal plates that formed our ship's hull, I knew this was truly a gale.

Troughs of waves rose and then spilled. Immense breaking water slashed across the deck. I wedged my body on my bunk, feet against the wall, my hands pushed against the lip of the bed, in utter darkness, facing the pitch-dark glass of the porthole. As the storm roared, I wanted stillness and quiet. I wanted the ship to stop this nightmare. Please, may I lie still and fall asleep? But I held on, awake. Then I remembered my great grandparents in their stateroom. I imagined their last minutes before the *Lusitania* sank. Their story had always ended when they walked into their stateroom, closed the door, and were never seen again.

As the metal hull groaned, I envisioned them lying together in their bunk, holding onto each other, bracing their bodies as the ship hurtled toward the bottom of the Irish Sea, gazing into each other's eyes. What would it be like to love someone so much that this is how you choose to die?

But I wanted to challenge their choice. Why didn't they fight for the slim chance to stay alive, for my grandmother, their daughter? The storm slammed me toward the bulkhead, and still, they lay in each other's arms. How long did they have? The sound of the sea was deafening, the pounding of the waves relentless. I held on. Could they have held on? I imagined the torrent of freezing water. How long did it take to drown in the tumbling darkness of a sinking ship?

Finally, I drifted exhausted into sleep, until daylight.

•

In the morning, it was silent in the maid's quarters. I wanted to hear voices, to know everyone had survived the storm. I pulled myself up the steep stairs, ground open the watertight door, and stepped gingerly onto the deck. Even though I was shaken and wobbly, I put my head back, nose in the air, like a dog leaning out of a car window, desperate for fresh cool air. I made my way forward, up the heaving deck. I lurched across the open space of the mizzen deck, a balancing act, until I sank with a sigh onto the deck bench bolted into the floor against the cabin wall. Only then did I look over the railing.

Our ship sank into a trough of waves while walls of water, stories deep, rose on either side of us, high above us. I shrieked, "Oh my God, the waves are going to crash onto us!" The wall of water moved so close to the railing, I could have reached out and touched it.

Zip flopped down on the other side of the bench and laughed. "This kind of looks like Moses parting the Red Sea." I was so frozen with fear, I could only glance at him in his greasy jumpsuit. Zip the rambunctious redhead, grinned like a farm boy. "Not that I read the Bible much these days."

I couldn't speak. My head whipped back to stare at the water high above us.

He was amused. "This will blow your mind. Keep watching!" I pressed my body against the bench, as the ship rose, riding a ridge of water with troughs as deep as our ship on either side of us.

I clenched onto the bench with one hand and flung my other hand out to grasp his freckled arm. This was not flirting, but utter terror. "Oh my God, our ship is going to fall over!"

"Don't you worry. Watch us ride this baby!"

My heart pounded as the ship sank on this elevator of sea back down into the trough again. I forced myself to breathe. Only after we had risen and fallen a few more times could I lighten my grip on Zip's arm. I finally believed our ship wouldn't fall over.

Other boys ambled up, leaned casually against the cabin wall, or sprawled on the deck to talk to Zip. A skinny, long-haired kid lit a cigarette. "God, was that floor slippery last night." They joked about how you were supposed to hold on with one hand for the ship and one for them, but they held on to greasy railings down below with two hands for themselves all night. "I made sure I didn't grab a high-voltage line."

I suddenly remembered the leak in the hull and the canvas patch. I asked, "Did the wooden plug hold, blocking the hole in the hull?"

"We kept the water pumps running, like usual." Zip said casually, "Not a problem."

Kim wandered down the deck, subdued and sleepy. As she approached, I wanted to ask if she was OK, but I couldn't imply anything about her not having slept in our cabin last night. She nodded towards me, like giving a signal. She was OK. I smiled back, signaling, *me too*. She joked. "Out for a stroll," as she wobbled down the deck toward our cabin.

Pogo arrived, wearing his yellow rain gear, looking sickly green. He squeezed in between me and Zip on the bench. I touched his arm. "How'd it go last night?" How could I have forgotten that he always got terribly seasick? My fears felt melodramatic in the morning light.

Pogo smiled weakly. "I roped myself to one of these deck benches, so I didn't have to go below. I couldn't see a thing." He'd been on deck all night in the lashing wind and rain, and now he was cheerful. "Aren't we like a rubber ducky floating on these waves?"

Ted stood at the railing, staring intently down into the deep valley of the wave below. I asked him, "How high are these waves over our heads?"

After much discussion, Ted said, "I guess these waves are at least twenty feet tall."

I stared into the wall of water. "It looks so solid, but the water is continuously moving. It's like it's held back by magic."

Ted shook his head. "Nope, just physics."

As the ship rose again to the top of the swell, I asked, "So why don't we topple over when we're up here?"

Ted considered this. "Buoyancy and momentum."

When I looked perplexed, Pogo smiled his comforting Hobbit smile. "The boat doesn't want to sink. You have to trust it." I suddenly understood that the Hobbits are the true heroes. Poor seasick Pogo, sick as a dog all night, yet with a twinkle in his eyes, he dispensed wisdom. My fear slowly diminished.

"I guess the storm is over," I said, "and these are rollers?"

Ted glanced around at the others. "Alright you Salty Dogs, was that a storm or a strong gale by the Beaufort Scale?" I knew this was a scale for rating wind speed and seas. They debated how many knots per hour were the winds and what the characteristics of the wave crests were. I shook my head and ignored them. The sun might actually break through the heavy grey sky. Nothing terrible was going to happen.

Pogo asked cheerfully, "Breakfast anyone? I think tea and toast would be perfect."

As I followed the boys to the mess, I saw Woodie. I leaned against the rail next to him, holding on securely as I watched the wall of waves soar above us. I stared into the layers of deep green-blue water. I said, "I start to think I can see tuna and sharks and maybe even," I smiled, "mermaids swimming by."

He nodded and kept watching the water intently. Then I remembered the storm and how I held on in my bunk. "Woodie, do you ever think about our great grandparents? Out here?" He turned and looked at me. I added in a rush, "I imagined what it was like when their ship sank." The deck jolted with the next plunging wave, and I gripped the rail.

Woodie stared down into the water, his hair pushed behind his ears, his face softer than the older boys, a few soft hairs clustering on his chin. He said, "I think I came to sea to bring their ghosts home." He looked at me intensely before he strode down the deck, swaying with the ship.

The Mexican coast was thick and green, with snowy mountains hazy in the distance. Wooden fishing boats chugged out to sea, cargo ships blared their horns as they arrived. Massive old tugs maneuvered us into port, with shouted volleys of directions from their crews to our bridge as their tire-covered bows jolted against our hull. Students and crew worked together to secure the lines of the ship when we reached the dock.

The captain called down to us from the bridge. "Students, teachers, and most of the crew: You are on leave tonight at 1900 hours." We cheered and dashed to our quarters to clean up. Back on deck, I hardly recognized some of the boys after they'd scrubbed off a week's worth of dirt and washed their hair. I was carried along in the excitement, not holding back, not staying on board to write or read. Maybe Ted was right about the storm. Maybe we had bonded in a new way. We were all going out for a party together, and I was wearing my yellow, very short culotte dress with sandals and silver earrings. I'd slipped on my fool's gold ring, admiring its sparkle again.

My brother shouted to me. "Looking good!" He'd spruced up in clean jeans and a wrinkled white shirt, clearly from the bottom of his duffel bag. I grinned. "You don't look too bad yourself!"

The cooks stuffed us with a dinner heavy on pasta before they let us off the ship, so no one would drink on an empty stomach. Stephanie arrived before we left. Like Mrs. Claus, she hugged students and handed out allowances in pesos as we lined up. At dusk, the old port town was decorated with strings of lights looping between the white colonial buildings. We signed off in the log and streamed down the gangway.

But the moment we reached the concrete pier, the strangest thing happened. I staggered, like I was dizzy. Other people stumbled, or leaned over and held onto their knees, like we'd gotten drunk in a minute. The crew members laughed. "Look at you guys, you are so land sick!" Fortunately, each step was steadier, and we were relieved to feel it clear quickly.

Everyone from the ship wanted to find a bar. I guessed this is what sailors did when they landed, and I reluctantly followed the crowd to the town square, where we crowded into the first bar in the plaza and filled the tables. A band played—guitars, a violin, and trumpet—as our group called out for *cerveza* and tequila. I squeezed into a chair in the midst of the girls. Kim was across from me, Pogo a long way down to the left, my brother off to my right.

Waitresses wielded trays of glistening bottles of beer that they plunked in front of us. They brought bottles of tequila with a worm floating in each bottle. I grimaced. Woodie teased me. "Time for *you* to have a drink." I shook my head and took a sip of Kim's beer. But I could feel my brother's unspoken message: "Don't be such a goody-goody. Loosen up!"

The oceanography teacher, Peter, held up a little glass with salt around the rim. He instructed, "Lick some salt off the back of your hand or off the glass, take a sip of tequila, then suck on the *limón.*" Like a chemistry experiment. Lick of salt, quick sip, suck the lime, and grin. "It cuts the tequila taste." He raised his glass and invited us to follow.

The waitress brought tiny glasses encrusted with salt around the rim. Someone filled the glasses and passed bowls of cut limes. "OK, take a sip!" The girls around me plunged in, their heads tilted back, they sucked the limes, and erupted laughing. I gazed at the grains of salt stuck to the rim of the glass. This little glass meant the difference being boring and uptight, or loosening up and having fun. My brother, even my mother at home, said, "Can't you lighten up and have fun?" I thought of how Kim had said to me, "You're too couth." I glared at the little glass and ignored the preserved worm in the bottle. A voice in my head shouted, *"Enough!* Take a fucking sip of the stuff. It's no big deal."

I tilted back for a fiery sip, then sucked the life out of the lime. Heat flushed my face. I'd done it. I'd passed the bloody rite of passage. I assumed

I'd suddenly be less uptight. Everyone talked a mile a minute, while I felt like I'd climbed the rig alone. "Don't be ridiculous," my inner voice chided me. "You simply took a sip." I glanced toward my brother, who grinned like he saw right through me. I stuck my tongue out at him. "See Woodie, I tried it."

Around me, my crewmates chanted, "Take another sip, take another sip." They pounded on the table. "Drink it!" I closed my eyes and washed down the whole little glass of tequila, crunched the salt, sucked the lime. My eyes teared, and my whole body melted and loosened. I shook my head from side to side so my long hair slipped across my face. I felt sexy and actually cool. When I glanced at my brother, he lifted his glass to toast me. He joked with his friends. "My sister's finally letting her hair down."

The trumpet pierced through the guitars, the violin chased the colorful lights sparkling above us. It was a crazy scene. I sipped a second glass of tequila that had magically appeared in front of me, between smooth sips of chilled beer. I talked to the cluster of faces from the ship. We were all unwinding from months of hard work—motoring here, the storm, and the constant uncertainty. When would we ever sail? It all dropped away, and we were surrounded by music. I kept taking sips of fire. I seemed to be funny, as I gestured with my hands. My life suddenly seemed full of good stories to tell. I took another sip.

A couple of girls were going to the bathroom, and when I followed, my legs wobbled. Each of us leaned against the wall, waiting for the next girl to go in. "How is it?" we asked the first girl as she emerged. She wrinkled her nose but shrugged. "Not too bad." I swayed into the white-tiled room, and time slowed as I unbuttoned my yellow culotte dress, pushed it back over my shoulders. I wriggled like Houdini, trying to slip out of my dress and underwear. I held onto it to keep it off the wet dirty floor, when I sank onto the sticky seat to pee with a sigh. But then my knees shook, and nausea scalded my throat. I turned in time to vomit wave after wave into the toilet.

One of our girls opened the door and said, "Elizabeth's sick." I slid down next to the toilet, and leaned against the white-tiled wall. Their voices talked about me. "Oh no, she's naked."

My brain grasped that I had to get my yellow dress pulled back on. The girls tried to hold me up, tried to pull up the dress from my ankles to my waist, but they couldn't get my arms down the sleeves. My body, like a wooden marionette with the strings cut, kept sliding to the floor. Someone said, "We need help. Get her brother." I disappeared against the tiled wall.

My brother shouted, "What the fuck is going on?!" as I drifted in and out. "Why is she naked?" They tried to pull me to my feet and wrench the dress up to my waist, but it was impossible to get my arms into the sleeves.

Woodie growled, "Somebody get me a shirt to put around her. You, get a taxi. Get some napkins so we can clean her up."

I was limp, held against the wall, while someone tied my dress sleeves around my waist. My head lolled, hair in my face, and my brother was furious, muttering. "They dump my sister on me to come to the rescue." He wiped vomit off my face. They wrapped and buttoned a long-sleeved shirt around my chest. Arms carried me out through the bar's roar of music. In the chilly night air, they pushed me into the back seat of a taxi. People crowded around, voices and confusion as they shoved my bare feet in before slamming the door. A couple of boys slipped into the front seat next to the driver, giggling about lightweights like Woodie's sister who'd never gotten drunk before. The taxi drove through crowded streets the few blocks to the ship. Woodie was swearing. "Her goddamn friends went back to the bar, and I'm left with my stupid sister."

Arms lifted, walked, and dragged me up the gangway. Woodie ordered, "Hold on tight. Don't want her to go overboard." They hauled me down the deck to the stern. When they stopped, I tried to stand but my legs buckled. I crumpled into a heap on the deck. My brother rolled me onto my sleeping bag.

The boys called, "Come on, man, let's go back to town. Come on, Woodie. She's fine."

He shook his head. "Go on without me. I'll hang out here a while." A wet cloth wiped my face and hands. He mumbled, "Keep the airways clear," and lifted my head onto his lap. His determined words drifted into my foggy brain. "Someday I'll learn to do this shit right. Things go wrong all the time." He was not the devil-may-care fifteen-year-old boy anymore. Then heavy sleep engulfed me.

I woke slowly in the grey light before dawn, slightly chilled under a sheet. There was warmth under my head. I opened my eyes to find my head on my brother's lap, his legs outstretched on the deck as he leaned back against the stateroom wall, asleep. I caught a whiff of a sick, sour smell. Yuck, it was me. Suddenly the night came back to me. Oh my God, what had happened? I sat up quickly, my vision blurry. I reached around for my glasses. Oh no. Where were my glasses?

Woodie jolted awake, his voice groggy. "How do you feel?"

"What happened to me?! I'm a mess!" A shirt was wrapped oddly around my chest, my yellow dress knotted by the sleeves around my waist. "Did I get drunk?" I grimaced as I found dried vomit on my clothes.

"Yep. You passed out."

I blushed. "You had to carry me back? God, that's so embarrassing."

He was dead serious. "Fuck being embarrassed. Be glad you're safe and fucking alive. Jimi Hendrix died from choking on vomit. I made sure my smart *stupid* sister didn't die."

I was startled by his intensity and sensed a danger I hadn't imagined.

Later with his friends, he'd tease me, "You've definitely improved your reputation." But now he stood, his voice tired. "Time for me to get to bed."

The realization dawned on me. "You stayed with me all night?" My eyes teared up. "Oh, Woodie." I felt a wave of tenderness for my little brother, but when I looked up at him, I saw a serious, determined young man.

He answered flatly, "It's what you do if a buddy gets drunk." He walked away toward the bow, shaking his head. He looked back again with a wry smile. "You probably won't even have a hangover. Beginner's luck."

•

I slipped into the girls' quarters for a shower and clean clothes. Up on deck, I wandered around the quiet ship, disoriented without my glasses, and only scant memories of how I'd gotten back on the ship. It was early Sunday morning, the city quiet and the docks dormant.

At the gangway, a bleary-eyed boy looked at me hopefully. "Are you relieving my watch? No one's shown up."

I smiled. "Sure, I'll take it. Let me find something to eat." I dashed down to the galley, filled a glass of water and peeled an orange. I relieved him from his watch and he limped off to sleep. Leaning against the railing, I watched the pattern of erratic rooftops of the old city, and even though I couldn't see clear outlines, I drew the city in the logbook, silhouettes of stone buildings, smokestacks, church towers. I was so focused on my drawing that I didn't notice Pogo until he was leaning over the book admiring my efforts.

"Nice," he said.

"Just coming back on board?"

"Yup."

"You were out all night?" After he nodded, I added, "I've never done that before."

"I love being out in all the stages of a night. Did it in Paris, too. Can you believe it, on a school field trip." He pulled up a chair.

He looked at me closely. "You aren't looking too bad."

I blushed. "You didn't see me when I left the bar, did you?"

"Uh, yeah. I helped you into the cab."

I had a vague memory of my feet being pushed as the door was slammed shut. Now it was his turn to blush. "Sorry I didn't come back with you. I felt a little guilty that I didn't."

"That's OK. Woodie stayed with me all night. So, what did you do?"

He gazed out over the city from our view on the ship. "I listened to the mariachi band for a while. Incredible acoustic bass guitar."

I hardly remembered the music. It was so stupid that I'd gotten drunk.

"The town square, the *zócalo*, has such a beautiful feel to it. It's the mixture of architecture, the lights, the people strolling. There's something dreamy about it. And yes, the *cerveza* is good. *Negra Modelo*. It tastes old-fashioned and soulful." His presence was warm. We watched the city as the church bells rang.

"Were you there all night?"

"Ah, no." An embarrassed smile crossed his face. "A group of boys from the ship were talked into going to, oh, dear, what should I call it, a house of ill repute." He looked at me. My eyes were wide open, incredulous. "Yeah, shocking. But it was like being in a movie. We walked upstairs and entered a smoky room with red lights, a little bar, and girls coming on to us. I can tell you one of our youngest students is already quite smitten with one of the girls." He shook his head. "I tried out my beginning Spanish, had another *cerveza*, and then I slipped out. It was the middle of the night."

He described how a bus came by, lit up, almost empty, with only a tired, older woman dozing on a seat carrying market bags. "My dad always said the best way to get to know a city is to hop on a bus and ride to the end of the line." So Pogo stepped aboard and rode, out through the dark streets of multicolored little houses and shops boarded up for the night. Scrawny dogs slunk out of the way. The bus finally stopped and turned off the engine. The woman got off, carrying her bags. The driver said, "*El mar, aquí.*" And he waved his hand toward the slowly brightening light in the east. The sea.

I listened to Pogo like he was reading to me from a novel. He walked until the street turned into sand, then followed a path into white dunes as the sun slowly rose. He said it was like stepping into Frank Herbert's book *Dune*. He almost expected to feel the sand rumble and see the giant sandworms moving toward him. He climbed up a ridge and slid down, the sand ran in streams around him. He paused to empty sand out of his pockets and cuffs.

As he approached the shore Pogo found, scattered in the dunes, driftwood shacks and fishing boats pulled up on the shore. Morning fires on the beach, women cooking. Children spotted him first and came running. They were playing in the waves with little crabs skittering along on string leashes. They took him to the fire. A fisherman and his wife offered him dark smoky tea and a hunk of dried fish. He sat with them and watched the sun rise. He gestured with his hands that he'd sailed here in a ship. They nodded and smiled.

Then Pogo looked as me, as if coming out of a dream. "I'm crashing. My head doesn't feel so great. See you after I get some sleep."

I stayed on watch as the ship came to life with groans and complaints. Later I walked to the bar to ask if they'd found a pair of glasses or shoes. No, no. So sorry. The next day I would pick out new aviator metal frames like Gloria Steinem. As I walked back to the ship, I noticed someone familiar walking in the same direction. Was it Zip? I hadn't seen him all day on the ship. I called out, "Hey Zip, wait up." I walked back with him. He was quiet, unusual for him, and almost bashful. He didn't ask why I was missing my glasses and I didn't ask where he'd been.

Years later, Zip told me a story he'd never told anyone about what happened to him that night—when Stephanie arrived in Veracruz with a beautiful woman with wavy blond hair. "As we were getting ready to leave the ship, this gorgeous woman walked up to me and said, 'You must be Zip.'" She was clean and smelled beautiful, not like us. She asked for a tour of the ship, saying, "Stephanie thought you'd be a good person to show me around."

She invited him to her hotel. She opened the door to a suite with a table covered with bowls of fruit, bottles of wine, cheeses and bread, and flowers. She sent him to take a bath first. Long distance, on the phone Zip still sounded a little amazed. "This woman 'queened me' you might say.

I don't think we came out of the room for at least twenty-four hours. For some reason she took to me. Maybe Stephanie arranged it and I was too naive to understand or question. I did enjoy it though!"

•

We'd been in Veracruz a few days when all students met in the mess with Ron, the tall history teacher with long black curls. He dumped a bag of maps and travel books on one of the long tables. "Sorry I'm late. I've come from a meeting with Stephanie and the captain. More delays."

A chorus of groans moved around the room. A negative voice snarled. "We're fucked. Nothing good ever happens on this school."

It was time for us to plan our field trips, but the mood wasn't good. The climate on the ship was always an uneasy balance between the negative complainers and the positive people. But the negative voices were gaining momentum, threatening to pull us under.

One of the older students in the back said, "Shut up. Let Ron talk."

"OK guys, I'm going to tell you the inside story instead of leaving you in the dark." The muttering increased. He raised his voice. "Listen up, here's the situation." Stephanie's ever-positive pep talks had made us crazy because we knew something else was going on. Finally, Ron was going to tell us the real story.

"Remember how in Key West we were waiting to find where we could get into dry dock?" We nodded wearily. "So, just as we were about to leave for New Orleans, where Steph had made arrangements, the owner showed up and said he had us all set up in Veracruz. It was cheaper, and a berth was arranged so that work could start on arrival. But when we arrived here, no arrangements had been made. They'd never heard of us."

A rumble of swearing erupted around the room. "We are so messed up. Those owners are out to fuck us over." Some kids sank their heads into their elbows on the table and didn't bother to lift them when Ron laid out our choices.

"Steph's been working her butt off getting us into dry dock, and she's lined up a berth in two weeks. So here's the deal. We have time, now that we are here in Mexico, for two trips. You'll form groups and decide what you want to do. Write up your plan and who's in your group. You'll come back in ten days to check in—to hear about each other's trips, regroup with new people, get out of your cliques, plan another trip. Your traveling allowance is $2.50 a day. It will take some planning to make it work." He looked expectant, as if hoping we were going to shift gears to excitement, but most of the students were still slumped around the benches.

One whined. "Wasn't there some guy who was going to organize our trips?"

Ron shook his head. "It turns out he didn't speak Spanish. But he found us these maps and books."

Complaints ricocheted around the room. "This whole program is fucked up." "Chick and Stephanie aren't pulling through." "This is not the incredible trip they said it would be." "It's a flop." "No, it's you guys that are bringing down the trip, with all your bickering and complaining." "We have the right to complain about how for shit this school is. I told my parents and they've called Stephanie." "My parents called her, too. Maybe we should leave? Nothing's ever going to change."

It seemed we'd hit an all-time low, although we were on the verge of an adventure off the ship. We were stuck and miserable; even the positive kids were floundering.

Kim stood up, and shouted. "We have to fucking wake up!" She looked around at everyone. She was probably the only one who knew all of us—the stoners, the Deadheads, the Salty Dogs, the readers, and the journal writers. "Do you know who's really the problem?"

"Yeah!" Voices rumbled. "Take your pick." Like popcorn around the room, a chorus of blame: "The owners, Stephanie, the teachers, this stupid ship."

"No!" she shouted. "The problem is us."

Pogo nodded and quietly recited, "'We have met the enemy and he is us.'"

I glanced at him. "What?"

He whispered, "It's from the old comic strip Pogo."

More kids sat up to listen to Kim.

"*We* are our problem," Kim emphasized, "not Stephanie. Sure, she makes business stuff happen, but she doesn't say whether we pick up our clothes, or clean up the mess, or be considerate of each other."

Someone groaned. "So, are you Mom, telling us what to do?"

Kim ignored him. "Do you know the truth about this trip? If anything's gonna happen, it comes from us, the students." Heads were raised, kids were listening. "Not Chick and Stephanie, the crew, faculty, nobody. It's up to us."

"Yeah, we're the ones who really do the work."

Zip stood up. "I get it. If we want these trips to work, it's up to us." He was beaming, his red hair and freckles standing out. "No one's telling us how to do it!"

Kim nodded. "These trips are really ours. What we do depends on us."

I said, "Our family traveled all over Mexico when I was fourteen."

Someone shouted, "Speak up!"

I raised my voice: "There are so many cool things we can do. We can go to markets and pick out food we want to eat. We can go to Mayan ruins in the Yucatan, or go to museums in Mexico City."

One of the younger guys asked, "But where do we start? How do we know where to go?"

Ron stepped forward. "Form teams. Who do you want to travel with? You younger kids, team up with one of the teachers. Here are maps and books, train and bus schedules." We looked around the room. Suddenly we felt awkward about who to travel with. We didn't want to get stuck with people we didn't like.

As if Ron read our minds, he said, "You'll be with a new group the second time. So jump in and try out different combinations of friends. Make sure your teams aren't too big, they're ungainly to organize. But you need to be more than two for a team." We looked around, scanning the faces of our close and not-so-close friends. Some were already clearly a group. Of course, Zip and Lisa. Pogo studied a map with Ted, Jane, Phil, and Daniel. They were always together. I was disappointed.

Ron called out. "One more word from Stephanie: Don't do any drugs, 'cause she can't get you out of jail. OK, jump in."

Kim, bashful Bruce, and I gravitated together, and a quiet serious kid, Ben, asked if he could join us. "Sure."

Students grabbed books and maps and headed up on deck. All over the ship, groups huddled together with notebooks and pencils. We planned and packed their backpacks. By the next day, teams were waiting on deck for our trip approvals, to get our pesos for ten days, and then head down the gangplank.

•

Two days later at midnight, the four of us stood on a crowded train platform in the small city of Xalapa, in the foothills above Veracruz. The train we were waiting for had just been cancelled, again. Kim was furious after six hours of delays. "What are we going to do?" She looked like a little general from the Spanish American War, in her riding skirt, army canteen belt, wallabies, brown knee socks, and the huge, belted wool sweater she'd bargained over with a street vendor. Tall Bruce and skinny little Ben both wore blue jeans and jackets, while I wore an embroidered blouse and a thin leather jacket from the market. We circled around Kim, all of us weighed down with heavy backpacks, all of us bewildered.

We'd been standing here on the train platform since the end of the market day waiting for the 6 p.m. train. Farmers lugged crates of chickens and sacks of oranges and vegetables, leading goats by ropes. We towered over black-haired farmers with sun-weathered faces, their profiles like the Maya on ancient sculptures. Kim chatted with teenaged soldiers carrying guns. She pointed to things, and they said the words in Spanish. Kim repeated *el caballo*, horse. *La cabra*, goat. *La nube*, cloud. The station filled, but still no train. Delayed until nine, then again until midnight. Then an official emerged from the ticket office and shouted, "*No hay tren hasta las cinco en la manana.*" No train until five in the morning.

The three of us stood silent in the face of Kim's fuming, since she seemed to be our leader, until she asked, "Where'd everyone go?" Everyone had seemed to vanish. But, actually, the waiting crowd had settled down onto the train platform, like a great sigh or a call to prayer. Families leaned together, women held children in their arms, and men leaned against crates and boxes and animals. Everyone seemed to be settling in to sleep, holding their place for the train on the platform.

We wondered, "What do we do now?" We'd been learning to make decisions together.

I spoke tentatively. "I think we need to sleep right here, like everyone else, until the train arrives." I was so tired. I didn't like when Kim was angry, but I wasn't shrinking back.

Kim was still pissed. "We've waited all this time already."

Bruce wondered, "Should we unroll our sleeping bags?"

I glanced around at the crowd sleeping on the dirty concrete platform; some sat on folded blankets, some on cardboard. Their coats and shawls were pulled tight against the chill. "I don't think we'd have time when the train arrives. We'll have to be ready to run." The others agreed reluctantly. I pulled the pack off my back and the others followed. The boys leaned their packs against each other. To escape the cold platform, I pulled my knees to my chest, curled on my side on top of my backpack, on top of the lumpy rolls of sleeping bag, clothes, and journal inside the pack.

It wasn't until I shifted awkwardly on my backpack that I remembered my camera was gone, stolen from our hotel room that morning when we were at the market. I felt grief for losing all I wanted to photograph, like

I'd lost the future of our trip, the photos I would take of sails billowing in the wind, photos of my friends on deck. All those photos were gone. As if the year ahead had vanished, and I was left with only my pen and journal.

Then I remembered our time at the market. Kim had bought lots of chocolate and an etched silver ring. She held up her hand to show me. "I always thought wearing a ring was a sign of women being subservient to men. But I love how your ring is a symbol of your independence. I'm wearing mine for the same reason." We'd put our ringed hands together and crowed, "Independent women!"

I lay awake surrounded by sleepers, a cough, a baby's cry, clucks of startled chickens. I remembered traveling with my family around Mexico in our campervan, when we'd bought a kilo of tortillas, made a huge bowl of guacamole, and climbed Mayan temples. I missed my family, even my dad. I wanted to write to them and to find them treasures in the markets. I drifted off into a dream where I ran for the train. I woke up with heart pounding. I lifted my head to listen, touched my ticket and passport in my pocket to reassure myself, and then drifted back into sleep until the dream repeated. I practiced all night in my sleep to jump and run for the train. When the rumbling train actually arrived in the grey dark, we startled awake, grabbed our bags and ran, clambered on, and found four seats together before every seat, overhead rack, and aisle became jammed with people, animals, and produce.

We hugged each other, as if we'd had a great success.

I said, "I kept dreaming I was running for the train."

Kim said, "Me too. I'd hear the train and was so afraid I wouldn't find my stuff and make the train. The dream kept repeating. I'm exhausted."

"We were dreaming the same dream! Are we in a dream right now?" We pulled from our packs dried figs, nuts, chunks of chocolate. Kim grinned.

"I don't think this is a dream if we have chocolate!"

I peeled oranges and passed around slices as the train thumped its way slowly toward the mountains. A couple of little girls asked to touch Kim's blond curls before they ran back to their mothers, giggling. Kim and I tried to write in our journals but the train jerked too much. We gave up, leaned against each other's shoulders, and fell asleep.

•

We arrived in Mexico City that night after our long, slow train ride, and found a hotel room. After a day exploring Mexico City, we crashed in our dreary room with one lamp between two beds. We were ready to get out of the city.

"The air's so dirty from exhaust," Bruce said. His confidence was gaining on our trip. His Spanish was good enough to get us around.

Kim griped again. "I can't believe I came all this way and didn't have enough money to go to the Anthropology Museum."

We decided we had to find a small town we could afford that would be fun to explore. Not too far away, and a train to get us there and then back to the ship after a couple days. As I studied the guidebook, Kim dashed to the bathroom and repeatedly flushed. Bruce rushed in as soon as she was back. Then she dashed to the toilet again. The thin walls dissolved any privacy. She came back demanding, "Who has the diarrhea pills?" Bruce tossed her the pill bottle, and she gulped down a couple.

She said the word *diarrhea* over and over like it was a joke. Then the two boys and Kim bounced on the beds, munched on chocolate, and compared notes on how addicted to chocolate they were, and all the while I was trapped in my own straitjacket. To me, this was not funny, but they found it uproarious. "Oh Elizabeth, why can't you loosen up?"

I used to believe that one day I'd be a fun person. I'd know how to have a good time. I'd be like Kim. But Kim somehow made this all worse, because she was so out there, and crazy fun. If I were with Bruce and Ben on my own, we'd probably all be reading and talking quietly about where we'd travel. We'd be happy in a reserved kid's quiet way.

I buried my face in the map, scrambling to find the place for us to go. Finally, I called out a name of a town. "Toluca, I think we should go to

Toluca. It's a couple of hours away, near the mountains." Even though I was someone who'd studied the books and figured out a plan, they looked at me like I was from another planet.

•

The train deposited us in Toluca at midnight. We followed signs to El Centro by the strings of bulbs drooping between buildings, passing dogs as they nosed through trash on empty streets flanked by low, cracked plaster walls. We were four teens, weary under heavy backpacks, uncertain where we'd stay, and scared to be so alone in a small city in the eerie silence. I reached out to Kim, linked my right arm through hers, and just like that, we all linked arms, Bruce on my left, and Ben on Kim's other side, and everything changed. I felt warm and connected.

We chanted, "*Lions and tigers and bears, oh my!*" over and over. We glanced at each other and laughed as we walked down the middle of the street. We broke into a chorus of "We're Off to See the Wizard," as our voices echoed down the empty street.

"What if someone hears us?" I asked. "They'll think it's a rerun of *The Wizard of Oz*."

Bruce looked toward Kim and me and asked, "So who's Dorothy?"

Kim and I looked at each other. I wanted to say I was Dorothy. I wanted to claim that I was a girl on the adventure, but I didn't. Instead, I turned to Kim, "You're Dorothy, of course. But then I don't know who I am."

Kim was fierce and fair. "We're both Dorothy."

I beamed. She let me be Dorothy, too! We were both brave, in different ways. Then Kim nodded to the bashful Bruce. "And you are the Cowardly Lion. Getting braver by the minute." We smiled down the line of our linked bodies as he blushed with pleasure. Kim and I knew that Bruce had a crush on both of us. With some people this could be annoying, but with Bruce, it endeared him to us.

Awkward, skinny little Ben asked, "Am I the Scarecrow?"

Kim declared, "Nope, you already have brains. You're the Tin Man because you need a heart." I glanced at Ben, who nodded thoughtfully. Kim understood him.

Our lumpy packs dug into our backs, our footfalls the only sound on the silent street, our bent arms warm against each other's chests. Brave and connected, we murmured the words, *Lions and tigers and bears, oh my*. Then Bruce asked, "So what does Dorothy want?"

I spoke first, a rare event for me when Kim was around. "Maybe all Dorothys are trying to find their way home." Kim and I glanced at each other, sobered. Home was such a loaded issue for us. Did we really want to go home? I changed to a lighter tone, grinning at Kim. "Right now, the Dorothys just want a warm bed!"

We entered an enormous, deserted, sparsely-lit square, edged with arched walkways, a massive stone cathedral towering above us. The first two hotels turned us away, the clerks implying that they didn't want hippies with backpacks. On a side street, warm light streamed out of a doorway onto the stone street. "Look, our yellow brick road," Kim whispered. It was an old hotel, with green plants in the interior courtyard and rooms on a balcony. We were led to a room with four double beds and real blankets. We collapsed into sleep and didn't wake until hours later in a deluge of sunlight.

Had we ever felt so good, or smiled so much? In the cobblestone square, we discovered a cart lined with jars of jewel-bright fruits for drinks, *aguas frescas*, each name on a smudged, handwritten tag: *Papaya, Melón, Tamarindo, Piña, Banana, Mango*. There were plates on top of each jar, and everything was sticky, with bees crawling, flying, drowning in sweetness. We pointed to the fruits we wanted blended with ice and lime. A smiling woman with gold-covered teeth handed me a tall glass, like a benediction, and we each carried our fruit filled glass to sit on the stone steps, sipping in the bright, sunlit day.

A week later, back on the ship, planning our next trip, I came up with the crazy idea of a hitchhiking race to Mexico City. Had I ever hitched a ride before? Never, but lots of students told us they'd hitchhiked on the first field trip. I was tired of getting stuck on trains, and buses were too expensive, so I convinced my new team that hitching would be faster and cheaper.

The *Antarna* still hadn't gone into dry dock. But work on the ship was scheduled to start any day. Ron greeted us as we clomped up the gangway on the return from our first trip. "Form new groups, tell us your plans, and you'll get your next travel allowance. This is a quick turnaround."

People were psyched. "Alright. Let's do it." All over the ship, wet clothes hung to dry. Students and teachers compared notes, what they'd bargained for in markets (hammocks, leather jackets, sweaters), what they'd eaten. We studied maps, where to camp, where to stay, how to go farther on this trip. We'd learned: pack lighter and wear warmer clothes. New groups formed. After a night's sleep in our bunks, we were ready to go. "Come back in ten days," they told us. "The ship will be ready," they assured us.

I looked for Kim to say goodbye. "What are you doing next?"

She smiled mysteriously. "Still figuring out the details. See you when we all return."

My new group gathered on deck, stuffing wads of pesos into a variety of hiding places in our packs and clothes. Then everyone looked at me, the unexpected leader of our next adventure. "OK, supposedly girls get the rides, so we divide up the girls with each group to get us rides."

Ted pointed out the obvious. "The only problem is that there are only two girls, Jane and you. And how many boys?" We looked around and counted. Yikes. Seven boys. Ted, Pogo, Bruce, Daniel, and Chris, as well as Woodie and his snarky sidekick Jake, who'd latched on with our team at the last minute.

"Okay," I said. "We'll do it. Four boys with one girl and three with the other. Let's walk to the highway."

I gave everyone a piece of paper with the address of a cheap hotel I'd found in a guidebook. I admonished them. "Don't lose it. Put it in your sock. We'll wait for you all to arrive." We hoisted our backpacks, and our motley company walked for an hour to reach the highway out of town. I handed out hitchhiking signs: *Ciudad Mexico.*

Despite being organized, underneath I was nervous, afraid I was blushing because, when we'd divided up the groups, I would be hitching with Daniel, as well as Woodie and Jake. I had developed a crush on the intellectual, serious Daniel and I felt tortured by a hyper-awareness as I noticed everything about him. He was wearing khakis and a blue-and-white striped button-down shirt with the cuffs rolled up. His thick brown hair was pushed back off his forehead. I was wearing my wraparound leather mini-skirt and embroidered blouse with gold stitches in the bodice. The little boys looked grungy in dirty jeans and faded T-shirts. Hadn't I said it was important to dress nicely to get a ride? But if I said anything now, I'd sound like a bossy older sister.

As we walked out of Veracruz, we joked, "Who's going to get to Mexico City first?"

Ted was certain. "Our team's going to win. What's the prize anyway?"

Everyone agreed: "A round of *Dos Equis* for the winners!" We arrived at the highway entrance and clustered in two groups, Jane and I standing conspicuously in front of the guys. I didn't even have a chance to take off my backpack, because in one minute, a brand-new Mercedes sedan with German plates stopped in front of me. An elegant older guy in a suit leaned over and called out through the passenger window in a German accent, "You two." He pointed at Daniel and me. I thought he was holding up two fingers, like he was giving us the peace sign, but no, he was taking two. I looked back at Woodie and Jake. "Sorry guys."

They laughed and pointed at the Mercedes. Woodie acted like it was a great joke. "My sister always gets the cool car."

I was caught up in the excitement of our race, the car, and my crush. I never once thought to say, "I can't leave my little brother behind." Daniel and I carefully set down our packs in the spotless trunk; Daniel sat in the front and I in the back. We slid across leather seats, closed the beautifully engineered doors, and left the rest of them behind, laughing and waving at us.

The smoothness of the ride was astounding, as the car drove effortlessly from the coastal plain up into the mountains. My ears popped from the change in altitude while Daniel and the driver talked. I tried to join in the conversation, but the German man glanced back at me, "You don't articulate clearly like your friend." Daniel didn't glance back. They conversed as if I was not even there. I didn't try to say anything after that. I watched the road, the mountains, studied the map, and calculated where he could let us off in the city and how to get to our hotel. Then I slept on those smooth leather seats.

I awoke with a jolt when we arrived in Mexico City, less than six hours later. We'd arrived faster than I thought was possible. After walking half an hour, we arrived at the modest hotel. We had definitely won the hitchhiking race. But there was no thrill, when no one else was there. After we'd settled into the hotel room, each of us reading on one of the four beds, I worried how the rest of them were doing.

A good way to get over a crush is to wait in a crummy hotel room for friends and a little brother to arrive. Crushes feed off watching from a distance and chance encounters, but having too much time with someone you don't really know rapidly wears it out. Daniel and I didn't have much to talk about. We read, wrote in our journals, wrote letters until we fell asleep. In the morning, waking up and seeing only him was a disappointment. We didn't want to explore the city when we thought the others might arrive at any minute. We grew bored and restless and self-conscious.

On the afternoon of the second day, heavy steps and laughter in the hall startled us. I threw open the door, elated to see familiar faces so far from the ship, and hugged adorable Pogo, funny Ted, giggling Jane, bashful Bruce, and quiet Chris, laden with packs. Daniel lit up—finally his friends were here—and I was not really one of his friends. That was fine. After twenty-four hours, we were relieved to have a break from each other. They wanted to know when we'd arrived. "You guys sure won the race. Got to get your *Dos Equis!*"

I looked down the hall before I closed the door. No one else tumbled into our room. "Where are Woodie and Jake?" That was when I found out they were traveling on their own, two fifteen-year-olds, whom I'd left behind. Fear clenched my belly. I felt sick while I tried to enjoy the new arrivals telling us about their rides, about the Cadillac with Texas plates, crazy guys claiming they were banditos, who gave them boiling hot Cokes to drink. They were starving, and ready for dinner. I said, "I'll stay here, bring me something." I couldn't leave my post, hoping the "little" boys would arrive any minute.

When I woke to the third day, I was slammed with fear and guilt. How could I have left them? What if they never arrived? How could we ever find them? There was nothing to do but wait. The others explored, and I was relieved when they left. Because of a stupid crush and a fancy car, I'd left my brother behind. I was ashamed of myself.

At the end of the third day, we were eating bread and cheese in our room when there was a knock at the door. It was the guy from the front desk. He gestured suspiciously toward two filthy, scrawny, long-haired boys in oil-stained jean jackets, as if to ask, Are these yours? "*Si, si, es mi hermano!*" I lunged past him to hug my brother, crying with relief. "Oh Woodie, I'm so sorry I left you behind."

Woodie and Jake pushed past me to dump their packs on the floor, uninterested in an apology. Everyone patted them on the back, and everyone laughed with relief. Woodie beamed, happy to see all of us, and basked in the attention. After they took a hot bath and changed clothes, they gobbled down all the food we had. Then my brother told the story, and Jake tossed in details, of their days on the road.

"After that Cadillac took the rest of you, we walked back to a two-lane road." They patched together a series of rides in funky trucks on hairpin turns and steep roads into the mountains.

"The first night we slept behind a billboard. We kicked around in the dark to make sure we didn't lie on cactus. Our sleeping bags are those pathetic quilted bags kids use for sleepovers. We shivered so bad." Woodie paused to laugh. As I watched my little brother, I was struck by what a comic storyteller he had become. He told us about how a big truck pulled over, and the driver gestured to a warm cab. He tossed their packs in the back of a greasy truck full of boxes and barrels and closed the doors on the back. They were nervous about leaving their packs, but no one was back there. Before we'd left the ship, Woodie told me he had a small stash of cash hidden in his clothes and shoes, but I knew his camera, which he'd bought with his savings, was wrapped up at the bottom of his pack.

The truck struggled up steep roads, across vast desert plateaus, past small villages of stone buildings and rusting metal roofs. Men clustered around the truck when they stopped for gas. Woodie said, "We pissed in the dirt and bought meat tacos from a girl with a basket. Brain, intestines, tongue. They were so spicy they burned all the way down." When they climbed back in the truck, he glanced in the crack between the doors at the back. Their packs were still there. But he thought he caught a glimpse of movement. Was someone back there? He gestured to the driver, who shook his head: "No, no," and pushed them back toward the cab.

The truck kept driving until dark while the boys dozed. Suddenly in the middle of a desolate plain, the driver stopped, engine running, and pointed for Woodie and Jake to get out. Woodie said, "My heart was pounding. What was happening?" The driver opened the back of the truck and a couple of guys crouching back there handed down the packs, smiling broken-toothed grins. "*Adiós, amigos!*" The guys climbed into the cab. The truck turned off onto a rutted side road, their headlights disappearing out of sight.

Woodie spoke slowly now to emphasize the vast empty plain. "Then it was silent. So empty it seeps into your bones. Remember in Castaneda's *Journey to Ixtlan*, when he's taught to face the dark? It was like that." He described the rim of the mountains showing the last edge of light, and we could see it. His pack was lighter, and he knew his camera was gone, but that wasn't important anymore because it was so cold. They had to do something. The ground was frosted, their hands and faces were growing numb in the wind with only one light in the distance. "We had to get there."

He held us in a spell with his story, as I kept shoving down fears of what could have happened, while I reassured myself that they'd gotten to the hotel.

Jake groaned. "I'm sure we walked for hours."

Woodie said they finally arrived at a small stone building with one lit window and knocked on a board door. "I'd practiced over and over, '*Hola, buenos noches.*'"

The door cracked open and a man looked at them suspiciously. "*Gringos?*"

"*Si. Estudiantes.*" The man studied their faces and gestured them in. His family sat around the fire, where a pot of soup and a skillet of tortillas were cooking over the flames. An older woman patted out more tortillas. Children in ragged clothes moved aside and made a place for them next to the fire, staring. Bowls of spicy, hot soup and spoons were pressed into their hands, with tortillas for dipping. "I'd never tasted anything so good." They slept in their sleeping bags on the floor in front of the fire, and the family slept on mats around them in the dark. At dawn, the man drove them to the highway. My brother ended his story. "They had so little but they fed us. I'll never forget that family."

Pogo said, "You guys definitely deserve the prize in the hitching race!"

Woodie grinned. "So what about those *Dos Equis*? It's time to celebrate!" We headed out to a local bar. I was relieved to get out of the hotel.

But after one beer, I was tearful and apologized to Woodie, "I should have told our driver that I needed my little brother to come with us. I am so sorry."

Woodie waved me off. "Hey, we had a blast."

"But if something had happened to you, I couldn't have lived with myself."

"It's OK. We got here. Get over it."

After that we stayed together. We filled bags with food from a market and then took a local train as far as we could go to the end of the city. All of us climbed onto the back of a big open truck driving into the mountains to a national forest south of the city. We set up camp near a stream crashing over boulders. I woke to the canopy of pines overhead, their needles shiny in a bright blue sky. I washed my face, cupped my hands, and drank cold water from the stream.

For five days, we read, rested, and ate near the stream. We hiked on steep woodcutters' paths into the mountains, and dreamed under star-filled skies. One night as we sat around the fire, I asked, "Have you seen your hands in a dream?" Everyone was working on it, but no one had been able to do it yet.

When we left the mountains, we divided into teams for hitching back to Veracruz. On our last ride, Pogo, Bruce, Woodie, and I crowded into the cab of a huge semi, shoving our packs behind the burly driver. Pogo and Bruce squeezed onto a narrow ledge behind the passenger seat. As my brother moved forward to climb up into the seat, the driver grinned and pointed to me, "No. Chica." He patted the narrow seat next to him; the gearshift handle was where my legs would be. I climbed up and squeezed in. In front of me on the dash were crosses and images of saints, and through the windshield were the mountains we had to descend to reach the coast. We needed this all-night ride.

Woodie climbed up next to me and wedged the heavy door shut. I asked, "Veracruz?" again to make sure. The driver answered, "*Si, si. En la mañana.*" In my short leather skirt, my bare legs were too close to where he was shifting gears. The truck descended from the mountain plateau as dusk sank, the engine deafening, and as he shifted down to handle the steep grades, his arm and hand kept bumping against my knees and legs. I leaned against my brother, trying to slide my legs farther toward him.

After the truck shuddered downhill, precipitously, around a series of sharp turns before a flat patch of road, Woodie leaned forward, and with as much authority as he could muster as a fifteen-year-old, knowing he was risking our ride, he eyed the driver fiercely and pointed to me. "My sister, *mi hermana!*"—implying: "Don't mess with her"—and hoping that the protectiveness of brothers for sisters would strike a chord with the driver. It worked. The man nodded, and his hand on the gearshift didn't brush across my legs again all night. My little brother was watching out for me better than I had watched out for him.

The semi rumbled on, the driver pressing down hard on the brakes as the engine bucked and roared, and we descended from the mountains, four American children drifting in and out of sleep in his care all night. He dropped us off at the edge of the industrial wasteland outside of Veracruz in the grey dawn. We clambered down from the truck cab, stiff and blinking. We called to him over and over before he drove off. *"Muchas gracias."*

We scanned over the town to the docks until we spotted her. The four masts of the *Antarna* rising above warehouses. We shouldered our packs and trudged in her direction, as the magnetic connection to the ship pulled us back.

•

We reached the long dock where the *Antarna* gleamed luminous white, freshly painted in dry dock. Paper covered the portholes, and workers were still busy on the ship and hull. We climbed the gangway, dumped our gear, and raced around the ship. "Who's back? How was your trip? Where'd you go?" The ship was alive with stories and rumors, confusion and excitement. I couldn't wait to ask Kim, "How was your adventure?" and tell her about mine.

All day groups of students returned. Students and teachers clustered around the deck and in the crew mess, comparing notes. Some had camped in mountains and almost froze. Harry, from Alberta, and Brian, a black kid from the Bronx, laughed. "We were afraid we were in for a shotgun wedding!" In Xalapa they met some college girls and stayed with them for a week in their apartment. They were terrified when the girls invited them home, but the families gave them lots of food and weed.

On the first trip, Stephanie sent Richie and Freddie (the youngest and perhaps the richest and the poorest kids) with teachers Karl and Simone, and they rode horseback through lava fields that had smothered a whole town, except the church tower, decades before.

A big team back from the Yucatan showered and put on clean clothes, before they collapsed in the crew mess, ravenous for dinner. The rest of us jammed around them to hear about their trip. Mike, the Mythology and Dreams teacher, wore a white polo shirt that didn't hide the scrapes and countless bites on his arms and neck. "We met a guide who said he'd take us through the rain forest near the Guatemalan border to the rediscovered Mayan temple city of Bonampak." We knew he'd been reading all about Mayan beliefs and history to prepare his students for the Yucatan. "I'd heard about this temple where the interior was covered with painted murals. I convinced everyone to go." He snorted with laughter. "But the guide forgot to tell us it was the rainy season and we'd be sinking into deep mud with every step for the first half of our three day walk into the jungle."

Zip said, "The second night we were sleeping in a remote Indian village, on the ground around a fire to keep warm. The guide had said that red ants come through about once a month and devour everything in their path, but we didn't take this seriously." He shook his head. "I think Grant was the first to wake." He glanced at Grant, the skinny silent kid who usually hung out in the rigging. "He was jumping and screaming as he tore at his pants and shirt. Within seconds the rest of us were tearing at our skin."

Grant grimaced and talked for the first time. "You had to remove every ant one by one 'cause their jaws lock into you." He pulled up his shirt to show his torso covered with red lumps and scratches.

"We retreated into a church hut and stood on benches," Peter, the oceanography teacher added. "We watched as armies of red ants kept coming, pouring over the floor, eating everything in their path. All night."

Richie held out a small polished skull on a leather strap fastened at his waist. "This was one of the spider monkeys we'd eaten for dinner. I'd left it on the ground. It was gross with hairs and skin, but those ants ate it clean."

Someone asked, "You ate monkey?" I suddenly realized they all looked thinner, their cheeks hollow, and Richie had lost his baby fat.

Peter groaned. "We ran out of granola and trail mix after a day. We were guests of the chief of the village, and he cooked groundhog and spider monkey, which tastes like chicken except with chunks of black hair cooked into it."

Then thin, quiet Phil spoke, his eyes more deeply shadowed and he looked alarmingly skinny. "The chief watched me as I took one bite. I gagged and almost vomited."

"Disgusting!" the chorus of kids cried.

Zip chuckled. "We haven't told you about the black widows falling on us."

Around the room, we shivered, our eyes opened wide. "Oohhh!" But one kid said, "Nah, you're fucking with me, man."

Mike was dead serious. "Our third night, we stayed in a big screen tent where the gum harvesters sleep. We climbed in our hammocks and drew the mosquito netting around us. Just as I was falling asleep, I saw dozens of black widows dropping down towards us on their webs. I saw the red hourglass in the firelight. They crawled right on the other side of the netting. I was too tired to care."

I felt almost embarrassed. Our adventures seemed so tame in comparison.

Richie grinned. "The only thing that helped was smoking weed, so I could zone out." Even though he was bitten and scratched, and his hair nearly covered his eyes; he looked older, different from the boy who'd arrived by limo. I was impressed he'd persevered on this trip.

Mike ruffled his hair. "You did awesome, Richie." But then he scoffed. "Nina was so terrified she had a plane come and get her out of there."

We glanced around the room, amazed. Nina, the girl with the black ponytail, who'd come late to host guests. She was Mike's girlfriend, but she glared at Mike. "That's not true. We walked in the rain, with mud to our mid-calves. I got a second wind, like going into a trance, putting one foot in front of the other. By the time we arrived, I was so sick. The closest doctor was in Palenque. So, I had to fly out." She glared at Mike. I was impressed with her.

Zip picked up the story. "We reached a dark green river, about a hundred feet across. And the boat to cross it was on the other side. How were we going to get that boat? Mike was worried about snakes and piranhas, but Peter just dove in and swam across. Crazy!" Peter's face and arms were red and peeling. "Later we found out the river was full of alligators!"

Mike shook his head. "It really was like Conrad's *Heart of Darkness!*"

Nina told about the first night, when a jaguar paced nearby, growling, a strange sound like a grinding sawblade. "It was pouring down rain, we couldn't start a fire. We hung our hammocks close together about three feet off the ground. Our guide went to sleep right away. I guess he was used to the noise. Grant climbed up high in the tree to hang his hammock, thinking he'd be safer."

We looked at Grant who shook his head. "In the morning, the guide started screaming at me. Jaguars climb trees when they hunt. He could have gotten me."

"Crazy, man, crazy."

Then quiet Phil spoke up. "On the trail I was walking ahead with our guide and he suddenly stopped and put up his hand. Before I could see what he was doing, he brought his machete down and killed a snake, a fer-de-lance." He looked around as if expecting us to know it. "It's a pit viper, one the deadliest snakes in the world. Fatal if it bites you. It's brown with black edged diamonds." I stared at him, chilled, remembering my childhood nightmare of the snakes in the roots of trees. "We were ahead of the others, so Peter and I curled the dead snake and placed it at the foot of a tree beside the path. Then we hid to watch everyone's reactions. We thought this was funny, that it would freak people out."

Kids voices joked. "You must have scared the shit out of people, man!"

Phil shook his head. "But nobody even saw it. Nobody."

Some kids swore. "Crazy, man." But there was a hush around the room, before everyone started talking.

A few of us clustered around Mike, hungry for more. "We climbed out of the mud onto a rocky trail as we rose higher in the jungle. It was so quiet in the jungle and we didn't hear anything until we heard a hum, that kept getting louder and louder. We came into a clearing and there on a cliff about a hundred feet high were thousands of colorful blooming orchids. The hum was a sea of bees and butterflies flitted everywhere. I'll never forget it."

After the others left to get dinner, Pogo asked Mike, "Did you ever get to that room full of Mayan murals?" I leaned in to listen. Mike explained it was a little temple looking down on a plaza, surrounded by jungle. The walls and ceiling were covered with murals, painted orange, blue, and red. The guide said a ceremony took place in the plaza. One person was chosen to dress in a sacred costume made from red and emerald green iridescent feathers from the sacred quetzal bird, the god of freedom and wealth. "They tied a rope around the person's waist to lower him from very high pole, and set him spinning faster and faster. The guide said, 'This is the flight of our dreams.'" I felt a chill go through me.

Mike stroked his chin. "You know how I said in class that when someone tells a dream and we listen to it, that it becomes our dream too." He paused to look around the room at the kids lining up for dinner. "Our journey into the jungle was like a dream, and now that we've told all of you the story, it's become everyone's dream." Pogo and I nodded.

I struggled to put something into words. "I can't shake the story of that snake. What is so dangerous, and hidden in plain sight, but we don't even see it?" Something felt so obvious but I knew I was missing it. I think that was how I felt most of the time.

Mike grinned, "That's the question really, isn't it?"

•

Across the room, I saw Kim for the first time, leaning in the doorway, her face almost a scowl. When I tried to catch her eye, she backed away and disappeared down the hall. When I climbed up on deck to find her, I saw her run up the ship's ladder toward the bridge.

After dark, I finally found Kim alone on her bunk. I pushed my backpack off my bed and sat down to face her. "So where did you go on your field trip?"

She glared at the ceiling before she sat up abruptly. "I didn't go on a second trip, because of Jakob." I held my breath. She was finally speaking about her secret relationship. "As first mate, he had to stay close to the ship. He promised me that we'd spend time together, and go away to a little cabin or something. But all we did was walk around the city a few times." She finished, angry. "That did not feed my soul."

She kicked the edge of my bunk with her sneaker. She punctuated her words with each kick. "I didn't go fucking anywhere. But boy, did I learn something. I will never, ever, relinquish an adventure again because of a guy."

After Kim lay down again, I asked, "What was it like on the ship through dry dock?"

"Loud, twenty-four hours. Spotlights on, banging metal, blowtorches, stinky smell of paint. After dry dock, they tied us up next to a bauxite loading zone that covered the ship with white dust." Her lips were pursed, and her eyebrows pinched toward deep furrows.

She hunched over, putting her weight on her fists on the bunk. Then she looked at me. "Remember Larry, one of the engineers?"

"No." I didn't really know the crew. But Kim knew everybody. While the students were gone, she'd worked in the galley and eaten with the crew.

"He almost died."

"When? On the ship?"

"Almost. When he didn't show for dinner, we thought he'd gone on a bender. Oh God, he ate shit, lots of candy bars and sausage sticks. Emil and I checked in on him. He was in agony; his skin was yellow."

I grimaced, thinking about this sick old man.

"He was moaning. It was stifling in his cabin. The portholes were closed because we were in dry dock. They called the hospital on the ship's radio. They shouted down to us: 'Where's the pain? Left or right?' I felt around on his belly until he screamed. I shouted up to the guy. 'Right lower.'"

I reached to my own belly. Right lower. I remembered my biology textbook with the transparent pages and organs in different colors. I asked Kim, "Was it the appendix?"

She nodded. "They called an ambulance. I hoisted one arm over my shoulder and Emil took the other. It was a nightmare, squeezing him through the narrow cabin door and down the hallway. We dragged and pushed him up the ship's ladder onto the deck. He screamed in pain. He looked almost dead. The guys carried him down the gangway. I wanted to go in the ambulance, but Jakob rode with him to the hospital. His appendix ruptured in the ambulance."

She leaned back against the wall, wiping sweat off her face. "It was touch and go. They let me go see him in the hospital, when the doctors said he was going to make it." She spoke slowly. "The hospital was so quiet, and he lay on white sheets." She was quiet, like a storm had passed. Then she jumped up. "Gotta do my watch," and she raced out, more a woman of the ship than before. My camping in the mountains seemed almost silly compared to what Kim had lived through.

Several days after we returned to the ship, I joined a crowd that leaned along the railing, looking down at the harbor activity. My brother pointed to a boat farther down the dock. "See that battered old Navy ship? The sailors challenged us to a game of football."

"Are you going to play?"

"Nah, not me. I'm a little squirt. But Ron and Zip play football. I bet they're good!" A bunch of our big guys and mates clomped down the gangway, wearing an array of faded blue T-shirts, with their long hair tied back. We cheered them on. "Go Oceanics!"

The Mexican Navy guys with sharp haircuts showed up wearing crisp white T-shirts, bouncing soccer balls.

Our team called, "Football?"

"*Si, fútbol*," they said, holding out the soccer balls.

Not only did our guys not know how to play, many had never even seen a soccer game. Running up and down the concrete dock, kicking the ball toward makeshift goals, the Mexican Navy trounced our guys, like a choreographed comedy. And we cheered for all of them.

Before dinner, we were ordered to stay on board the ship. A gaggle of brightly dressed women in high heels arrived from town to flirt with the Navy guys and our boys on the railing. They must have been the "ladies of the night" Pogo had mentioned. A young one waved to the railing. "*Adiós, mi amor, Richee!*" She seemed to assume we'd be leaving soon, like sailors always do. Maybe she knew something we didn't.

Richie ran down the gangway and threw his arms around her. He clomped back up the gangway quickly, calling to his friends, "I'm leaving. I'm tired of the ship." He wanted to stay with her in Veracruz. "I'm done. I'm getting my stuff." Someone warned the teachers, and he was restrained at the gangway when he attempted to leave with his backpack and fishing gear. He stomped back toward the boys' quarters, his cheeks streaked with tears and frustration.

Having flown down from New York, Stephanie arrived in a taxi at the dock. She stepped out in her red power dress, her long black hair gleaming, held by a barrette at the nape of her neck. She called out to some students to haul a stuffed duffel out of the trunk. "Is that a body in there?" the kids asked when they tried to lift it.

"It's mail for all of you. I keep telling your parents not to send packages." Shouts of "Mail Call" rang down the decks, and everyone came running. Stephanie looked intent and fierce as she conferred with Jakob and Captain Floden, before she strode back down the gangway. She didn't stop to wave. Students nudged each other and whispered, "She's off to dinner with the owners, finalizing details for our departure."

A few of us clustered on deck and pieced together what we knew. Kim growled. "The owners are keeping our papers and not letting us leave port."

I didn't understand. "But Stephanie leased the ship for a dollar a year from them, and she's paid all the bills, including dry dock. And they won't let us leave?"

Zip was pissed. "They'd agreed, a gentleman's agreement. If they didn't want to lease the ship to the school again next year, they had to reimburse the school for all the paid bills. We've worked like dogs, and now they want to take back the ship?"

Kim mapped out the details no one had told us. "Stephanie signed the lease in Florida, but her lawyer found out weeks later the owners never signed it. They want her to sign away the right to be reimbursed for all that work she paid for." Her eyes narrowed; her lip arched. "They want to hold the ship, and us students, in port until she agrees and signs. Those bastards."

A sense of anticipation ran excitedly all over the ship. The gangway wasn't raised, but the railing doorway was latched shut. Something was in the works.

After dinner, I went back to my bunk to read, with the porthole and door closed, to keep out the bauxite dust that insinuated into every nook and cranny on board. I'd become an optimist again, somehow believing that everything would work out. Perhaps my optimism was built on naïve cluelessness. I read the letters that Stephanie brought to the ship, from friends at college, and a letter from home. I opened the family letter with trepidation, but after my mom's newsy report, there was a warm enthusiastic letter from my dad appreciating the letter I'd written about sailing to Mexico. Once again, I'd revived my hopefulness about him, that maybe we could get along better. Then I fell asleep.

•

Early the next morning, I was jolted awake by the rocking of the ship as sunrise streamed through the dusty porthole. I bolted up the stairs and pushed open the watertight door to let in the fresh sea air. I was instantly ecstatic when I saw Kim leaning on the rail, watching the sun as it cleared the horizon.

I threw my arms around her. "Kim, we're at sea! How did this happen?" Kim's face looked tired in the bright early light, but she beamed a rascally, thin smile.

I pushed her. "You know something! How in the world did we leave Veracruz?"

With unusual reserve, she answered carefully. "It happened after dark when everyone was asleep."

"Tell me more!"

"It was planned for after midnight." Kim leaned dreamily against the rail. "Sails are getting set!" She yawned with gusto, stretching her arms as far as she could. "I'm off to sleep. See you later." She headed down the steps to our quarters.

•

It would take decades for me to squeeze the whole story out of my former shipmate, and piece together more details from a few teachers, Stephanie's letters, and an interview years later with our Swedish captain.

Stephanie had written that the harbormaster of the Port of Veracruz informed her that the owners had asked him to hold the ship. After she left us that afternoon, Stephanie quietly paid the final dry dock bill, $25,000 in cash, and she worked with the officials to clear the ship to sail for Panama. Then she went to dinner with the owners to negotiate a contract.

Late in the evening, after the students were below decks, the captain ordered the gangway raised and secured. Tugs arrived, and the *Antarna* cast off lines, leaving behind the docks of Veracruz, the lovely old city, and the snowcapped volcanos to the west. The tugs proceeded to leave tire marks from bow to stern along the freshly painted hull. Nearly everyone on board, as if under a spell, slept through all of this.

In the 1990s, our captain, Stig Floden, was interviewed for a book on the ship, now known as the *Sea Cloud*. He must have been nearly eighty, and he recounted many lively, embellished accounts of his time on board. This was his account of our departure from Veracruz:

> The shipyard was paid off, and [the Owner] who had fruitlessly tried to prevent the ship from leaving, was left on the pier watching it continue its school cruise. As the *Antarna* left harbor, Stephanie kissed the 63-year-old captain and jubilated: "We've done it again."[1]

Except that Stephanie never sailed with the ship.

Fifty years after our departure, Kim and I were talking to each other on our computer screens—Kim in England, I in Maine. I asked questions. "Did you watch us slip out of Veracruz? Did we really fly a pirate flag?" We were in our mid-sixties, remembering ourselves at sixteen and eighteen.

"We flew the pirate flag 'til dawn. Captain's orders," she responded calmly. "I was present for the entire process. I liked being as close to those in the know as possible. That's what I wrangled by hanging out with the

1. Kurt Grobecker and Peter Neumann, *Sea Cloud: A Living Legend* (United Kingdom: Collectors' Books Limited, 1991).

first mate. I remember radio messages not being answered by anyone on board until we were quite far out beyond Mexican waters." She added, "I stayed up all night. The pleasure of the dawn at sea was a delayed climax to the buildup and success of leaving."

Months later, I wrote to Kim to tell her I was going to sail on the *Sea Cloud*, now a cruising yacht, on its most affordable sail for four days around the Canary Islands. I wanted to remember the smells and sounds of the ship at sea to write this story. She wrote back, "Where on the ship are you going to sleep?"

"We'll be starboard side, an officer's cabin, original teak bunks. I think it's the old radio officer's cabin."

She wrote back, her email erupting in caps: "I REMEMBER the radio office!! We were there when pirating the ship!!!"

"Did the ship really refuse to answer messages?"

"Yes, we kept getting messages as we raced toward open water. The radio officer kept sending static feedback. Jakob was standing outside, because he had to not know this was going on, so he couldn't be charged with piracy." She described how she'd used her voice, crumpled paper, and twisted dials to create static interference, to convince the shore that we couldn't hear their messages until we reached international waters fourteen miles offshore.

•

That morning, I stood at the rail at sunrise after Kim went below. The ship motored over a gentle sea, out of sight of land. The bell rang and sleepy students emerged on deck, stunned and amazed. On my way to the mess for breakfast, I looked toward the bow where the two jib sails I'd bent onto the bowsprit caught the wind—and a colorful Jolly Roger flapped in the wind.

In the mess, I told my brother Woodie. "Get your Polaroid camera and follow me."

Fifty years later, studying the photo album I made the summer after the ship, I found a faded black and white photo of a small flag to the right of the bow. In my eighteen-year-old handwriting, I'd penciled in the only documentation that any of this tale is true: *Pirate flag (made by students) flown on order of Captain.*

What moves me now is to imagine what the ship looked like that night, when it motored out with no lights, like a ghost ship, a bright white hull, four masts rising far into the night sky. She carried sleeping children and teachers, as engineers worked below and a few officers and Kim kept watch all night on the bridge as the pirate ship sailed into the open waters.

•

At muster that first day of sailing, Jakob announced, "We're on our way to Panama." He was interrupted by cheers, buoyant *yahoos*, and "It's about bloody time!" After a stiff smile, he explained. "This is a voyage that would ordinarily take four days by motor, but we're going to take about ten days. You will finally have your sail training." More cheering. Our escape seemed to have stirred up an excitement in everyone. "We will start with calisthenics on deck, and then lay aloft." When we looked confused, he clarified. "Climb the rigging, up and over the second platform. We will speed up bending on the sails. Our goal is to sail with no engines for a week."

We motored around the Yucatan peninsula, past the low, dark shore of Cuba where fishermen ventured far from land in wooden boats. We rounded the mountainous emerald island of Jamaica before setting our course southwest for Panama. And all the while we hauled, hand over hand, heavy canvas sails into the rig and bent them onto the yards. I gazed up into the rig of the main mast, I recited the names: mainsail, lower and upper topsail, topgallant, royal, and skysail.

Once we were given the order to set sail, the students and teachers worked aloft in teams, spread out along the yardarms. And I was one of them. I had become less afraid. I didn't know how it happened. I was stronger and braver, but it was more than that. My mind stopped cruelly attacking me the way it used to. I was not hearing my dad's voice browbeat me. I climbed steadily aloft, with great concentration, as we sailed over smooth waters. I made my way up to the second platform on my own. And then, I edged slowly out onto the second yardarm, my feet on the footrope, my arms leaning over the yard. I was part of the team that loosed the first square sail. I felt brave and proud of myself, and truly happy when we let go the lines. The sails dropped unbound until they filled, finally restored to life. As I looked down over the linen sail, it glowed with light as it caught the wind.

•

With sixteen sails bent on, the captain set a course so they'd fill with a steady following wind. My brother sat down next to me on the deck when he came off watch. "We're sailing at seven knots solely powered by the wind." The ship cut through the water peacefully without four 1500-horsepower engines rumbling below decks. The ship sailed, and when we were not on watch, we rested. I fell into deep naps, alongside my friends and teachers on deck, where we read and slept in the shade on long, slow, hot afternoons.

One afternoon, I startled awake. A voice in my dream announced, "It's time to go out on the bowsprit net." I lay there in the heat and rocking of the boat, feeling almost drugged. It was hard to imagine getting up and doing anything.

I said out loud, "It's like we're in the land of 'The Lotos-eaters'." I'd memorized the poem by Tennyson in fifth grade. I recited the poem: "*In the afternoon they came unto a land.*"

Nearby, Ron joined in: "*In which it seemed always afternoon.*"

"Like today."

Ron and I recited the stanza together: "*All round the coast the languid air did swoon, / Breathing like one that hath a weary dream.*"

I laughed. "You never know who's memorized their English Romantic poetry!" When I looked over at Ron, he'd slipped back to sleep again. These seductive endless days. It would be so easy to fall back into a nap. I could wait for us to pass through the canal. But I had a strange feeling that I'd regret this the rest of my life if I didn't go now, even though it seemed like I had all the time in the world. The urgency of the voice in my dream compelled me. I pulled myself to my feet.

As I walked toward the bowsprit, I glanced up at the bridge. The windows, like silvery mirrors, reflected the sky, and the room behind was in shadow. No one seemed to see me. We were in wide open water, no ships in any direction. We had not seen land for days.

I climbed over the rail at the bow and onto the bowsprit. Then I lowered myself down into the bowsprit net, a triangular safety net reaching from the hull to the end of the bowsprit. The grid of thin taut cables printed squares into the flesh of my bare legs and feet, as I sat cross-legged on the net, my breath caught in my chest. I dared myself to look down. Only twenty feet below was the bright ocean, the ship's gleaming white bow, and there they were—the dolphins! Four or five or six silvery sleek bodies flew through white-foamed waves; they leapt and dove and shot forward. Their bodies rocked from side to side, showing the whites of their bellies, as they crossed from one side of the bow to the other, at the cutting edge of our ship's hull.

Slowly I stretched out, belly down in the net, and I was held, suspended, for a long time, floating above dolphins.

•

On an evening that the full moon rose at sunset, the captain ordered all the sails to be taken in. I edged my way out to the end of the bowsprit to pull down and stow the jibs. When I turned around, our glowing ship looked like she was sailing right toward me. Below the bowsprit, the splattering white foam of the sea parted at the bow, misting me from the breaking wave. Students in the rig hauled up and secured the white sails to each yardarm. They looked like shadows as they descended. That night we feel asleep on deck as moon shadows scattered across the waves.

Another moonlit night, I was on the midnight-to-four-a.m. watch, keeping an eye on the glow of the compass and the bow light as we sailed with canvas sails taut in the wind and darkness above us.

After our watches that night, a few of us sat in the dark, listening to each other's voices. Zip spoke enthusiastically. "It's so awesome to steer the ship. It's almost like our ship is seducing the wind and the waves." Then he laughed at himself. "But I'm still basically shit steering the wheel, wandering to and fro on the compass heading." As he looked around in the dark, he spoke to me and Jane, who sat next to Ted. "But you ladies hold a near steady course."

I confessed. "At first I felt like a nerd, focusing so hard on a straight line. But now, I'm connected to the ship when I'm steering. It's like I become the ship and I can feel the wind in the sails. Especially at night, when I come off the wheel, I'm floating." Jane giggled shyly and nodded her head. She knew that feeling too.

Zip said, "Captain Stig and I talk after I make the engine room report." Then Zip lowered his voice. "Tonight, he told me this was the first ship he ever sailed on."

I startled wide awake. "That's crazy. How old was he?"

"He was fourteen, a sailor in the rig, when Marjorie Merriweather Post sailed this ship as a private yacht for six months every year in the 1930s. The captain said they sailed places not even on charts, and he perched in the rig to watch for rocks. He eventually became third officer, and when they went ashore, he was bodyguard to Marjorie's daughter Deenie, with a pistol in his pocket, to prevent a kidnapping. They captured a giant turtle in the Galápagos and kept it as a pet on deck, caught a manta ray fifteen feet long, and held costume parties. The past felt so close when he talked."

I was amazed, imagining that Stig had been Richie's age when he began his career as a sailor and now as he neared the end, he was captain on the same astounding ship. Stephanie must have known this. How many other secrets had she hidden from us?

When the breeze picked up before dawn, I was rocked awake each day and became a connoisseur of sunrises. I'd slip out of my sleeping bag and climb the ladder to the upper deck to watch.

One morning from my perch, the ocean rose and dipped, a rippling grey silk coverlet. The dark rim of the sea looked like stone, an edge as sharp as if cut with a knife along a carpenter's level. A pale lemon light seeped along the horizon.

Dawn illuminated the edges of things, the sails lightly filled with wind. Everything else was in shadow. The web of lines climbed the mast, like the taut black threads my brother stretched on the ship model he'd built years ago.

Each dawn I watched the transformation of one thing into another, of night into day, as it spread and expanded. Each morning was so different. Would the yellow light grow stronger until a brilliant sun broke across the stone horizon and bombarded us with light? Would there be clouds, or fog at the horizon, or would the sky redden and streak the undersides of clouds as we sailed into the dawn?

One morning, I remembered a Narnia book, *The Voyage of the Dawn Treader*. We truly were a Dawn Treader as we stalked the rising sun. So many sea journeys in history and literature had been so dangerous, but our journey now was peaceful. I soaked in the light as it changed, moment by moment, until dawn dissolved into day.

One morning, Kim looked up from the deck below. "There you are. Whatcha doin'?"

"You sound like Piglet."

"You sound like Pooh."

"I feel like Pooh. I'm watching the sunrise."

She climbed up and squeezed in next to me. We put our arms around each other, leaning our heads together. The light changed. The disc of the sun rose above the water, and a brilliant heat filled the sails. Then we climbed down and walked to the railing.

Then I remembered. "I flew in my dream." The words poured out of me. "I had to work hard. I tried putting my arms in different positions. I stretched my arms forward like Superman taking off." I laughed and showed her the different ways I tried to fly. I tried jumping to take off, or flapping my arms. "I knew I could fly. I finally found the right position and took off." I held out my arms as if they were angel wings.

I leaned against the rail and closed my eyes to remember. "At first I flew low to the ground, inches above people who wanted to catch my ankles and pull me down, but then I flew higher and swooped around the branches of a huge oak tree and through the open courtyard of a grand house, and then I flew on until I landed safely in a meadow." I sighed and looked at Kim. "I've never felt so happy."

•

A day before we approached land, Woodie found me reading. He said, "OK, let's do it." He'd promised he'd climb out onto the bowsprit net with me. I'd actually done something brave that Woodie hadn't done yet. We slipped off the railing of the foredeck onto the bowsprit. I went ahead and slid down into the net and Woodie lowered himself down after me. Carefully we stretched out side by side on the net, lying on our bellies, so we could look down to the water. His left hand held onto the top of the figurehead eagle's wing, my right hand held onto the cable at the far edge of the net.

Woodie joked. "Isn't there some movie where guys get caught in a cargo net and are suspended over pirates with swords? Or maybe we're hanging over a lagoon full of lunging sharks, or piranhas?"

"Don't freak me out, Woodie. Just feel it." The ship's bow charged through swells of waves twenty feet below us, stronger swells than when I had been here alone. The spray tingled across our faces and arms and legs. Sunlight spangled across the surface of the waves, and the dolphins appeared, leaping through the bow wave.

Woodie howled. "Can you fucking believe anything can be this beautiful?"

My smile stretched until my cheeks hurt. I closed my eyes to feel it. My body was surfing on the wind, riding the waves, with my brother.

Woodie called out. "Let's roll over and lie on our backs."

We rolled toward the eagle's wing, and rolled onto our backs. We stared up into the rigging and masts with clouds racing above. The ship looked like it was chasing us.

Woodie pointed to the main mast. "See that sail, the main topgallant?" I followed his finger up the mast. He described how they were taking in a reef, tying up half the sail. The students up there were swinging back and forth as the sea swayed the mast. But they got into a rhythm. They grabbed the sail when they swung backwards and they pulled the sail up, gathered it on the top of the yardarm, moving forward and back, before they fastened it. He lay there in the bowsprit net, smiling. "I feel so safe and happy in the rig."

•

After our two weeks at sea, a group of us leaned on the railing sniffing the air. I asked, "Is it true that you can smell land before you see it?"

Pogo nodded. "Supposedly, but I can't smell anything yet."

I sniffed. "The air smells clean."

Pogo pointed to gulls following small fishing boats in the distance. "Our first birds in days!"

There was a smudge on the horizon, and Daniel asked, "Is that land?"

We studied the horizon and the airy mass. Ted said, "I think it's clouds clustering over the land."

I scanned the horizon, straining to see. When I glanced down into the ocean, it was suddenly a lighter blue, almost turquoise. "Is the ocean getting shallower?"

Kim came by and sniffed the air like a hunting dog. "I smell something swampy."

"I bet you're smelling the boys." I pushed her, and we tussled and laughed. By the time I turned back to the railing, a dark smudge appeared above a narrow green line at the horizon. Above us on the bridge, a voice called out, "Land ho."

"They really say that?" I was cracking up. "It's like we're in *Kidnapped!*"

Kim squinted. "Are those mountains?"

Ted nodded. "Yeah, and jungles and swamps. When they built the canal, so many people died of malaria."

I grimaced. "Do we have to worry about malaria?"

Ted said, "Nah, I bet they spray the Canal Zone swamps with shit-loads of DDT."

"Gee, that's comforting. Hey, I smell something." I paused, trying to discern the faint, warm odors coming across the water. "It smells green, kind of swampy."

Kim bumped against me. "See, I told you. I've got a good nose."

Traveling under motor power once again, we headed toward the land-mass on the horizon, watching the land come into focus as layers of color turned into white beaches and jungle with mountains above. At a distance, a line of cargo ships emerged at regular intervals from a bay, like traffic released from behind a traffic light. This had to be the entrance to the canal.

"We won't be in here long, before we proceed to the Pacific," Pogo said. He'd studied the charts on the bridge. The isthmus of Panama is about fifty miles across, with three sets of locks and a few lakes to get to Panama City on the other side. And then off we'd go, to the Galápagos Islands.

As we approached port, the long breakwaters on either side were mas-sive. We motored through a narrow passageway to enter Limón Bay, with the cities of Colón and Cristobal on our left, where the old city was built by the French on dredged soil. Our ship dropped anchor near Cristobal harbor as the sun set, blood orange. The steady breeze from the trade wind had vanished, and stagnant heat surrounded us—it was suddenly stifling.

We didn't know that our progress through the Caribbean had been tracked. Before we left Veracruz, the captain heard the owners had made it known that they would do *anything* to get the ship back, kick off the kids, and sail with a professional crew. Our captain knew what was at stake.

On our first night at anchor near the city of Cristobal, where we waited to be cleared to proceed through the canal, the captain called an evening muster. All the students and teachers stood in formation on the foredeck. The ship's whistle had to be blown several times before we settled down from our festive mood. Stephanie, who had arrived before dinner, looked somber as she stood next to the captain.

He spoke sternly. "We have been informed by the Panamanian government that our ship will be searched tomorrow. This is most likely a drug search. Possibly with dogs to check every single nook and cranny in the ship." He paused when some students giggled. "I must impress upon you this is very serious." He commanded. "There must be nothing found." He chose his words carefully, and scanned our faces. "If anyone knows of any drugs that are on board, it is essential that they are disposed of tonight. Tomorrow, dress in your cleanest work clothes and stand at attention at 0745 to receive our guests."

I could see how sad and worried he was. "Our safe departure for the canal depends on each of you." He stopped again after more giggles from the back. I glared at those jokers. He said, "If you can't take this seriously, you must know that if they find any drugs, they could remove my captain's license. They could impound the ship. They could put you in jail. Our ship—and the school's fate—is in your hands." He turned abruptly and walked off to his cabin.

The air caught in my lungs, and my legs nearly gave way. But some boys clustered around Stephanie, like this was a big joke.

"So hey, Steph, what's happening!?"

"Is this for real?"

"He sure was uptight!"

Stephanie's face was pinched with worry, her voice tremulous. She appealed to the students, begging, "Please throw anything you have overboard. We could lose the ship."

Some joked. "We better see if there's any drugs on board." Soon, pot smoke drifted from the boys' bunkroom.

I was shocked and hurt. We'd been told months ago of the dangers of sailing with drugs aboard. I was so stupid. I hadn't known anyone was getting stoned on the ship.

It was a strange night on the ship; the deck lights were off, as if to stay hidden. Students and teachers and crew wandered restlessly and leaned on the railing to watch the city lights across the water. There was a shadowy parade of container ships headed for the canal, passing by other ships as they emerged from the canal to head into the gulf. They never stopped coming.

None of us could settle, not knowing what would come in the morning. My friends and I cast frustrated glances at the stoned guys as they giggled. Our safety depended on their following orders. Could we trust the druggy kids to take this seriously? Would they still treat this like a joke? Would they get rid of their stash? A pall came over me. Our journey was at risk, not from a storm but from a betrayal among us. Now moored in an active harbor, I felt exposed and it took a long time to fall asleep on deck.

The bosun's whistle came early, as a somber weight spread through the ship. Without saying a word, everyone hurried to pick up their bedding and store it on their bunks. Kim and I dressed and made our gear shipshape. As I looked at my clothes, books and journal, I murmured to Kim, "Where can we keep our journals safe?" We grabbed them and shoved them under our mattresses, not knowing how we could keep anything safe if things got bad. We ran to the mess for a quick breakfast of stale, cold cereal and dried milk. Food was running low. Stephanie had promised we'd take on fresh food and milk as soon as we reached port.

Sweat slid down my neck in the tropical sun as I stood at attention on the foredeck with the other students. Boats approached. Students near the railing peered down and shouted back to us, "Machine guns and a shitload of soldiers!" Our captain, in full uniform, waved them back and gestured to us to be silent.

Rumbling engines of boats idled on both sides of our ship. My belly clenched. Officials streamed up the gangway: a pack of dark-suited lawyers and two men we assumed were the ship's secretive owners, fifteen uniformed Panamanian soldiers with rifles, a military commander. But no dogs. Thank God. So this was a drug search at sea. I tried to take a full breath but couldn't. I glanced at Kim. As usual, I was scared but she glowered furiously, her dirty blond curls held down with a red bandana.

We stood at attention as best as fifty teenagers could, in our jeans and blue shirts with our long hair held back in ponytails. We watched them play out a kind of theater, with our captain in full uniform and Stephanie in her red dress, as they greeted the men who boarded the ship. We scanned their faces. Who held our fate? After the polite welcome, the conversations grew more heated. Fortunately, we students didn't know why our captain was furious.

Fifty years later, one of the teachers told me that the Panamanians informed the captain that the drug search would include searches of what they called "the cavities" of the women students and teachers on his ship. The owners and their lawyers stood by, making no protest, while our slight older captain, a father of girls with Stephanie at his side, furiously refused to comply. We couldn't hear his words and didn't know he was fighting for our safety. In the face of over a dozen armed soldiers, on a ship surrounded by two armed war boats, our captain somehow prevented this from being carried out. The Panamanians conferred, waved their arms, and let it go.

"Students and teachers, you are to remain on board in my sight," the captain ordered, and the soldiers descended into the ship.

Boots stomped down the metal ladders into the crew quarters. Kim and I grasped each other's hands, moving our heads like antennae to search for sounds from belowdecks. Were they ransacking our things? Where were they? I imagined them in the galley, mess halls, companionways, sail locker, engine room. Metal doors slammed, muffled insistent steps vibrated through the ship. Then a mate led a group of soldiers toward the stern to the girls' quarters.

We girls clustered, silent and waiting. I swallowed; my mouth parched. Sweat streaking down our faces in the sweltering heat, we met each other's eyes, caught fingers, and leaned shoulder to shoulder. I leaned back and looked up at the rope ladders of ratlines climbing the masts. We had to keep sailing.

A few soldiers came up on deck with a prescription bottle and asked whose locker was number 34. Rick, a shy and really good kid, stepped forward, gulping. "The pills are antibiotics the ship's doctor prescribed for a bad cold."

"We'll see," the officer said, pocketing the pills. I glanced at the officers, owners, and lawyers as they talked with the captain and Stephanie, taking papers and shoving them in their briefcases, while we wondered what was going on.

But then a strange thing happened. The drug search ended abruptly. The soldiers returned, shrugging their shoulders. They smiled at us, and suddenly it all seemed like a joke the Panamanian soldiers had played on the American owners, who had wanted to kick the student crew off the ship. By the time the angry owners and lawyers moved down the gangway, the Panamanian officials were laughing with the captain and offering cigarettes to our crew. As they gunned the engine of the launch, the soldiers waved the peace sign to us long-haired kids gathered along the railing, staring down at them. The other two boats followed the launch, machine guns no longer pointing our way.

Our scuba teacher Karl nodded toward the military boats. "PT boats from World War II."

"They were guarding us with World War II boats?" one kid joked. "Oh, gee, I'm scared."

Karl flashed him a look. "Those boats are no joke."

We looked at each other and at our captain and Stephanie.

Someone asked, "Did we pass the drug search?"

"Were they really looking as hard as they could've?"

A shiver of relief spread through the students, followed by a strange elation. We were going to be OK. Then we laughed and goofed around— even the more serious students like me, all of us released our pent-up fear, our strange sense of disorientation. What do we do now? Someone yelled out, 'We've got to check out our quarters!"

The girls ran to the stern, dashing down the ladder into our quarters. It wasn't terrible. Clothes and sleeping bags were scattered on the floor. The weirdest thing was that all the tubes of toothpaste had been squeezed out.

"Hey, you didn't tell me you were smuggling diamonds in our toothpaste."

"How are we going to brush our teeth now?"

One girl repeated what Stephanie had said to the captain: "Thank God they didn't plant drugs on the ship and get us for that." A new wave of fear surged through my body. What could have happened now scared me more than what actually had happened. We'd dodged a bullet I hadn't even considered, but an ominous chill lingered.

A kid shouted down into our quarters. "Stephanie says we're going to have a party!" All our faces lit up. Our cheerful shouts cleared the lingering presence of soldiers and guns. A party! I admired Stephanie's quick thinking. What a brilliant move to lift our spirits and diminish fears. By the time we raced up on deck, the crew had lowered our small launch.

•

Stephanie, still in her red dress, gathered a team of students and asked, "Who speaks Spanish?" Kim rushed down the gangway, crowding in next to Stephanie to go to town.

I joined students and teachers to haul folding tables to the fantail, then spread out white tablecloths, cake plates, and silverware. The shore team was back faster than we expected, waving like returning heroes. We set up a chain of students to haul coolers filled with boxes of ice cream, drinks, and ice up the gangway. I dashed down the gangway to help Kim carry a long white box up to the deck. We walked side by side down the deck as Kim bubbled with excitement.

"I practiced my Spanish on the boat but in the bakery my brain froze up. '*Necessito una muy grande...*' I blurted out in French, '*gateau.*' They laughed and corrected me: '*pastel.*' But they only had little cakes. *Muy poquito!* But," Kim's face lit up, "someone hadn't picked up a huge birthday cake in the refrigerator case. Stephanie convinced them that we needed that cake."

A parade followed, people chanting, "Cake, cake, cake!"

At the fantail, we opened the lid. The cake was decorated with flowers and butterflies with *Feliz Cumpleaños* in fancy script. Some kids sang the Beatles song: "*So you say it's your birthday...*"

From all over the ship, from the bridge, engine room, kitchen, and all quarters, everyone came, over seventy-five people crowding around the curving stern of the ship. From the captain to the Mexican oiler man, the entire kid population, the teachers and crew, the radio officer in his sarong, the new doctor and his wife, all stood around the jigger mast in the golden late afternoon light of Cristobal harbor while massive cargo ships moved by in their steady march toward and away from the canal.

I cut the cake into enough pieces to feed everyone, as a couple of teachers served the plates. Kim liberated boxes of melting ice cream from the coolers and passed them out along with handfuls of spoons. She scooped out a big bite of strawberry ice cream and offered it to one of the younger boy students. She explained, "This is what I do with my little sisters at home."

Inspired, all around the deck, people scooped a spoonful and looked for someone to feed the scoop to. It became a game, and everyone played. I went up to people I didn't know, an officer I'd never talked to, and an engineer in a blue jumpsuit. I gave them bites of ice cream. I'd never laughed so hard. I hadn't ever looked at this many people directly into their faces before.

I went up to the captain, and he accepted my bite of ice cream. Looking him in the eye, I thought of him standing on the deck surrounded by soldiers. I teared up. "Thank you, captain."

He looked at me kindly and patted my back. "We are safe now."

After emptying my box of ice cream, I stepped back and scanned the crowd. Stephanie, still fresh and unwrinkled in her red dress, her long black hair smooth, her sunglasses pushed up on her head, chatted in the midst of all of us, the weight of the day lifting. She was finally enjoying this crazy school she'd created.

It dawned on me that we were all sober. No one was zoned out. Over the months of working together, we hadn't had a moment of unified connection like this. Finally, after all the long meetings about community spirit, feeding each other became a kind of communion, a salve to our spirits. We were sure this was the beginning of everything. The canal and the Pacific were ahead of us.

·

Two days later, we were given a shore day in the town of Cristobal. Sixty students and teachers strolled through the old city, which looked like a funky New Orleans town of three-story colonial buildings, their porches edged with wrought-iron railings. Some people shopped for clothing, for food delicacies, for uncut semi-precious stones. Woodie replaced his stolen camera, so he could photograph the ship under sail.

I finished a cheerful letter home while I ate a Chinese lunch at the YMCA. I didn't mention that the city was under martial law, with young soldiers on every street corner holding semi-automatic machine guns, or that they looked like the soldiers from the drug search two days before. I mailed my letter, assuring my parents that all was well, and that soon we'd be on our way to the Galápagos. I wonder now who else also sent home cheerful letters, protecting our parents from concern about us. But I was uneasy; I wanted to get back to the ship.

Pogo, Daniel, and I waited at the docks and admired our ship as a tug moved her across the bay. Pogo asked, "Remember the night we took in the sails in the moonlight?"

We nodded. We were ready to leave, ready to sail. We took the first launch ride back to the ship.

While we were away, the captain and Stephanie prepared a formal protest to the U.S. State Department about an illegal drug search inside the U.S.-controlled Canal Zone. When they attempted to restock our stores, they discovered the local ship chandlers refused to stock us with food and water, and wouldn't explain why. Soon after, the harbor master ordered our ship moved to a new anchorage in a backwater. The head of the canal police informed the captain over the radio that any crew member of our ship would be arrested if they set foot on land.

Once the students, teachers, and crew returned from shore, Stephanie took her assistant ashore to protest to the authorities and demand that our purchase orders for food and water be filled.

Later, as we lingered after dinner in the crew mess, the captain asked the teachers to join us. He put up his hand for quiet, and his voice was somber and weary. "I was informed by radio that Stephanie and her assistant were arrested this evening when they arrived on shore. They have been taken to jail in Cristobal." The room was stock still, all of us staring at him. He added, "The PT boats are back, guarding the ship, so we don't attempt to escape."

In the stunned silence, through the open portholes the throaty gurgling of high-powered engines idled on either side of our ship. The reality sank in: we were trapped.

Our questions ran wild. "Are we being held hostage? Who is doing this? Who brought in the Panamanian navy for the drug search? Who are these owners?" The captain said he had to return to the bridge and would attempt to answer more of our questions soon.

Left on our own, students clustered all over the ship and tried to make sense of what was going on. Did the owners sweep in, bribe some officials to take the ship from the school, and use the Panamanians to carry out the dirty work? But how could they kick us off the ship?

Then I wondered, "Wouldn't it be crazy if the Panamanians decided to steal the ship from the owners?"

Ted asked, "Who was really in charge when the Panamanian officers came on board to conduct the drug search?"

Woodie grumbled. "The man with the gun always seems to be in charge."

Kim was furious. "But we're in the U.S. Canal Zone. This was an illegal act for an American chartered ship to be boarded and searched by the Panamanians."

"But the ship is registered and flying under the Panamanian flag," Ted countered.

It was like a puzzle we couldn't solve. Pogo brought in our current historical context. "Don't forget the U.S. is in the midst of negotiations for the peaceful transfer of the canal to Panama." None of us could know that the canal transfer would not be resolved for another six years. None of us had any clue about the politics of a country under martial law, or who might be in control of our fate.

Stephanie and her assistant returned to the ship after twenty-four hours in jail. We had no idea why they'd been arrested or how they'd been released. Stephanie was wound up as she talked to us at dinner. "The jails are full of Americans, people passing through on sailboats or traveling across Panama. They told us the U.S. Embassy is not answering their calls for help. They don't want to disrupt the canal negotiations."

I was confused. Who was holding us hostage—the owners or the Panamanians? As I wandered that night along the decks, I was aware of the ominous weight of history. Here we were on a ship built at the bottom of the Depression as the largest luxury yacht in the world, for the wealthiest woman in the world. Later, when her husband was the American ambassador to Russia in 1938, this ship sailed to St. Petersburg during Stalin's reign of terror, for grand dinner parties and to haul home the Tsar's jewels, which she'd bought at bargain prices. The ship had been purchased by the dictator Trujillo during his murderous reign of terror in the Dominican Republic. Now it had become tangled in another international power play. Were the American owners bribing the Panamanians to steal the ship to break our school's lease? Perhaps Panamanian officers and American owners both hated long-haired hippies and wanted to get rid of us? Or had the tide turned, and were the Panamanians finally having their day, turning the tables on the American lawyers and ship owners? Was this a joke on the owners? But no matter who was behind all this, the joke was on us. And it was no joke.

•

Woodie and I lay on our bellies under a lifeboat on the upper deck. A mirage shimmered over the scrubby marshlands that extended to the horizon. I closed *Moby Dick*, rolled on my back, and stared up at the hull of the lifeboat hanging a foot above us. "Ishmael drives me nuts. He's like a guy on a bus who won't shut up." Woodie focused his binoculars on the parade of container ships steaming toward the Canal Zone while we sweated in the heat of this backwater, where we'd been left at anchor for over a week.

All over the ship, everyone—students, teachers, and crew—clustered in the shade, reading or sleeping. Our sea watches, scrubbing the decks, work in the rig and in the engine room, had all stopped. We floated in limbo. Meals, or rather odd collections of food, were set out for us to graze.

Woodie poked my arm. "Another Liberian flagged ship. What a piece of shit that one is." He handed me the glasses and pointed out the oil-stained rusty hull. "Look at the way that boat is listing to port. It's amazing they let it go through the canal." He showed me the Liberian flag, red and white stripes with one big white star on a blue field.

I handed him back the binoculars. "How'd you get so smart?"

He shrugged. "You just never noticed." I could tell from the little curl of a smile that he was pleased.

I rolled on my side and looked at my little brother. He had some peach fuzz, his hair had grown to his shoulders, and he was deeply tanned from our six months working in the sun. We both wore dirty, sun-bleached T-shirts and shorts. I gave him a little shove. "You know everything about boats and you haven't read *Moby Dick* yet? I won't leave the ship until I've gotten through it."

"We'll be completely out of food in days. You'll never finish the book in time."

He turned the binoculars on the PT boat at anchor less than a hundred feet away. About eighty feet long, built for World War II, the boat was quick and fast, looking just like the boat from the TV comedy *McHale's Navy*. Except at the bow of this boat, the machine gun pointed toward our ship, toward us. Holding us hostage. The Panamanian Navy crew rested in the shade, feet up, hats down, fast asleep. It was kind of weird what we'd gotten used to.

I looked at my brother. "Do you ever think of going home?"

"Nope. Never."

"Me either," I said, but without his anger. Sometimes I thought about home. But after living on this ship for six months, I couldn't imagine leaving.

Kim appeared and plopped down on deck next to me. She scraped at a nearly empty jar of honey with a spoon.

"Not much left?"

She scowled. "Not much of anything left to eat, period."

The refrigerators had stopped working again and when the stinking food was tossed overboard, sharks lept and thrashed, ripping open the rotted chunks of meat and cheese. For two weeks, the Mexican and French cooks prepared what was left in the stores, mixing orphan cans of soups and stock, serving us paltry bowls of mismatched pasta stuck together from cooking in too little water, until the stores were nearly empty.

She peered down at the PT boat, the sleeping soldiers, the machine gun. "Still there? Fuck. I keep hoping they'll take off." She ran her fingernail along the last honey under the lip of the jar.

Pogo slipped in to join us in the shade. "I'm worried about our drinking water. It's starting to stink. We could get really sick."

We looked at each other, like this was a riddle we could somehow figure out. I asked, "So what are we going to do? I wish we could sail away."

"It sounds like a joke," Kim said, "but Stephanie brought that up with the captain last night. 'Why can't we just try to escape?' The captain had to show her the narrow channel out of this harbor on the chart. 'It's fourteen miles to international waters. We could never start our engines and make it out of here.'"

"We'd never shake the PT boats," Pogo groaned.

Woodie added, with a wry smile, "Did she forget to notice the machine guns?"

"You don't think they'd ever shoot at us?" I shivered. "We're American kids."

Woodie growled, "I wouldn't put it past them. Even though we have no idea who they're really working for."

"Do you actually think somebody's trying to starve us off the ship?"

My brother and closest friends looked at me like I was clueless. Woodie said, "Isn't it kind of obvious?"

Feeling foolish, I asked, "Who's going to get us out of here?" All over the ship, we were trying to answer this question. Some hoped their senator would intervene, and one kid was sure the U.S. Navy would fly us out. But we kept coming down to one name. Richie. I hadn't seen him for days, but in our clusters of survival units, his name became a kind of currency. We were betting on Richie and his mom and Hollywood to be the ticket to getting us out.

Kim lowered her voice. "I was on the bridge when a call came through. Arrangements were being made to remove three VIP students. The captain was firm. 'If we allow them to separate the *important* people, the rest of us might rot here for a very long time in that godforsaken jail. The answer is no. We stick together. We all leave together—or no one leaves!'"

This news was sobering.

"Who are the other two VIPs that could be plucked off the ship?" I asked.

Kim snorted. "I'm sure Marjorie Merriweather Post called about her granddaughter."

"Who's her granddaughter? Someone on the ship?"

"Nina. That fun girl in charge of the staterooms. Didn't you know?"

"Nina with the long ponytail? No wonder she had the bucks to get flown out of the jungle. No one tells me anything!" I gazed across the bay from our perch. Puddles of oil shimmered on the murky water.

Pogo asked, "Do you think our parents know what's going on down here?"

Kim shook her head. "I wonder if Stephanie called all the parents, or only the ones who have clout?"

Woodie put on Stephanie's super positive voice: "We seem to have a temporary little problem that I am going to fix really soon. It's just a little . . . " He paused. "Now how do we describe this? Hmmm, just a little international incident."

I looked at him. "Are we really in an international incident?"

"I think we qualify for that. Except, where are the reporters?"

Kim frowned. "Good question. Do you think there are any articles in the papers about us back in the States? Isn't Mary Tyler Moore's husband head of NBC? Why aren't they covering this?"

Pogo mused, "Maybe they don't want this covered?"

Kim leapt up. "I better get back to the bridge to keep an eye on what's happening." Her feet pounded down the deck.

Pogo stood up slowly. "I need to tell Ted and those guys the news." He smiled at me before leaving. "I'm going out on the bowsprit net to watch the sunrise tomorrow."

"Finally!" I'd been urging him for weeks. He climbed down the ship's ladder to the deck below.

Woodie looked at the soldiers in the boat. "I know how to wake them up." He yanked my red leather journal lying next to me on the deck, miming that he'd throw it on them.

I seized it back. "You're not funny!" I clutched my journal, the most precious thing I owned. I was more afraid of losing it than I was of those guys with guns. They seemed unreal, but my journal was everything. After almost six months of writing up to ten pages a day, I was almost out of pages. I slid the book under my belly to keep it safe, and we both read again.

•

Something happened the next day that made the captain know he had to surrender the ship and get us students to safety. I never heard about shots fired at the ship until fifty years later when I read an interview with our captain when he must have been in his 80s.

> "Later we were informed we could get water at the Delta Line Terminal. So we ordered a harbor pilot and weighed anchor. Two Panamanian gunboats which threatened to open fire on us if we attempted to leave harbor accompanied us. One of our boys played a prank and hoisted the pirate flag. The gunboats opened fire with their machine guns and raked the ship with bullets. Everyone dived for cover behind the gunwales. Luckily nobody was injured. But we were very frightened."

I was sure our captain was exaggerating. His accounts of our time on the ship in the book were rife with mistakes, so I assumed this must have been a tall tale. I posted the quote to a dozen Oceanics students on our private online group. "I'm sure they didn't shoot at us."

Ted responded from New Hampshire, where he designs software, "Never heard about any shots."

Also in New Hampshire, Woodie, now a retired ship's engineer, wrote, "That couldn't have happened. An exaggeration."

Then Zip, who lives in Costa Rica and installs solar panels, wrote to us:

"I was there. I was the reason they shot. The captain decided to try to pull the anchor up to move us a short distance away from the much larger cargo ships at anchor that could have swung into us. They wouldn't pay attention to ramming a "little" boat like us. So Stig decided we had to do something. He gave me orders to raise the anchor. I descended from the bridge, crossed the forward deck, climbed up the ladder to the foredeck. The captain sent me to single-handedly work the anchor winch as discreetly as possible. But there's nothing quiet about pulling the anchor up, so as soon as the chain started clanking, suddenly the gunboats approached and started shouting at us. And then, as I continued to run the winch to lift the anchor chain, they started firing warning shots just above my head!! I could hear and even feel the bullets passing in the air above me. This scared the crap out of me and immediately Stig ordered me to drop anchor again, but we at least shortened the chain a bit to give us a little more buffer from the other ships."

I was stunned. I'd never known about any of this. Soon afterward, Kim wrote from England, where she works as a therapist with abused women:

"I was on the deck off the bridge standing with the captain, watching Zip on the forward deck, raising the anchor chain. I saw it all, the boat below in the water, the shots, Zip crouching. Getting shot at sobered me about the severity of the siege. After the shots, the captain said, 'We aren't going to get out of here on this ship. This is serious. I have to get you kids out of here alive.'"

Then Pogo posted his response from China, where he works as an architect:

"I remember it was almost dawn when I climbed out onto the bowsprit. I was lying in the net below the bowsprit watching the light change. A PT boat floated in the morning fog out beyond the bow.

I'd decided to hang out there for awhile, suspended over the water, since it was probably my last chance to do this.

I was hanging there like a fish in a net when one or two shots were fired and I thought I was done for, that this was it, I would be killed. I lay there and waited, but nothing more happened.

I was traumatized. I'd been shot at. I realized: this was serious. What kind of power did the owners have over the Panamanians to do this to us?"

How could something this unimaginable happen and the rest of us hadn't known? How was it that my two closest friends never told me about the shots across the bow until fifty years afterwards? Did they all decide on their own to keep it a secret?

•

On the day that Stephanie and the captain finally surrendered, when the captain told us, "We must prepare for our evacuation," the cooks set out all they had left. Small glass jars of caviar, cans of smoked fish, pâté, and pork schnitzel, and the last boxes of crackers from our elaborate buffet in Miami, when the Panamanian consul had celebrated the raising of his country's flag at our stern.

The captain told the cooks to open the liquor cabinet to the students, teachers, and crew. He said, "It will be left for the Panamanian Navy or the owners, so why not let the children have a party?"

Some joked, "If we don't have water to drink, we can drink alcohol." I skipped out on dinner and the drinking, fell asleep early on my sleeping bag on deck.

My brother told me the next day what happened. Late that night a group of boys had set off emergency flares, streaks of orange smoke that rose off the bow. A Panamanian boat arrived from shore, and officers in a fury shouted up to our ship, demanding to speak to the captain.

The officer shouted, "What is the meaning of this?"

The captain said, "The children set them off."

"These are only for emergencies!"

"We have an emergency. We have no water. We have no food."

The next day, we were not allowed to start our engines but instead we were towed to the dock to take on a few large containers of water and a small amount of food staples. What made them change their mind? International law? Pressure from above? Shame?

•

A couple of days later, the community met on deck with Stephanie. The students and teachers sprawled around her, disappointed, frustrated, angry, and sad. Ever the optimist, she was looking forward. "When we get out of here, will we stay together as a school? Or are we done? I need to know. How do we go forward from here? I can find another sailing ship to finish the year. But I have to know what you want." She painted a gripping portrait of a next ship. "We could still sail, a modified itinerary. Chick is looking for another boat at this very moment." My old loyalty was still there to follow Stephanie's vision.

Some students gave impassioned declarations of wanting to stay together, and Stephanie passed out sheets of paper and pens. "Will you stay or go? I have to hear from each of you."

Later, back at the New York office, the notes—some small and torn, some one word, some a page long—were pasted onto sheets of paper, xeroxed, and sent to parents along with Stephanie's nine-page letter, written from jail in Panama, describing the whole history of Oceanics' dealings with the owners. In jail, she'd finally conceded, "We chose the wrong ship for our school this year."

We poured our hearts into our anguished decisions. Nearly all said they would stay on with the school. Most everyone wrote how school meant so much to us. Steph moved ahead and located a place we could stay until she found another ship to finish the school year. She set her new plan in motion, little realizing how quickly the decisions of teenagers can change.

•

After Stephanie and the captain agreed to surrender the ship, we faced the immense job of packing up everything we'd brought to the ship. The armed PT boats left. Launches were allowed to move to and from shore. And Stephanie came up with a last-ditch inspiration. Maybe if she sent two students from the ship to appeal to the owners, maybe they would remember and understand this was a school and that teenagers were being impacted, and maybe our students might touch their hearts, and maybe they might reconsider.

She chose the sweetest most adorable girl, Lisa, with her shy flash of smile and Minnesota accent, and, of course, Zip, the most engaging charming boy, with his freckles and red hair. She asked them to meet with the owners, took them in the launch to shore, put them in a taxi, gave the address, and told them to return immediately afterward.

We clustered around Zip when he returned. He was skeptical that they could make a difference. But the owners had greeted them politely, and even offered tea and cookies. They had their brief meeting, and were promptly dismissed. "What was intense," he said without his customary grin, "was how many military police types were stationed in the streets. Each one seemed to be taller, more muscular, and scary looking than the last, with those caps with very high crowns. Those stoic, hardened faces . . . " He shivered.

Nothing came of Stephanie's last attempt.

The shrill, silver bosun's whistle blew, and word flew around the ship. Captain Floden called muster. We were dirty, weary, and ready to leave. We'd been packing for the last few days, and we would leave the *Antarna* in the morning. As I walked through the milling students, I looked toward the bowsprit and into the rig above us, the sails on the yards overhead. I wanted to memorize how it all looked, to carry every detail so I wouldn't forget. But it was only when I looked at Kim, tears streaking down her cheeks, that the dam on my emotions gave way. "This is our last muster."

As she nodded, our faces crumpled into our grief. We slipped our arms around each other but had to draw back quickly to laugh.

"You're so stinky!"

"You're so sweaty!"

But we kept our arms thrown around each other's shoulders, heads touching as we stood.

When the captain emerged from the bridge, he addressed us with great respect. "One of my last acts as captain of this ship is to give each of you signed ship's papers stating that you have been an admirable crew member on the *Antarna* sailing under my command. You have done well." He handed a sheaf of papers to Jakob to hand out.

The captain walked down the line and looked directly at each of us. "You have worked so hard packing and preparing to leave. But I have one last request for you. We must leave the ship in impeccable order. I ask you to clean the ship and polish the brass one last time so we are ready to go in the morning." I looked around—a quiet nod that rippled through us. A tired nod. "Yes." We would do this for our captain.

When I held my ship's papers and ran my finger over the hand-typed and signed statement. A chill raised the hairs on my arms. Despite the tropical heat, when I held my seaman's papers, from a captain of rare capability, that I could present at another ship as proof of my training and experience.

•

This was how we left the ship: the Panamanians would not let us motor
to the dock to disembark with all on board and our gear. The school had
to pay for over twenty trips on launches that swarmed back and forth to
ferry everything off the ship. We were up at 4 a.m., working as a chain of
arms, lowering hundreds of boxes down the gangway—every single duffel
and backpack from the ship, every box of the five-thousand-book library,
the film equipment, the scuba and snorkeling gear. Then we unloaded on
shore, hauling everything up to the customs officers on the docks.

Jakob and his brother, Emil, had already lowered his small Viking
sailboat from the deck into the water. Loaded with their gear, once
the ship was surrendered, they would sail through the canal to the
Pacific Coast.

At the end, when the decks were empty, the launches filled with students. As the last boats pulled away, we stood and faced our ship—one
last time as we moved closer and closer to land and away from the *Antarna*.

It was like a camera pulling away from the last scene of a movie I didn't want to end. I didn't want the lights to come on. I didn't want to leave the theater. My eyes blurred with tears. Others turned toward where we were going, but I gazed at where we'd lived. Many photographed their last view of the ship. But I had no camera, no lens between me and the ship as I studied each detail one last time. The sparkling water reflected on the gleaming white hull and the golden eagle at the bow, the masts rose high above, and the rigging and lashed sails shone luminous in the morning light. We students were still and silent and numb, standing sentry to honor our ship.

On the dock, I was wrenched into action. The students, teachers, crew, and officers worked together to lift and carry our gear, boxes, duffels, to the customs officials, while teenaged soldiers with automatic weapons cradled in their arms watched us as our bags were inspected and sealed on long tables in the broiling midday sun.

Stephanie was a blur, a fury, a dervish moving from everything we carried to the customs officials, as they opened and inspected every bag, box, item of clothing, before they stamped in red, *Inspected*, and then sealed to make sure no one tried to plant drugs on us. Stephanie moved faster and faster as if this would somehow keep us safe. She would later write to our parents that the customs check was "conducted on our behalf to ensure that Panamanian officials would not attempt to accuse anyone in the group of possession of contraband, hence jail . . . " I can't imagine our parents felt reassured reading this weeks later. The dire implications of a drug plant in our bags had been hidden from us.

After our gear had passed customs, students, teachers, and crew carried every bag and box to the sliding doors of an open cargo train car. We stacked everything that made up our school, while young men holding machine guns, like the ones used in Vietnam and war zones around the world, eyed us. Why did armed soldiers surround us every step of the way? Were we a danger? Were we suspects? Were they ready to imprison us if anything illegal was found? Is this the way of martial law, where everyone is considered a danger? The illusion that we American children had always carried—that we were safe and had rights—dissolved. The soldiers waved their gun barrels to direct us toward the train. The metal barrels were feet away from our bare legs and sandaled feet. We dutifully climbed into old passenger cars and slid into our seats. But I was still aware of the soldiers who stared at us from the platform.

Stephanie charged down the aisle, counting and recounting to make sure all her charges were present. She was wired and radiant once everything was sealed. She was sure she was extracting all of us safely out of the country. She was filled with the excitement of new plans and promises, for a new ship, the rest of the school year, and everything was going to be great! Just you wait! The Panamanian officials informed her in somber, menacing tones that we were "very lucky to be released," yet she was elated. She was getting us out.

The rattling old train carried us through dense green jungle. Occasional openings between trees revealed the concrete-walled canal, where huge ships like giant toys seemed to float effortlessly through. One of those ships could have been us. We could see ourselves lining the railing of the *Antarna*, back when we were still innocent and expectant, when we might have been heading to the Galápagos to study biology, on our promised free passage through the Canal Zone. We passed swamps in the jungle, and overflowing vegetation hung close to our wooden train car.

Overwhelmed, oppressed by the heavy weight of it all, I was also strangely thrilled. Ships appeared between trees for another moment before the jungle closed in again as the train carried us across the isthmus of Panama, the waist of the world, where commerce carried on without interruption.

Red-tiled roofs of towns appeared, then rows of American military barracks, before we passed the old Spanish buildings of Panama City with the Pacific coast in the distance, and finally we arrived at the airport. Now our gear was loaded onto a parade of luggage carts and driven toward the plane on the tarmac.

Before the train discharged us at the Panama airport, we were still a sailing school with students and teachers, crew and staff, a medical doctor and his wife, and our captain. But on arriving at the airport, a great dissolving commenced. Those of us who didn't have a plan were herded along, still naïve ducklings following our leader, Stephanie, as she directed us toward the plane.

But a great dispersal had begun, though most of us didn't realize it. The long-unpaid crew took off for the next boat, the next job, and left our disastrous adventure behind.

The airport was our first access to phones and to the world in the two weeks we'd been held hostage. Some headed straight to the pay phones, never to be seen again. The math teacher and art teacher, who'd made the pirate flag, walked away with Mike, our Dreams teacher, and Nina who bought them first-class tickets, to fly to Florida to stay at her grandmother's estate, Mar-a-Lago. Students disappeared. Rick reached his parents by phone; they told him to come home right away, and he was gone. Familiar faces for six months suddenly vanished, most never to be seen or heard from again.

In Passport Control, I held out my passport, my weary arms shaking, while we made it through the last checkpoint before we were free. My passport was stamped—March 23, 1972. Below the date, handwritten: M.V. (Merchant Vessel) *Antarna*. I was a sailor who had arrived in and left from my ship.

We boarded a plane someone's father had chartered. Fifty years later, Kim said on the phone, "It was the only time my dad really came through for me." Her father, who often skipped out on paying tuition bills and cried poor for much of her life, had somehow negotiated and arranged this chartered plane to fly us to Puerto Rico. He and some others arranged for us to stay on a remote farm on the south coast of the island, where we would wait for the next ship. Kim added wryly, "He liked playing the hero."

We collapsed into the plane's upholstered seats. Stephanie was lit up, her smile beaming, thrilled about the next ship, her black hair glossy, her dress remarkably fresh. She talked continuously. "We've gotten good leads on beautiful sailing ships. We could sail from the U.S. to pick up the students and gear in Puerto Rico." The school would finish out the rest of the year, could even have summer school. Piece of cake. No problem. This is so great. You'll love the new ship. Once we make all the arrangements, it won't take long. You'll get a rest in Puerto Rico. You deserve it. Perfect timing for a rest. Then time to start catching up on classes. She was spinning and happy, and swallowed another of her little red diet pills. "It's going to all work out."

But we were weary, in shock, and grieving.

Stephanie told the stewardesses to pass out little bottles of alcohol, plenty of bottles. I sipped scotch and orange juice while Kim and Bruce shared a rum and Coke. As the plane engine rumbled, brilliant sunlight poured in through the round, porthole-like windows, and we were momentarily illuminated. A strange, uproarious happiness spread through us, the laughter of release as the plane taxied down the runway.

Every moment took us farther from our ship, that glorious gleaming ship, the masts rising high above the deck, and our rig, every ratline spliced by us, all the polished brass and the varnished wood on deck, the bleached teak decks we'd scrubbed, the breathtakingly lovely ship, our ship. As the plane accelerated, our ties to the *Antarna*, like an umbilical cord, pulled ever tighter and thinner, until the plane took off, and the cord snapped, and we were severed, floating, and unimaginably lost.

•

I slept fitfully as our plane rumbled through the night, twelve hundred miles across the Gulf of Mexico, before we landed and stepped out into a muggy Puerto Rican night. Like long missing children, we were shepherded through a packed San Juan airport. Sleepy and confused, I observed as if lost in a fog: Pogo in his Mexican hat, Ted's unruly curls, and Jane's bowl haircut, packs on their backs as they dissolved into a crowd, vanishing. I had no idea if I would ever see them again.

We were distracted by a lively band and a small crowd that waved and cheered. I looked around. "Is this for a returning baseball team?" Friendly people surrounded us, asking, "Oceanics? Welcome! Welcome!" It seemed the music and cheers were for us. "We are friends of your school." Stephanie was in the center of it all, hugging and shaking hands. We followed them to waiting school buses. "We have dinner for you at the church." A supporter of the school had asked the church to shelter us, and the community had turned out to help. Friendly people wearing Red Cross and Lion's Club jackets formed lines to load our gear for us. We fell asleep sitting upright on bus seats at the end of that relentless day.

We arrived in the dark in front of a tile-roofed Sunday school next to a church. Tables were laden with pots of rice and beans, platters of fried bananas, hamburgers and buns, pudding and fruit—more food than we'd seen in a month. On a long concrete porch, the dark trees and grass hummed with the night sounds of birds and insects, as we devoured our dinner. We stumbled into children's classrooms with our packs, unrolled our sleeping bags on the floor, and spread out like castaways. The lights were turned off, and we fell asleep to the murmur of adults talking on the long portico.

•

I woke up on a linoleum floor, looking at the undersides of children's desks and chairs, glancing around to find Kim, her face buried in her sleeping bag near mine, in the next aisle of children's tables. Morning light poured in the windows, and I smelled food cooking. More food! Wide awake and energized for the first time in weeks, I whispered, "Hey, you awake?"

Kim growled "No," before she rolled over.

I'd stepped out of a fog. The world was bright, and I was ready to talk. I rambled out loud. "You know what this reminds me of?" No response. "It reminds me of sleeping on that train station floor in Xalapa. But we don't have to run for a five o'clock train."

Kim groaned. "Oh, God, I had terrible dreams. Nightmares. People trying to leave Oceanics. No water. No taxis."

I pushed away the memories of Panama and looked at this bright room, at children's artwork and tropical trees out the window. Curiously peaceful, I said, "Guess what? We're on land. We slept inside for the first time in forever."

Kim's growl came out of her covers. "I hate sleeping inside. If I can't be outside, at least I'll sleep on the floor."

I sat up and stretched. "I think sleeping on floors is overrated!" I stood and looked out the window to the porch and a long table where people were setting out pitchers of juice and milk, bowls of scrambled eggs, and bacon. "Hey, more food! These people are so nice!"

Kim snarled. "Yeah, it's pretty simple. Nice people feed children, not like the owners who starved us."

I pulled on a clean shirt over the T-shirt and shorts I'd worn for days. "God, I stink. Where's my toothbrush?"

We emerged on the long porch where children in plaid uniforms rushed about helping with the meal. In a few hours, their school buses would take us over the mountains to the south shore to the promised "farm" where we'd stay until Stephanie's promised "next" ship appeared.

After breakfast, Kim and I leaned against a tree in the churchyard, away from the others, who loaded gear and food for the farm into a school bus. It was a relief to talk freely, since she was no longer secretly spending time with Jakob or hovering near the bridge. We had so much to talk about, to try to understand about the school and Stephanie. Were we still with her or not?

Kim curled her upper lip in a look of concentration. "Jakob kept knocking me for my unfailing admiration for Steph. Last night I finally had a chance to talk to her." I imagined them sitting out there in the tropical darkness. "I was ready for a heart-to-heart. I was so distraught over how our Oceanics year got aborted." She looked at me, her face tight with fury. "It tastes sour, that taste of defeat, of being dumped and discarded."

I was shocked at the power of using *abort* as a verb to describe what had happened to us, the sharp truth. I picked a dried brown leaf off the cement porch and ran my index finger over its hard ridges.

Kim leaned forward, raking her fingers through the dry earth. "I don't have problems with things ending, school, camp, relationships. But when something ends with no awareness or responsibility, that leaves me feeling mad and sad at the same time." Her look at me was anguished. She shook her head. "I believed in Stephanie. I was astounded by how she could move heaven and earth to do what she believed in." Then she growled, "But the owners foiled her like big bullies."

I watched her face—the firmness of her resolve made her look older than sixteen. After so much confusion, she had cut to the heart of it. The owners had stolen our ship, our school, our year at sea. The promise of sailing. The promise of what we could learn. Our year had been amputated. Could Stephanie have dealt with things differently?

Then Kim looked down, before looking right at me. "I've made the decision to leave."

"What do you mean, you're going to leave? When?" I could hardly breathe.

"Today. I'm not going to the farm."

"How can you go?" Others had left, vanishing at the airport, but not her. I'd never imagined she would leave. Could she be enticed back? I tried to build a case. "The school depends on us." I meant to say the school depended on *her.* Words and thoughts erupted in my mind, shocked by this news, worse for me, than anything we'd lived through. "Have you told Stephanie?"

"She can shoot the shit forever, weaving brilliant dreams. I'm done with throwing all of me into Stephanie's school. I have to take care of me and my family. I told her I have to go home."

I couldn't say, *how can you pull us apart?* We were going to have months more to be together. She was severing us. I tried to appeal to her commitment. "What about rebuilding our community spirit?" But now this all sounded so lame.

I was trying to hold on to everything she said, to remember, so I could write it in my journal, but as Kim talked, my mind went numb. I glanced toward other students across the yard, carrying their backpacks to the buses. I glowered at them, willing them not to come near us.

We leaned against the tree that shaded us from the tropical sun. On the ship we'd had endless time to talk; now, with so little time left, she was putting pieces together. Kim said slowly, "I'm done with tantalizing offers of Never-Never Land and Peter Pan adventures from Stephanie. We've spent so much of this year waiting and waiting. I have to keep my life moving. I don't want to sit on some beach in Puerto Rico waiting for another ship. Other kids will love it. But I don't want to be bored. I have to get on with my life."

She imagined this would be a repeat of the Bahamas scene, of getting dumped on a beach to hang out and wait, for who knows how long, for another Stephanie pipe dream of the next ship. She had no interest in camping out with no purpose. "Aimlessness at sixteen is not my bag. Staying here feels like a bandaid. I have to rip it off quickly to look at the wound and expose it to the air."

Kim was resolved. "I have no school credits from this year and now I'm a fucking year behind in high school. At home my mom is going off the rails." I stared at her. I'd had no idea the responsibilities she carried, to take care of her mom and sisters. "I have to choose to help my family and my life, over Steph's school. I've given my all."

Had I given my all? I was still learning what that could be. I knew I wasn't done. The safest place for me was not going home. On the plane, Woodie and I had glanced at each other a few times, and we didn't even have to talk about it. There was no thought of going home, especially now when it seemed we were out of harm's way.

Kim looked tired and serious. "I didn't have anything left to say to Stephanie, except that after everything, at least we're safe. That much I thanked her for."

We glanced toward the voices around the buses. Our talk had been a eulogy delivered at our funeral for our school, but the school, or some version of it, was still going on. A group of students clustered around Stephanie, in sunglasses, her hair smoothed into a ponytail, wearing her blue dress with little white anchors, checking boxes of food before loading them. Stephanie was still upbeat and positive, keeping it going, stirring us into life, getting students loaded onto the buses.

Kim smiled, looking at her. "I still love her for attempting all she does."

I nodded. "Me, too."

Kim and I stood together near the door of the bus before I climbed aboard. This was harder than leaving the ship. Students climbed the steps with their packs. Many hugged Kim goodbye, saying, "Kim, you have to write to me," the way people do at the end of camp or school. But I was desperate. I had to give her something. What did I have that I could give Kim that expressed our depth of feeling at this moment of leaving? I looked at my hands and it was obvious. I pulled the fool's gold ring off my index finger and put it in her palm. We laughed through tears. "Our fool's gold year."

Kim apologized. "I don't have much to give. You are my other half." She pulled off the Mexican silver ring she'd bargained for in the market, back when I was too "couth" and she was too wild. Now these rings carried the essence of who we were. She said, "You'll stay and care about the people I can't."

Was I taking on Kim's mantle? "But what am I going to do without you?"

Her face was streaked with tears, and we held each other's hands. She said, "When I'm with you, I'm whole. We are like the symbol of yin and yang, we balance each other."

I was stunned. I knew the symbol, black and white comets with a contrasting dot. She saw us like this? I'd never known this. I'd always assumed that I was somehow smaller, less wise, less than her. Now, at the last moment, she was telling me I was her equal? That I balanced her? That I offered something to her? We threw our arms around each other, weeping, until we pulled back, laughing about streaking snot on the other's shoulder. I cried, "It's like we're being taken from each other. We had so much more to learn together."

Kim worried. "It'll be so hard to keep in touch."

"But we will," I promised, "we will."

I was the last one to climb the bus steps, and I stumbled to a window seat near the back so I could wave goodbye. Standing beside Kim was our Swedish captain, no longer in uniform, a quiet older man in a tan sports shirt and khaki pants. He had accompanied us to Puerto Rico, and stood there at the door saying goodbye to each of us as we climbed on the bus, an officer honoring his sailors, until the bus pulled away.

Writing this fifty years later, I break into tears.

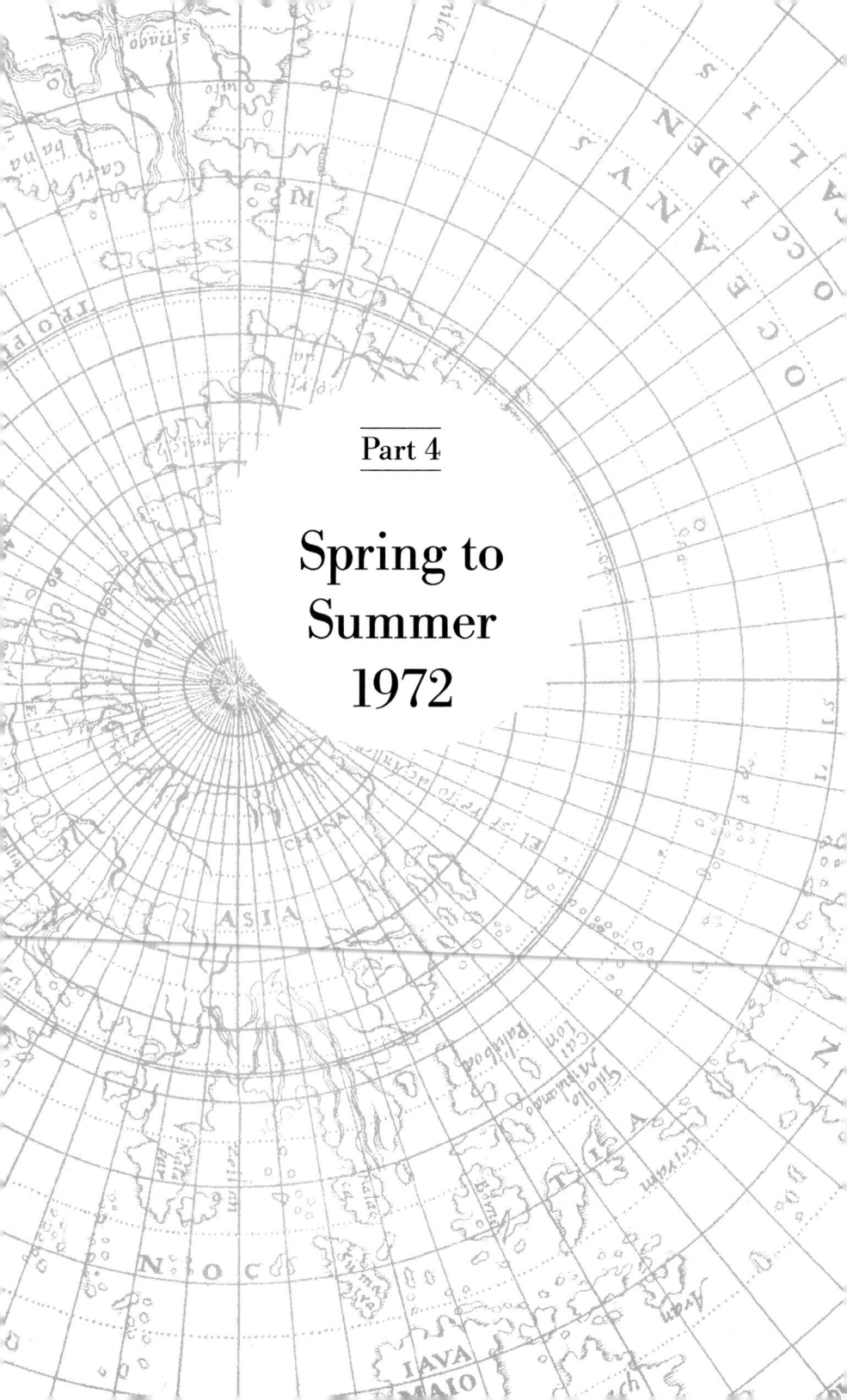

Part 4

Spring to Summer 1972

After the Ship

We're the Ones Left Behind
Written on the envelope of Woodie's letter home from Puerto Rico:

"There is no bad news in this letter."

Kim was right. On the farm in Puerto Rico, we became aimless. The "farm" consisted of a vast cow pasture with long-horned cattle, a line of coconut palms, and miles of beach. The farmhouse was a small concrete-block room with one hanging lightbulb and a four-poster bed. After we unloaded all our gear, which filled half the room, and after we set up an outside kitchen, and after Stephanie was sure we were settled in, she took the hours-long bus ride over the mountains and back to the airport and flew to New York.

I didn't even know how many of us were left. We seemed washed out, worn out, confused. Our life settled around the shady concrete slab where the cheerful Mexican cook boiled rice and beans over an open fire. We drifted into doing what lost teenagers do. Some wrote letters home, played chess or poker, smoked pot while hiding in the trees, swam on the beach, or read. No one talked about what had happened.

On hot days, I read and slept in a hammock in a cow pasture. At dawn and dusk I hiked across the meadow dodging cow pies and long-horned cows, thistles and thorns, to get to the beach where I stayed close to shore for a short dip. I was afraid to swim out through the waves. Then I walked to the farmhouse for meals.

Woodie joined the snorkelers who dove into a wrecked boat offshore. At first, he could only hold his breath long enough to swim down and look through the cargo hatch. The other guys talked about how they dove through the hull and came out through a hole on the side. He told me, "It's scary but everyone's doing it." He worked up his nerve. "I was swimming through the hull, when an octopus came out of the hole in the side and surrounded me in a cloud of ink." He still found the hole in the side and made it to the surface, gasping for air.

I was terrified hearing his stories, while he laughed. He body-surfed in rough waves, gripping the sandy bottom so he wasn't pulled out by the undertow. He lay on the sand as the waves crashed over him, too exhausted to move. He grinned. "I pretend to be shipwrecked." He sounded like Odysseus, wave-broken and salt-crusted, tossed up on shore.

Two weeks after we'd arrived, when the farmer took the cattle out of the field, I was sleeping on the ground in my sleeping bag, while my brother and a few other students slept nearby. One morning, I woke to find a young local man reaching his hand down inside my pants. I bolted upright, and whispered. "What are you doing?"

He smiled warmly. "Don't you want me?"

I spoke forcefully. "No. Go away." I lied. "I have a boyfriend." I gestured to my friends nearby.

He protested. "Why isn't he with you?"

I whispered, "Go away!" When he finally walked across the meadow, I pulled my sleeping bag down closer to my brother. I was flooded with embarrassment. I didn't want them to know. This event made it glaringly clear that I was a girl sleeping alone in a meadow. After all this long year—sleeping outside on the ship, in port with only an unreliable kid on night watch protecting the ship, and after our time at sea with leaks and submarines and soldiers with guns—all that time I'd felt safe. But now I lay trembling. Even though this young man had listened to me and walked away, my illusion of safety had been broken. I wanted to go home.

I rolled up my sleeping bag and found my journal, which bulged with drawings, letters, and photos. At the farmhouse, I found my backpack and duffel. At breakfast, I told Ron, one of the remaining teachers who was supervising the students, "It's time for me to go home."

Woodie walked with me to the pay phone in the village but said, "I'm not leaving. I'm waiting for the next ship."

On the phone, my mom's voice cracked. "I'll have a ticket waiting for you at the airport." I took the morning bus over the mountains to San Juan. I was numb, my mind blank, as if I'd left the ship all over again.

I made a collect call to Stephanie from the airport. She appealed to me, "Will you come back to the school on the new ship as a professional student in a leadership role? I'll make you one of the quartermasters. We are only a few weeks away."

"I can't think right now."

At the Cincinnati airport, when I found my mom in the waiting crowd at the gate, I threw my arms around her and sobbed and couldn't stop. She cried, too. "I didn't know if I'd ever see you again."

"Oh, Mom, it wasn't that bad." Then I laughed, already forgetting how dangerous it had all been. We lugged my stuff back to the VW bus for the drive home. Mom talked with excitement about finishing her degree in criminal justice. But when we walked in the house, she ducked her head down as if making herself invisible again.

My first night home at dinner, Dad was jovial. He'd been reading Stephanie's new parent letters. "What are Stephanie's plans for a new ship?"

I repeated news of different sailing ships she was considering, and her plan for a few students and crew to sail it to Puerto Rico from Florida to pick up the students on the island.

Mom asked in a small, worried voice, "What's Woodie doing on the farm in Puerto Rico?"

Dad barked, "He better not be drinking or smoking pot!"

I described how strong Woodie was getting. "He's learning to snorkel on the reefs offshore, and dive." I asked Dad about construction projects. Then I asked my little brother about school and sports. But I didn't say anything about myself, about how I'd been afraid to swim in the surf, afraid of what I might find below the surface. I didn't say that I'd read all day because I'd felt so lost and disoriented since leaving the ship in Panama, or that I missed Pogo and Kim so much my chest hurt. And I didn't say anything about the young man in the field, or why I'd come home.

After dinner, Mom typed a college paper at the kitchen table as my little brother worked on his homework, while Dad sprawled in his Eames chair, his legs across the ottoman, listening to a stack of jazz records. I lay on my bed and looked around at my stripped-down bedroom, which I'd dismantled before leaving for the ship. It looked like a guest room now. The tension in the house was palpable. There was nothing for me to do here; I couldn't let myself fall into the old muddy river.

After two days, all I wanted to do was return to the school on whatever ship Stephanie might find. I called her. "I'll be ready whenever you need me."

She was pleased. "I'll let you know when to come. I think it will be in about three weeks. I'm so glad. You have so much to offer to the students." Now I had something to look forward to.

Meanwhile, my grandfather was sick, and my grandmother needed help on her farm in upstate New York. I was relieved to have an excuse to escape from Dad, who by the second dinner home was back to lecturing Mom about everything she was doing wrong.

On my grandmother's farm, she and I tackled the spring chores, pruning the raspberries, preparing the brooder for baby chicks, and tilling the gardens. We gathered, sorted, and washed a hundred eggs a day. As we worked, I told her about writing in my journal on the ship, how I'd made notes through the day to remember what I wanted to write.

She lit up. "My father used to do that. We'd ride horseback every afternoon when we could, and he had to stop to jot down ideas he wanted to write about. He called it, 'putting salt on the tail of a good idea.'"

I never told her how aware I'd been of her parents drowning at sea, but one afternoon she said, "I want to show you something." She took me into her bedroom and pulled down an old, flat box from a high shelf. Inside were sepia-colored photographs of her parents before their death in 1915. She opened faded newspaper articles about the sinking of the *Lusitania*, running her worn hands over the paper, smoothing the creases. She handed me a black-and-white photo and a newspaper clipping. "This is the last photo of Mother and Father on board before they left the dock in New York." I put my arm around her as we gazed into her parents' brave faces.

It was May by the time Stephanie called to confirm my arrival on the second ship, but she failed to mention that it had nearly sunk two days before.

How often in our lives can we leave a place and still return? When I arrived at the second ship on the Jacksonville docks, I strode up the short metal gangway, dumped my duffel on deck, and took a look at the three-masted square-rigged wooden ship. She was a third the size of the *Antarna*. I scanned the thicket of rigging lines on the rail near each mast. I followed a line up into the rigging and it went right where I thought it should. I flushed with pride. I'd actually learned something. I followed the smell of lunch coming up from the galley and found friends and officers eating in the mess. It was a sunny room, bleached wooden walls with oak trim, bolted white tables and benches, with mostly familiar faces grinning at me, friends I didn't know if I'd ever see again when I'd left Puerto Rico. I'd come home.

My awkward friend Bruce blushed. "Hey, look who's here!"

I answered, "Quartermaster Garber reporting for duty."

Rick asked in his bashful way, "So Stephanie roped you back in? Me, too."

I smiled. "Yup! Of course. Stephanie enchanted me back, but I want to be here." It's where I was supposed to be, to help the school finish the year.

Zip was at another table in his oil-stained jumpsuit speaking intently to the new Mexican engineer. He waved in my direction.

Lisa slid down the bench next to me. I hugged her warmly, almost like Kim used to hug me.

Within an hour on board, I'd stowed my gear at my bunk and was in the rigging, knife on my belt, replacing frayed lines that held ratlines in place. I found my footing to climb up the foremast, and I didn't even think about it. I climbed, hands reaching up, my feet finding the next ratline on which to place my weight. The small scale of this boat worked for me. I was not afraid. By the end of two days of work, a small group of us had replaced all the ratlines on the foremast. Strangely, she was already our ship. We could make a difference in a day and could chart our progress. I'd never had this enthusiasm on the *Antarna*, where jobs had seemed endless.

Evenings in the fo'c'sle, I felt like Wendy having a blast with the lost boys and girls in Neverland. Lying in rows of double-decker bunks, we read and chatted before we slept. I was without my inseparable friends, Pogo and Kim, but I was becoming closer friends to everyone else. Most of us were in the same situation. We weren't with our old buddies so we were making friends outside of our groups. The old star leaders were mostly gone (except Zip). Those who were left were the quieter, or awkward ones, the younger, the less agile or noticeable teens. We were the B team, the junior varsity, who had been called in to finish out the game. And we were doing a good job, now that we had a chance to shine.

I was put in charge of making a bowsprit net. I figured out how to lash on more lines and splice between them to make a net. I worked in the sun, with the gulls wheeling by. I loved the smell of tarred line as I lashed the lines securely. I looked up into the rig and remembered Kim working high above me in Miami, when I was too afraid to climb aloft. On this ship, I clambered up and down without thinking anything about it.

I imagined Kim was working right next to me. She was back in high school, where they hadn't given her any credit for her year at sea. She was jealous that I was working on the ship. I had a conversation with her going on in my head all day, which I later wrote into letters. I didn't keep a journal anymore. I'd left the red leather journal at home, hidden in my closet so my dad couldn't read what I'd written about him. At home, I'd jumped back into my old strategy of trying to keep him in a good mood. He was proud of me now that Stephanie had made me a quartermaster, and when I called home, he wanted to hear about the work on this ship. His plan to disinherit us had never been spoken of since he'd left Miami.

I'd heard a rumor that this ship nearly sank her first day out in open water. Those of us who arrived two days later laughed as if it was the punch line from an old joke. What was a day at the Oceanics School without an emergency? Zip, Rick, and Bruce had been three of about five students who came on board early to ready the ship for sailing. They agreed to tell a few of us the story once the hull was fully repaired. Zip promised they'd get the pumps working this time. But the rest of us who arrived later didn't believe she'd nearly sunk.

A week later, when Stephanie arrived with the last students from Puerto Rico, she met with each of us individually in the officer's mess. She sat across from me in a new dress I hadn't ever seen, and my old love for her surged through me as I sat down to face her. I knew I was different than the girl at her office last summer and wondered if she'd notice. She looked at me closely. "You've really come into your own. You seem very nearly happy." I smiled. I was.

But she didn't stop there. "What are your plans for next year?"

That's when I drooped. I confessed that I'd put off applying to college last winter until it was too late because I'd been so distracted by everything going on with the ship. Now I wasn't sure what to do next. My parents never asked me about school, or made any suggestions. If anything was to happen, it would be up to me. But here was Stephanie, once again, thinking about me and my life. She stepped right in with ideas, writing notes and contacts on a yellow-lined pad for me. "I think studying in Europe is the next step for you." She encouraged me to live in France with a family the way she had when she was twenty. "You could take classes at a French university. And you'll have time for applications for the next year." Stephanie ushered me into a vision of a life beyond the ship. I left the room inspired.

Still loyal, I returned to my tasks, tutoring Richie with more success. After a bunch of us went to see *The Godfather*, Richie and I talked about it for his political science class. We talked about science fiction stories he liked, and what the author was trying to say. He was growing up. I still ruffled his hair the way Kim would, and he'd give me a smile, a genuine smile. I cooked healthy meals for the thirty of us on board. I'd stepped into Kim's shoes; encouraging the discouraged students, urging them to keep going to classes in the teachers' desperate attempt to make up for a lost year.

After seeing Woodie work aloft, an officer on a square-rigger tied up nearby invited him to join their ship as crew. Someone from a cruising sailboat asked me if I'd be a paid cook on their sail to England. A whole new world of possibility opened up, but we both said no. We were compelled to finish our Oceanics year.

•

It took me a few weeks to discover we were once again on a precarious ship. A few of us gathered on deck one evening. We were due to make a 24-hour sail to see how the ship handled, while moving to a cheaper mooring on our way to the Caribbean. Woodie looked at Zip. "Are you going to tell us the story of the near-sinking or do we have to drag it out of you?"

Rick looked very serious. "You need to know that this ship is dangerously top-heavy. She was a schooner re-rigged to be a square rigger for the film *A High Wind in Jamaica*."

Zip grimaced. "We had only a skeleton crew on board. This ship had been a museum in port for years." He explained how they'd worked nonstop for a week to get her ready for students and were exhausted by the time they motored her down a slow river to the sea. It was only when they passed the islands and hit the Gulf Stream that everything went wrong. Zip said, "It was some kind of squall. Waves pummeled the hull. The masts made extreme swings from port to starboard. Ferro-cement patches fell from the hull. Seawater poured into the ship."

Rick said, "We kept a bucket brigade going all night to empty the hull. The bilge pumps were jammed with debris."

"That was when the generators heated so hot that fires ignited in the engine room," Zip added.

Rick finally called the Coast Guard and declared Mayday. They towed the ship up the St. Johns River until it was beached on a mudbank to save it from sinking. "It was the only thing we could do, so we didn't lose her."

I was stunned. "That was two days before I arrived. Steph didn't tell me on the phone. She simply said that the ship needed a little updating after the sail south from Savannah."

•

The next day out on very mild seas, the ship rocked like an upside-down grandfather clock—a heavy, slow ticktock, like a toy boat rocking too far in a bathtub. From then on, we only made short sails down the coast on calm days, mostly motoring. When Stephanie heard about the sail from her New York office she decided we would concentrate on classes now, every day. Less than a month after we'd boarded, everyone already wondered when the school year would come to an end. Ron had a dime in his pocket to make regular collect calls to Steph. The three remaining teachers hadn't been paid since November but didn't seem to have homes to go to. The last time Stephanie wired money for groceries, it hadn't gone through. It seemed her attention was entirely focused on getting ready for next year's school. Classes ran six days a week for the students who showed up. By the end of May, people were slipping away, flying home. I cooked the remaining staples in the kitchen.

Woodie and I hung on, not ready to deal with our dad at home, until an outbreak of impetigo spread through the ship. I looked it up in the first aid book: highly contagious bacterial infection from unclean, hot, moist locations. We woke up each day and asked, "Who's got it today?" We scanned each other's arms and faces to see who had the latest oozing crusty lesions. One morning, Woodie and I looked at each other and made our decision without speaking. I walked down the dock to the pay phone and called collect. "Hey, Mom. It's me. We're ready to come home." She called the airline and had tickets waiting at the airport.

A couple of weeks later, when Stephanie stopped calling, the teachers decided the school year was done. They arranged for Driveaway cars that included money for gas, left the boat at the dock, and drove north, dropping off the last students on the way. They ended up at the New York office to write their student evaluations, where Stephanie added glowing recommendations that allowed several students to graduate; ensured that some, like Woodie, would get credit for a year of classes; and helped others, like Pogo, get into college.

•

From my journal, Summer 1972: "I am not as lost as I think. I've come home for a pit stop on my growing up. A quick reassuring check to see . . . where I am."

At the end of our first week home, Dad sat down hard in his chair at the dinner table and snarled at Mom. "What do you think you'll do with that degree?" as if he could shut down her joy.

We were celebrating Mom's college graduation, and she was not daunted. While I brought in dinner from the kitchen, she side-stepped his attack and announced with pride, "I'll be working full time with the Probation Department in Cincinnati. Here, let me serve you some chicken. This looks great, Elizabeth." Mom glowed. At forty-two, she was beautiful with her short haircut and colorful sundress.

Dad growled. "When are you going to get the garden in?"

I watched Mom lightly deflect him and not take the bait. I was impressed. I put butter on the steaming asparagus and passed it down to my brothers, who cracked up silently. I gave them the evil eye, but they ignored me.

Dad raged on as if in a tennis match, slamming another serve over the net. "I never should have allowed you to get a job."

Mom lightly lobbed back, as she tossed the salad. "You told me that I was costing you too much on your taxes, and that I needed to work. So I went back to school and found a job."

As she expanded, I watched my father diminish. At sixty, this brilliant, brutal man was losing his reign of domination.

I had made my own trajectory to leave home. I researched French study abroad programs at the library, typed letters in French, inked in the accents, and sent them off airmail. But I was also determined to document our year at sea. I developed the rolls of film Woodie and I had taken on the *Antarna*. I scoured the house and found the letters we'd sent home from the ship. I bought a big scrapbook and rubber cement, organized the photos and letters in order, and worked for hours at the long desk in my bedroom, using my project as a protective shield against the precariousness of life at home.

When Woodie signed up for his junior year at the high school, he ran into the guys who'd bullied him for years. He told me that night, "They took one look at me and realized that era was over." He laughed and ran his finger over his chin stubble. Tanned, taller, and muscular, he moved with confidence. His voice was deeper. "When I went into the office, someone grabbed my shoulder. It was that Dean who used to ride my ass. I whipped around. 'Don't mess with me, mother fucker.' He jumped back so fast!" Now Woodie was roaring with laughter. "He looked frightened of me, even though he tried not to show it." Then his face turned serious. "For the first time in my life, I've got some power. Things are going to be different around here."

•

At dinner Dad tried a new tack. "First thing tomorrow, Woodie, you'll get your ass in gear and work with me in the garden."

"Sorry, I'm hired at Country Kitchen. I start my training as a line cook tomorrow." He waved his hand like he was wielding a spatula and flipping burgers.

I stopped eating my salad. "Oh, Woodie, you could have worked on that sailboat crossing the Atlantic this summer."

Woodie held a spear of asparagus and ate it like a rabbit. "They changed their mind when they found out I was fifteen. I'll get some cooking experience, so I can ship out next summer."

I glanced at Mom, who was smiling to herself. Had she even heard that Woodie might have sailed across the ocean? Was I the only one paying attention to everything going on?

Frustrated, Dad turned to Hubbard, appealing to his youngest. "You'll work with me, won't you? You need to repair the clutch on the tractor."

My youngest brother sounded sincere. "Swim team training starts first thing in the morning for the summer. I'll be home by noon to help you." He nabbed another chicken leg from the platter.

Dad fumed. "How many times do I have to tell you boys to get your elbows off the table?" My brothers jolted to attention, pulled their elbows off the table, grinned at each other. Dad didn't notice. "Who's going to help me get the goddamn garden in?"

I jumped in. "Relax, Dad. I'll help plant the garden before I go to Grandmother's farm next week. With Grandfather sick, she needs help getting her garden in, too. I'm going to set up a farm stand so I can earn money for going to France in the fall."

Dad glowered. "No one told me anything about this."

"I wrote to you all about it from the ship. Stephanie helped me figure out a plan." I emphasized Stephanie's name to use whatever power her name might still have over Dad. "She encouraged me to live in France for a year—to attend a language program and live with a family. I sent off application letters to several French universities this week."

Mom sipped her wine. "I have a leadership training in Maine for two weeks. Elizabeth. I'll pick you up on my way home."

Dad's head nearly whiplashed. "You can't leave for two weeks. You need to be here for the gardens and the boys."

"We don't need her," Woodie and Hubbard said as they cleared the table, happy to slink away, and load the dishwasher.

I tried to distract him. "Maine!" My spirit soared. "Dad, remember my friend Pogo from the ship? I could go with Mom and visit him."

Dad lit up. "That Pogo, he was the best helper I had. Great guy. He has to go to architecture school. He lives in Bar Harbor. I visited a friend at his family summer house when I was in college." He launched into a long story of not having the right clothes for fancy dinner parties at the estate.

I interrupted for a moment. "Everyone, don't go anywhere. I've got a surprise for dessert." Mom headed to the kitchen with me. She split biscuits, one for each plate, while I added a scoop of vanilla ice cream. I whispered, "Tell me about the workshop."

She asked, "Have you ever heard about T-groups or Gestalt?" I shook my head while I added a heaping spoonful of sliced strawberries. "It's about getting out your feelings. You sit in a circle and talk." She added dollops of whipped cream on top of the strawberries.

"For two weeks? That's a lot of feelings. Is it really for your job?"

She waffled, moving her head, yes and no, and held her index finger to her lips.

My eyes widened. "Not a word out of me. But I can go with you to Maine, right? And take your car when you're in your group? I have to see Pogo." Excitement rushed through me when she nodded yes.

I called out, "Here comes dessert."

•

A month later, when I dropped my mom off in Bethel, Maine, for her two weeks of encounter groups, she was terrified. I gave her a big hug, and promised to return. She said, "Have fun finding Pogo."

I was on my own, with her car and a map of Maine. I had Pogo's address, and a postcard he'd sent a month earlier from the Black Hills: "I'm driving with my sister from Oregon home to Maine in her VW bug. Our fastest speed is 30 mph. We are too slow to go on highways. Hope we make it. Pogo." Suddenly my plan seemed a bit nuts. But I assumed I'd find him, so I drove east across the state.

When I arrived in Bar Harbor that night, a guy in a gas station gave me directions to a narrow two-block street. I drove slowly down the block to a streetlamp where I saw a large group of people in the middle of the road. Once I'd parked and stepped out of the car, I realized they were looking at the stars, calling out with *oohs* and cheers. I walked up to them, and said, "I'm looking for Pogo. Is this where he lives?"

A familiar voice called out to me in the dark, "I'm Pogo."

"It's me, Elizabeth."

He laughed. "Of course, you are." We hugged each other a long time, making up for no hugs at the airport in Puerto Rico. They were having a meteor shower party, and we watched, half-hugging, and glanced at each other between meteors, grinning, shy and bashful. He said, "I can't believe it's you. I didn't know if I'd ever see you again."

I looked at him carefully. "Your beard's longer, but you're still you." When I got cold, he took me by the hand and led me into his childhood home, a two-story wooden house, where the walls were packed with book-shelves, records, and art, a comfortable well-worn house that filled with friends, records playing, bottles of beer passed around. When I was sleepy, Pogo showed me to a single guest bed in his mother's sewing room.

The next day, he and I left for his family camp, a hand-built cabin, on a pond near the coast. We canoed in with food, clothes, and books, and stayed for days. We slept on separate bunks, swam in the still water, watched the light change. Somehow, after a few days, we found ourselves lying next to each other on his bunk. We noticed things, like the skittering of the squirrels across the roof and the loon calls from the pond, the light moving slowly across the wall. Pogo and I gazed into each other's eyes, for hours, and then kissed.

On the ship I had vowed to return to being a girl again, the way I'd been before sex had made it all complicated. I'd declared to myself that I wanted to become intimate only after I'd been friends with someone a long time. We lingered at that edge, until we fell into the comfort of each other. Not a loud, splashing fall. It was quiet, peaceful, and safe.

•

Two weeks later, when my mom and I returned home from Maine, Dad and the boys made us dinner. Woodie sliced ripe tomatoes, Hubbard shucked corn on the porch, and Dad ordered them around constantly while he grilled steaks and roared the blender to make fresh mayo. Mom and I glanced at each other and both wished the same thing: Couldn't we turn around and leave? My brothers' faces were hard and sullen.

She had concluded her workshop exhausted, and told me that she'd cried for days about my little sister, who'd died at age two, when I was six, from a heart defect. "I thought I'd grieved when she died, but I had so much grief bottled up in me, I couldn't stop." She'd slept like a child curled up on the backseat while I drove us home. I was leaving in a month for France.

As we ate dinner, Dad said, "We've been up 'til midnight the last few nights, canning tomatoes, and freezing bushels of corn, haven't we boys?" They nodded numbly and stared at their plates. Then Dad glared at Mom and me and snarled, "But now that you're home, you can finally lend a hand, if you aren't too busy." He launched into a list of what we had to pick and freeze. Then he turned on Woodie, "The groundhogs are getting out of control in the garden. You've got to have the .22 loaded and ready."

Woodie ducked his head like he'd been hit. His voice was low but steady. "I said before, I'm not shooting them."

Hubbard jumped in before Dad could launch an attack and said, "I've been finding their holes, it's a whole network. I made a plan to set traps outside of all of them." Dad told him when to set the traps, while Woodie and I slipped away to wash dishes and then disappeared into our rooms. Mom seemed frozen at her spot at the table until she said good night and went to bed.

I woke up in the night to the sound of Dad lecturing her in their bedroom. "If you think you can traipse around the country and leave us all at home, you are mistaken."

I pulled the pillow over my head and tried to go back to sleep.

•

From then on, each night at dinner, Dad let loose his worst in an unrelenting fury—no longer about Woodie's long hair and bad attitude, or me and my old boyfriend. Now he zeroed in on Mom, how she'd changed, how she was not being a wife and mother. Mostly Mom was silent, but when he accused her, "Who do you think you are, changing like this! You are not the girl I married," she seemed to wake up.

Her voice was small. "How could I be the girl you married? That was twenty-five years ago."

He slammed his hand onto the table. "Don't challenge me. Don't lie to me. You are changing and I don't like it one bit. You are breaking your vows to our marriage."

She looked confused. "What are you talking about?"

His head was gleaming with sweat from the overhead lights. "You know damn well what I'm talking about. I won't subject our children to your mental cruelty and lies."

My brothers and I slipped away to our rooms. We'd tried to step in to protect or defend Mom but that had only made it worse. But there was no escape from Dad's voice, and the three of us lay on our beds, held captive like our mom enduring in frozen silence at the table.

•

A week later, on a rare day Dad left for his office, his Jag roaring down the drive, Mom said, "This is a day off. No work. Do anything you want." My brothers and I were too tired and flattened to cheer. We disappeared into our rooms.

It was a hot August morning, and I slid into my chair to read my attempt at a poem in the style of R. D. Laing's "Knots."

I am going insane/ I am playing that I am going insane/ I see the game and I continue it/ I'm reading The Bell Jar and she is going insane . . . / The girl sounds just like me/ or better.

I put my head on the keyboard of my portable. How had I gotten back here so fast? Did the year on the ship actually happen? Was I still the same depressed girl reading Sylvia Plath that I'd been at the end of high school? Had I been here all along? What had happened to hurtle me back into this sarcastic, snarly, depressed girl? How could I have fallen so quickly?

Caught in the web of my father's cruelty, I anguished. Had nothing changed from our year on the ship? My brother and I were trapped in something worse than the storm at sea. This tempest of Dad's yelling and threats and fury blew every night. We were ensnared in the nightmare again. I was so profoundly disappointed in myself. How could I have let this repeat? What was wrong with me!? I'd thought I'd learned so much. Had I already lost what I thought I'd gained?

·

After another week of agony, Woodie couldn't bear it. He took the loaded .22 and lay down on our father's bed and lined up the barrel to point toward his head. Who knows what he thought as he lay there in the long, terrible pause with his finger on the trigger. I could only imagine he knew that the agony of his life, our family's life, could cease in an instant.

Later that afternoon, I walked into the house, finding him as he shoved the gun between coats in the hall closet. I stared at him. All he said was, "I couldn't do it to Mom." He raised his hand toward me, perhaps to make sure I didn't say a word or move toward him, or try to comfort him. He walked to his room.

He'd told me on the ship, "If they send me home, I will die," and I'd believed him. But something had changed in our year at sea. In the wreck on the beach in Puerto Rico, Woodie had fought for his breath to pull himself through to save his life. Here at home, he pulled himself through some internal battle, and he put the gun away.

·

When I drove into the city, a section of the highway with thirty-foot-high concrete walls was my siren song; singing to me to plow our VW bus into it at sixty miles an hour. I could vanish instantly from pain and confusion. But like my brother, I never pulled the steering wheel into that wall. Instead, I discovered my long-buried anger.

Did I ever get angry on the ship? My rage was so suppressed when I'd walked up the gangway, I could hardly feel it. I'd watched Kim with amazement as she'd spotted injustice, the belittling of us girls, seeing what was invisible to me. She'd taken action and climbed the rigging before any of us.

Even in Panama, when we were running out of food and water, when the ship was taken from us, had I been angry? No. When even Lisa, the nicest girl on the ship, sounded snarky and negative, I'd found her sarcasm shocking.

But back at home, after my brother and I had almost chosen to kill ourselves, after death felt so close we could smell it, only then did a cold fury build, a laser beam of anger that grew, making me feel strong and unstoppable. As I glowered inside during dinners at the long table in the glass-walled Great Room, a chorus repeated in my head: *I hate him, I hate him.*

•

One night in mid-August, I took my sleeping bag out on the porch to escape the yelling in the house. As I lay there in the dark, my father slid open the glass door and directed my mother to a chair on the porch not far from where I was trying to sleep out of sight. He paced and lectured and cross-examined her like a prosecutor, for her crimes, her changes, and on and on all night. At dawn, he directed her into the house and slid the sliding glass doors shut. That night something broke open. Someone had to do something to save our family. The answer floated clear and strong into my mind as two sentences. All I had to do was kill my father. Then the nightmare would be over.

A strange calm radiated through me. I was going do what I had to do to save my family.

Woodie and I knew about being held captive. We knew the relief that came when we were set free. Back in Panama, our freedom finally came from surrendering. We gave up everything—the ship, five months of our labor, the thousands of dollars spent, the possibility of the months of sailing. All that promise had been surrendered in exchange for us to be freed. I'd learned that liberation was sweeter than holding on. I would risk everything I had to save us.

It was simple. I would kill my father and then the yelling would stop. We would be free. I would surrender my life, go to jail, to free us. I felt lightened, almost peaceful. I examined his Japanese steel knives in the drawer in the kitchen. I would stab him in the chest. We would be able to breathe again. I wrote a list of all the books I'd finally have time to read. I slept and planned and set the table and cleared the dishes, and lived in this razor-sharp beam of anger. I was happier than I'd been since I'd returned home. Freedom from this nightmare was coming. I would stab him with his finest French steel carving knife. I would pierce the space between the bones and find his heart.

•

The day came, an ordinary day, as my brothers and I cleared lunch dishes and carried them to the kitchen. One of us had done something wrong again. It didn't matter what set him off. I knew this would be the moment. I stood in front of the wide drawer filled with his fine carving knives. I was ready. He stood a few feet away from me, yelling.

But at the moment when I'd planned to open the drawer of knives, something happened. We all turned and faced him, our eyes unified, glaring.

No one needed to say a word. Somehow, in that moment, my sixty-year-old bull-chested father collapsed onto the floor, his chest shuddering with a rapid heart arrhythmia that left him gasping for breath. He looked pitifully broken lying on the linoleum floor. One by one, my mother, Woodie, and I walked away, and Hubbard helped him to bed and found his heart pills.

I slid open the glass door and stepped out onto the porch, immediately engulfed by the muggy summer heat. I was trembling, and disoriented. I reached out to steady myself on the corner porch post. I didn't have to kill him. He didn't have to die. I never had to pick up the knife. I didn't have to sacrifice my life to save my family. I gasped, *We are free.* I stepped off the porch and walked with wobbly legs across the lawn toward the trees. I was barefoot and could feel every step. I realized I could just keep walking. I didn't have to stop.

I had become a girl who'd saved herself.

•

A few days after his collapse, my father was strangely elated, acting as if nothing had happened, and in this state of mania he gave me his XKE Jaguar convertible. His plan was for me to sell it to pay for my year in France, or to keep it and stay home. The choice was mine. He offered me the key and I took it.

The next day, I packed a small bag and drove east to visit Kim. I was eighteen years old, brave and daring and gloriously free. I was wearing jeans and my Mexican embroidered blouse, my long hair pulled back with a kerchief to keep it out of my face in the wind.

I found my way to her rutted driveway in rural New Jersey. We hugged hello, laughing and crying, holding out our hands to show we still wore each other's rings. We talked endlessly as we walked across pastures and down farm lanes. Kim sometimes broke into a canter, and I ran to catch up. Other times I drove, and we let our hair fly in the wind. We parked overlooking the river to talk. She took a photograph of me in the Jaguar in a meadow at sunset.

Something had shifted in me by standing up to my dad. Kim and I were done with talking about Steph. We were committed to being loyal to our own lives. We drove with the top down, singing *"We all live in a Yellow Submarine."*

Years later she wrote to me about that visit. "I felt torn away from you prematurely. Your coming to see me would feed my soul in the months afterward. Maybe you know how I suffered hearing about your return [home.] You don't know how much you were my anchor."

Three weeks after I walked away from my father on the kitchen floor, I flew to France. Within a few weeks of my leaving, my mother and my brother Woodie moved out. Hubbard stayed with my father.

What Are You Most Attached To?

Stephanie's letter, March 30, 1972: *When it is all over, and when we're able to look back objectively, I know that the events will come into focus, and the experience will seem very full and rich.*

Years later, we learned that after the Oceanics School left the ship, the *Antarna*, was abandoned, left untended by the owners in a bay near Cristobal, Panama, for six years. We don't know if they even went aboard after we'd left the ship spotless.

The miles of new rigging and the sails of Welsh linen rotted on the masts and yards. Moss grew across her teak decks. The sanded and varnished mahogany walls and deck boxes peeled, split, and rotted in the tropical sun. Her stays corroded, her brass fittings oxidized, her engines and systems fell into disrepair. The $400,000 Stephanie had raised from donors with the vision of a magnificent school ship—and the work done by students, teachers, crew, and engineers—all went to waste. Merchant ships and sailboats passing through the bay on their way to and from the canal noticed the square-rigged ship and paid attention to her over the years, passing along word to people who loved fine ships. Many of us assumed the Panamanians had confiscated the ship.

But what had happened? The mysterious owner (and his shipping agent), who had held us hostage, starved us out, and threatened to trap the students in jail, abandoned his prize in Panama and never returned. Couldn't an agreement have been made? Perhaps he had been bested too many times by Stephanie, he had to win their game. Had he written us off as hippie kids, having no qualms about holding us hostage and cutting off water and food?

And whose intervention had gotten us out? Fifty years later I learned another story.

When Stephanie left the farm in Puerto Rico, Harry, one of the First Nation students, said he was ready to go home to Alberta. He flew to New York with her. A friend of hers sent a limo to pick them up. Stephanie took the car phone and handed it to Harry. "Call your sister, let her know that you're OK."

When I talked to Harry, who lives on the reserve in remote Alberta, he told me what his sister said. She was working for the chiefs of the Six

Nations in Ottawa when Stephanie called to say we were in trouble in Panama. She had called the head of Indian Affairs, who talked to the prime minister. Harry told me about the trail of phone calls, the call to the ambassador to the UN, and finally to the Queen.

He said, "Remember, my people are children of the Crown, British subjects. Our treaty was with Queen Victoria, and now with Queen Elizabeth. My sister said the Queen called Nixon. She said we were prisoners of war according to the UN. Panama said we had contraband. But we didn't. The Canadian government believes we were a bargaining chip for the Canal Zone. But they didn't realize three Indians (who can travel unimpeded in and out of U.S. territory), as well as students and teachers from Canada, Denmark, France were on board. They were breaking a UN treaty in the canal. My sister heard that Nixon called Panama and said, 'Let them go. They are just students.'"

In 1978, the *Antarna* was rescued from disintegration by a German sea captain and investors. The ship was purchased from the owner's corporation—not from the Panamanians, as I had imagined. This captain and his crew managed to patch the ship together so it could motor at great peril and in precarious condition across the Atlantic to return her home to the shipyards in Kiel, where she had been built almost fifty years before, to be refurbished and resurrected as the *Sea Cloud*. Once again in her full glory, she takes on passengers to sail throughout the Mediterranean and the Caribbean.

Stephanie pursued the owner with legal suits for the next thirty years, long after his sale of the ship and long after the transformation of the *Antarna* into the *Sea Cloud*. I Googled the legacy of the court battles with the owner, and there they are, online, hidden in plain sight. One case is even used to teach lawyers a legal argument to prove when a solo owner is hiding ownership under the guise of a corporation.

Stephanie and Chick ran the Oceanics School until 1979. The year after the *Antarna*, the school had its finest year at sea. Mike, the Mythology and Dreams class teacher, returned as educational director for the next two years. When I tracked him down by phone fifty years later, he described the year that followed mine.

"The school was held on a Norwegian sail training ship, the three-masted barque, the *Statsraad Lemkuhl*, a 350' steel ship, with 26 professional crew, and 100 total with the students and teachers, and Stig Floden joined as Head Mate.

We were 10 months at sea, mostly under sail. The first month we went way up to the top of a fjord and did our rowing training there and running drills. The students had to learn all the ship's commands for sailing the ship in Norwegian. We got so good at our drills, including in the dark in the middle of the night, that we even beat some of the Norwegian sail training crews. We had three girls from the *Antarna* year, two returned as students, and Jane worked as crew. When we left that small town on the fjord, they turned on and off all the lights in the town to signal to us as we sailed away."

When I wrote to Jane recently about her two years with the Oceanics, she wrote back about being crew the second year. "I remember getting 'baptized' a 'salty puppy' and shaving my head when we crossed the equator. I loved being out at sea in the rigging. We polished a lot of brass and worked in shifts—everything was very organized compared to the *Antarna*. We didn't have to clean water tanks, scrub mold in the galley, or replace rotten rigging. But the *Antarna* adventure also had its charms—I can't to this day tell you which experience was the better."

•

After high school, Kim lived and worked on boats, installing engines and plumbing, eating what she could fish, and selling the rest of her catch. She lived for four years on a ten-ton ferro-cement ketch, up and down the East

Coast. Then she went to New York and on to Italy to work as a fashion model and to tutor English. She's now a therapist in England.

Kim and I have only seen each other in person a few times, but over the years we have written countless letters and emails, reporting on important dreams, what we're reading and thinking. In her work to empower women, she still belches and swears occasionally, now consciously with a therapeutic intent.

Pogo and I spent most of the 1970s together. He worked as a potter and carpenter, and he taught me to renovate houses in Ohio and California, before our lives took us in different directions. He became an architect and has worked in the United States, England, Eastern Europe, and China.

About twenty-five years after I'd last seen him in California, when we were both married with children, I was standing in an old-fashioned grocery store in Blue Hill, Maine. I looked down the narrow aisle and saw a man at a distance, and before my mind could say "This is Pogo," my heart said "This is someone I have always loved." I walked toward him with tears in my eyes, knowing it was my dear friend. We still write regularly.

Woodie arrived on the *Antarna* enthralled with the idea of going to sea. On board he became impressed by the professional mariners who were responsible for our setting sail: our engineer, Mr. Neilson, Captain Floden. A few years after high school, he went to a merchant marine academy to train to become a ship's engineer. Over the decades he moved up, from Third to Second to First to Chief. He sailed on every kind of cargo ship. He sailed on the Arctic and Antarctic, the north and south Pacific and Atlantic, and the Seas: Indian, Mediterranean, Black and Red. Twice his ship was in the still eye of a typhoon before it sailed into the wall of the storm, where winds over a hundred miles an hour made the entire ship hum. He was never on a ship that sank except one that had already reached dock. By the end of his career, he felt like a grizzled old merchant mariner training cadets. When someone might ask him how long he'd been shipping out, he'd chuckle "I've been sailing so long my first ship was a square rigger," which was true and beautifully misleading.

Retired now, Woodie once wished he could have applied all he'd learned in his career as a chief engineer to the *Antarna* back when we were on board. "I could have gotten that engine room running like a top. I would have loved that."

Zip left Nebraska for Stanford after high school, where he met up with Lisa again, and kept diving. After a decade in England, he's loved living in Costa Rica for twenty years where his company installs solar and wind systems. He's told me many stories, and sent me instructive emails and videos about the *Antarna's* engine room.

Richie lived close to the dangerous edges of life after Oceanics. His mother's memoir, *After All*, described him being pursued by drug dealers in high school. At twenty-four, he had settled down and was looking forward to a new job when he died of a gun accident. He owned and kept many guns in his apartment, and he was watching television while playing with one, putting the loaded hair trigger weapon to his head. Those of us who had known him at fourteen were saddened for that boy we'd known, wondering if we could have done more to make a difference.

A few years ago, I decided to contact Stephanie, wanting to ask her questions that still haunted me from our year on the *Antarna*. What happened in Panama, and how did we get out? I calculated how old she would be, six years older than I was. But when I Googled her name, I found obituaries from a few years earlier. First for Chick, in his mid-eighties, described as a famous World War II photographer and documentary filmmaker, and then, three months later, Stephanie's obituary. She had died at sixty-eight. The comments were from students of the Oceanics School about how she had changed their lives.

When I wondered who else might help me learn how we were released from Panama, I thought of Mary Tyler Moore, and her then husband, Grant Tinker, head of NBC, but they had both died. I didn't know who else might know.

I set out to find students and teachers on the *Antarna* to ask questions, to remember what happened, and to write about how that year changed each of us. I set up an on-line forum where we could post stories and photographs. We shared memories we'd never spoken of, as we still try to understand what happened. I've had many long phone calls, and emails, becoming friends again as I took notes.

So far, I've found twelve former students, and they have all followed varied creative careers. We did all kinds of work after the ship: fish packer, farmer, potter, carpenter, college grad and dropout, fashion model. We all traveled and have worked in many fields: mathematician, herbalist, tribal leader, acupuncturist, architect, diesel engine installer, attorney at the NSA, solar engineer, a dot.com billionaire, inventor, consultant with the White House, pediatric orthopedic physician assistant, realtor, yoga and meditation teacher, post and beam builder, chief engineer on container ships. Some still sail, and one teaches celestial navigation. We live in the United States, Canada, Costa Rica, England, Denmark, China.

Of our ten original teachers I've found Karl, Peter, Ron, and Mike. I sometimes feel like I'm still one of the students, bugging them with questions. Karl worked as a diver with submarines, and for many years lived and volunteered in the Caribbean. He spent hundreds of hours scanning slides from the year of the ship to make his photos digital. For fifty years Ron has taught and been a leader in independent education. Peter became a world-renowned expert on sharks. After Mike taught at Oceanics for three years, he landed at Dean Witter and eventually became a senior vice president.

•

In 1978, a flyer for the 1978–1979 Oceanics school year, the school's final year, showed up in my dad's mail right before he sold the glass house. He sent it on to me in California, where I worked as a carpenter and rented a little cottage on the back streets of Berkeley. I glanced at it with wearied humor, wondering what Stephanie was up to. I read the familiar invigorating promise, and studied the photos—the bow of a ship, sails rising above the deck, a grid of small portraits of students I didn't know looking like

"Salty Dogs" in foul-weather gear, in the rigging, washing dishes. Then I recognized in one photo: my long hair falling over my shoulder as I wrote in the red leather journal, the lines of my careful handwriting still visible on the lined pages.

How had my photo joined the publicist's repertoire? Had some sweetness still lingered in Stephanie for me, after all these years? Did she want me to know she still thought of me? Did she wonder if I might someday write about the school and all of us?

•

In the late 1970s, I still loved my red leather journal. I'd sit on the back stoop of my little cottage in Berkeley and get lost reading the pages of that year on the ship, my crushes, my struggles to deal with my father, stories of the students and the ship. I carried it with my subsequent journals in a metal file box along with letters from Kim and old boyfriends. I was so attached to my red journal, believing it was the most precious thing I owned.

In 1978, Kim, with her life in turmoil, sent me her journals from the ship, two black-and-white-speckled stenographer's notebooks—for safekeeping. I carried them for the next forty years through every move. Eventually she forgot I had them, imagining that they had been lost in a flood in her mother's basement.

In 1980, I studied meditation with a few teachers. One of the teachings I absorbed was that I had to let go of attachment—to the past, to my ideas of myself, and to objects. We were admonished to free ourselves of the old stories of our life so we could step into who it was possible for us to be. The teacher asked, "What are you most attached to?" I knew instantly. It was my red leather journal from the ship. We were told to explore where we were holding ourselves back, what was blocking us from having the life we dreamed of.

There came a day when I decided I had to burn my red leather journal, to free myself of my attachment to the year on the ship. I lit a little bonfire in my little garden plot in the flatlands of Berkeley down near the highway and the bay. I ripped chunks of pages from the red leather-bound book, but they didn't catch and burn until I pulled them further apart to single pages. So many names and days and stories caught flame, and still I ripped and tossed them into the fire—until I saw a sketch of Kim and me, walking in Mexico, carrying a bag between us. I reached into the flames and pulled out that page and saved it in the metal box along with Kim's journals.

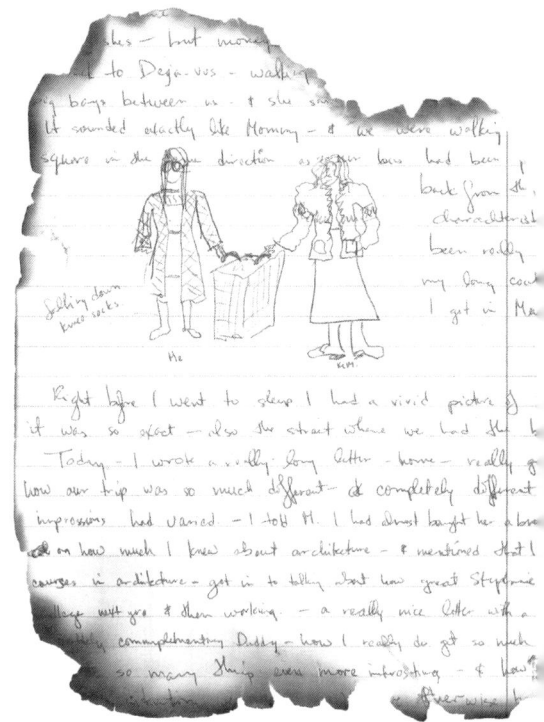

A year later, I started a new life in Maine with a family, and a practice of acupuncture, putting the world of the ship far behind me. But I never forgot the ship and I kept writing. Years later, on a writing retreat, I skinny-dipped in the ocean, twirling my arms in the silvery phosphorescence, gasping with awe and wonder.

•

In 2019, I sailed for four days around the Canary Islands on the flawlessly run and professionally maintained *Sea Cloud*. The moment I saw her proceeding toward the dock, I wept, watching her come toward me, looking like she had when we'd motored away from her in Panama nearly fifty years before. I explored her decks, remembered my old hiding places, and took notes about the feel of a ship under sail, how to walk the deck in rough seas, the sounds of the engines, how the captain stood on the bridge and called out orders. I kept hoping Kim or Pogo would turn the corner or appear in the rigging along with the rest of the Oceanics kids and teachers.

I still dream about the *Antarna*. I am on her deck in a crowd of students looking up into the rig. I walk down the gangway to the dock to run an errand, but I can't get back. The dream hurtles me farther and farther from the ship, but I keep trying to return. I see the masts across the harbor, then from a window in an old bookstore, the dream taking me farther away, up cobblestone streets, finally into a forest where I find two lost children—a boy and a girl. I remember I'm in a dream, and just as it begins to fade, I look down and see my hands. I know what I need to do. I reach out to the children, take their hands at the last moment, and we lift off into flight so we can return to the ship.

Acknowledgments

I could not have written this story without my friends from The Ship. I started planning to write the story the summer I returned home. Through fifty years of countless moves, I carried the photo album filled with letters and photos, Stephanie's parent letters, as well as Kim's journals. Without those archives, I couldn't have reconstructed our year at sea. My gratitude begins with Kim, who gave me access to her journals, hours of long conversations, and emails. I used her words for most of her dialogue because no one can talk like Kim!

My profound thanks to all the Oceanics students and teachers that I was able to locate from our year on the *Antarna*. Your patience with all my questions and notetaking and your willingness to share your stories so generously made this story come alive. Thank you for all your vivid lively stories: my brother Woodie, Pogo, Kim, Zip, Ted, Bruce, Mike, Karl, Harry, Jane, Rick, Ron, Phil G., Phil P., Nina, Ethan, and Jill. Thanks to Mike for many long conversations and clarification of what happened in the Yucatan. Thanks for Abe Goodale's beautiful watercolor of the Sea Cloud under full sail.

I am so grateful for all the photos that we shared with each other on the ship and recently, especially Karl's digitizing his vast collection of slides, and photos from Ron, Rick, Woodie, Ghislaine, Bruce, Nina, and probably others I've forgotten. I'm so grateful for my cousin Helen Garber's recently discovered and digitized slides from her hard-working visit to the ship with my dad to build bookshelves.

Once I'd gathered all the stories and reconstructed what happened, it still took years of writing to find the right voice for these 1970's teenagers and how to tell our stories. My first editor, Baron Wormser, read my big messy first draft, and directed my attention to some big picture issues. During two Covid years, the remarkable teacher and writer, Susan Conley, inspired me to write scenes with immediacy and teen energy and worked with me closely through two drafts. I jumped into several intensive seminars with wonderful teachers who helped me keep the story moving. Thanks to Steve Almond, Melanie Brooks, Elissa Altman. As I pitched the book, I learned to write essays and pitch letters in the high-energy classes with the empowering teacher Susan Shapiro. I also learned so much in classes with Ryan Britt, Susan Conley, and Wendy Call. I thank you all!

Working with editors throughout the process was invaluable. Thanks for Polly Bennell's coaching on structure, for Tanya Whiton's developmental editor's big picture feedback, and for the close attention of my copy editors, Sally Jaskold and Chris Daly. It is so important to have different skillful sets of eyes on a manuscript! Thanks to my amazing nautical reader, Hila Shooter, who between sailing gigs on square riggers, updated my ship's language and reminded me of the Beaufort Scale to determine whether we were in fact in a "storm" (more than 48 knots of wind) or in a "strong gale." Thanks to generous editors of my query letter and book proposal: Molly-Ann Leikin and Arielle Greenberg. I had invaluable assistance from the "Title Doctor," Kristen Paulson-Nguyen, as we explored until I found the right title. I thank you all!

My biggest fan and encouraging reader has been my mom, Jo Garber, who laughed at the crazy stories and was relieved she didn't know even the half of what happened on the ship.

I'm grateful for dear friends who have read and cheered me on, for Vicki Pollard and Martha Derbyshire who so often responded to brand new pieces; for my writing buddy, Linda Buckmaster, as we kept steering through years of work on our books; for my amazing Ladies Pandemic Writing group when we wrote, listened, and encouraged each other through the tough years: Kathleen Robinson, Kathleen Sullivan, Kelli Thompson, Mary McCann, Johanna Franzel, and Andrea Hanson; and writing friends in other groups and classes over the years: David Lyman, Linda Bowie, Colleen Bogner, Monica Van Peski, Jennifer Craig. I am so happy to have reconnected with an old friend, Kate Sheridan, decades later, and for her generous close reading of the manuscript.

In November, 2019, I was so grateful for the four engrossing days my husband and I spent sailing on the *Sea Cloud* around the Canary Islands. Thanks so much to Lisa Huijsers, Tom Hood, the keeper of the ship's history, as well as the captain, officers, engineers, and crew who sailed the ship so skillfully. We were honored by Chief Mate John Svenson taking us an out-of-bounds of tour of the engine room, the galley and crew messes (my dad's bookcases are gone now), and a special tour of hidden places on the ship.

After a year's search for the right publisher, I was blessed with finding a publishing team whose first words were "We love this story. We want to publish your book." This is what writers dream of. The Toad Hall Editions team—Amy Tingle, Maya Stein, and Liz Kalloch—made me feel at home as we met around their "center of the universe" kitchen table work space. How extraordinary to work with such a devoted, skilled, creative, think-outside-the-box team in Maine, who are determined to bring out women's voices in beautiful books. Maya's editing has been sensitive and wise, Liz's designs are poignantly beautiful, and Amy oversees the whole magic-making container. Everything they do is a class act.

My husband, Dirk, has been a steady source of encouragement and humor. He can't get over how dangerous our year at sea was. He's always willing to hear another story, and offer me the right nautical vocabulary for ships, knots, and scuba gear, and he was invaluable as a researcher when we visited the *Sea Cloud*. I'm so grateful for how he's kept the woodstove warming the house, as I worked on the book year after year.

Elizabeth's reading list — Sept 1971 - 1972   The OCEANICS School

(Would you believe - I kept thinking I hadn't read very much!)

1. Zelda - Nancy Milford - (read this right before I left for Oceanics - excellent especially on schizo-personalities)

2. short stories by F. Scott Fitzgerald

3. Vonnegut — Cat's Cradle
4.   "   Welcome to the Monkey House   ⎫ I have no idea why I read
5.   "   Slaughter House Five   ⎬ all these. - fun reading - but
6.   "   God Bless you, Mr. Rosewater   ⎭ impossible to remember

7. (½) Moby Dick - Melville - (really enjoyed it - but it sure is long .....)

8. Heart of Darkness - Conrad

9. Catch 22 - Heller   (wow! this really hits you!)

10. Hesse's   Knulp - very simply written like a folk tale
11.   Demian - confusing & un-understandable to most -   I felt that I really
                                                                      could see what he was
                                                                      talking about
12.   Siddhartha - had a profound affect on me
13.   Narcissis & Goldmund - not his best but also great

14. Jung — Memories, Dreams & Reflections (autobiography) good but unsure about
                                                           how coherent the book...
15. articles & lectures by Jung

16. The Little Prince   — (I love it)

17. Winnie the Pooh - series (I especially love these!) - as if you didn't know.

18. Old Man & the Sea - Hemingway - fairly good

19. parts of the I Ching - really magnificent book

20. Strawberry Statement ⎫ both crudy!
21. Good Times / Bad Times ⎭

22. Man's Search for Meaning - Fromm - good

23. Brave New World - Huxley - (I really got into this)

24. Summerhill - Neill - (not too great - fairly ambiguous - not what I expected
                          at all - disappointed)

25. What the Trees Said - (about a commune - no really new ideas)

26. A Separate Peace - Knowles (not really anything great - but I still like it)

27. 1984 - Orwell — (good - not great - the subject seems like old hat)

28. The Reivers - Faulkner (I saw the movie in Panama - fun but not
                            much - difficult to read - reading his writing is fascinat...

29. Waiting for Godot - Beckett   (I didn't really get that much out of it)
30. Portrait of the Artist as a Young Man - Joyce - (excellent - fascinated by his style)
31 The Phantom Tollbooth - Norton Juster (fun kid's book)
★ 32 Laing - Knots - poetry (in paperback for only #1)

in the past few weeks
33 Islandia - Wright (good) (I especially loved this - very emotional crutch for awhile)
34. The Fox - & short stories by D.H. Lawrence
35. Winter's Tales - Isak Dinesen (Great! (some))
36. a few stories from Slouching Towards Bethlehem Joan Didion (hmm... not bad)
37. How Children Fail - Holt
38. One Flew Over the Cukoo's Nest - Kesey
39 Childhood's End - Arthur C. Clarke

About the Author

Elizabeth W. Garber is the author of *Implosion: A Memoir of an Architect's Daughter* (2018). She has published three books of poetry: *True Affections* (2012), *Listening Inside the Dance* (2005), and *Pierced by the Seasons* (2004). *Maine* (Island Time, 2013) is a collaboration of her poetry with paintings and photographs by Michael Weymouth. Her essays and excerpts have appeared in *Salon*, *Maine Homes*, *Johns Hopkins Magazine*, and her poems have been included in several journals and anthologies. Three poems have been read on NPR's The Writer's Almanac.

She received an MFA in Creative Nonfiction from University of Southern Maine's Stonecoast Program, was awarded writing fellowships at Virginia Center for Creative Arts and Jentel Artist Residency, and received a BA in Humanities from Johns Hopkins and a Masters in Acupuncture from the Traditional Acupuncture Institute. She has maintained a private practice as an acupuncturist for nearly forty years in mid-coast Maine, where she raised her family. Visit her at elizabethgarber.com.

About Toad Hall Editions

Toad Hall Editions, a small press founded in 2021 and located in midcoast Maine, offers an alternative publishing platform to those who struggle to find themselves represented in more traditional publishing models—women, LGBTQIA+, minority, and gender-diverse writers and artists.

Find out more at toadhalleditions.ink.